50

作者:卢卡斯·奥托
主译:方华文
译者:孟祥春　张立蓉

英汉对照
Greatest Modern Heroes

50+1位

最有影响力

风云人物

安徽科学技术出版社
Encouragement Press, LLC

B

图书在版编目(C I P)数据

50+1位最具影响力的风云人物 ／（美）奥托著；方
华文译. -- 合肥 ： 安徽科学技术出版社，2009.06
（50+1系列）
ISBN 978-7-5337-4437-3

Ⅰ．①5… Ⅱ．①奥… ②方… Ⅲ．①名人－生平事迹
－世界 Ⅳ．①K811

中国版本图书馆CIP数据核字(2009)第079291号

50+1位最具影响力的风云人物

(美) 奥托(Otto,L.)著 方华文 译

出 版 人：黄和平	
责任编辑：付 莉	
封面设计：朱 婧	
出版发行：安徽科学技术出版社(合肥市政务文化新区圣泉路 1118 号	
出版传媒广场，邮编：230071)	
网　　　址：www. ahstp. net	
E－mail：yougoubu@sina.com	
经　　　销：新华书店	
排　　　版：安徽事达科技贸易有限公司	
印　　　刷：合肥瑞丰印务有限公司	
开　　　本：787×1092　1/16	
印　　　张：14.75	
字　　　数：406 千	
版　　　次：2009 年 6 月第 1 版　2022 年 1 月第 2 次印刷	
定　　　价：39.00 元	

(本书如有印装质量问题，影响阅读，请向本社市场营销部调换)

译 者 简 介

　　方华文,男,1955年6月生于西安,现任苏州大学外国语学院英语教授,著名学者、文学翻译家及翻译理论家,被联合国教科文组织国际译联誉为"the most productive literary translator in contemporary China"(中国当代最多产的文学翻译家,Babel.54:2,2008,145–158)。发表的著、译作品达1 000余万字,其中包括专著《20世纪中国翻译史》等,计200余万字;译著《雾都孤儿》《无名的裴德》《傲慢与偏见》《蝴蝶梦》《魂断英伦》《儿子与情人》《少年维特之烦恼》《红字》《从巅峰到低谷》《马丁·伊登》《套向月亮的绳索》《君主论》《社会契约论》以及改写本的《飘》《汤姆叔叔的小屋》《查特莱夫人的情人》《大卫·科波菲尔》《苔丝》《高老头》《三个火枪手》《悲惨世界》等;主编的译作包括《基督山伯爵》《红与黑》《简·爱》《汤姆·索亚历险记》《茶花女》《金银岛》《鲁滨孙漂流记》《巴黎圣母院》《莎士比亚戏剧故事集》《精神分析引论》《论法的精神》和《国富论》等;并主编了多部英汉对照读物。以上均为单行本著作,所发表文章不计在内。

Everyone needs a hero. Heroes are people who make the news and are larger than life. They are the men and women of action, who think great thoughts, have nerves of steel or who make personal sacrifices—who prompt generations upon generations to speak of them in that very special way. We hold up heroes as models for our children—idols of what we want them to be like and how we want them to act.

A modern hero is not always a great general or statesman (although there are some of them in our contemporary pantheon), but more often men and women who have influenced society, changed its views, sought to make the world a better place, entertained us or made us laugh or, even, given their lives for their ideals and their values. Our heroes are men and women from all walks of life, from all around the world, who through science, politics, war, letters, music, sports or the media stood head and shoulders above the rest of us. Heroes speak to us, sometimes directly but often indirectly, of the things that are most important in our own lives, and they challenge us to be like them, to follow them, to act like them and ultimately to respect them—even if we do not always agree with them.

Many of the heroes in this book are household names, recognized immediately for their presence on the world stage and for their accomplishments. But some of our heroes are not household names—9/11 victims and survivors and the veterans of World War II, for example. Some are from earlier generations, but without them, the lives that our generation has lived would have been significantly different. Some heroes are not people at all, but animated figures from comic books or characters from television and the movies.

Whatever you think a hero is, it is my hope that you will find this collection fun, entertaining and interesting. I also hope that one or two of these profiles will make you think about someone you thought you knew well in a new way. Or maybe one of these profiles will inspire you to take some actions to develop a great idea of your own. Every effort has been made to make the people real, showing both their admirable and less flattering sides. Even though they are our heroes, they are often not without controversy. After all, this is not a book about saints, but real people and real events.

Enjoy our heroes for what they are, learn from them, be inspired by them and most of all appreciate them for their contributions and their courage.

Happy reading!

Lucas Otto

风云人物充满了传奇色彩,造就了新闻。他们是实干家,有着伟大的思想,具有钢铁般的意志,或者作出了个人牺牲——他们促使着一代又一代的人以一种特殊的方式去追述他们。我们把英雄人物奉为子女的楷模,期望子女像他们那样,并以他们的方式来行事。

现代风云人物并非都是将军或者政治家(虽然本书内不乏其人),而往往是这样的人,风化社会、改变社会观念、努力让世界变得更加美好,或者娱乐我们、让我们发笑,抑或为了自己的理想与价值观献出了生命。他们来自全球,遍布各行各业,通过科学、政治、变革、文学、音乐、体育或者媒体脱颖而出,高人一等。他们向我们言说,多为间接,有时直接,言说我们生命中最重要的东西;他们激励着我们向他们看齐,追随他们、如他们一样立世处事,并最终尊敬他们,即使有时我们对他们并不认同。

本书中的风云人物大多家喻户晓,他们出现在世界舞台上,成就非凡,立刻可辨认出来。但有些英雄的名字并却非妇孺皆知,如"9·11"事件的罹难者与幸存者以及二战老兵。有些属于上一代人,但如果没有他们,我们这一代人的生活与现在将大不相同。有些英雄人物并非真人,而是连环漫画中的动画形象,或者是影视中的角色。

不管您认为风云人物是什么,我希望您会觉得该书读来饶有兴味,怡人耳目。希望其中的一两篇勾勒剪影会让您对业已熟悉的风云人物有新的认识。更希望其中某一篇会激发您采取行动,衍生出自己的伟大想法。该书力求真实勾勒,既呈现英雄受人尊敬的一面,也不粉饰其不算美好的另一面。尽管他们身为风云人物,但有时并非毫无争议。毕竟,该书呈现的不是圣人,而是真人真事。

希望您能喜欢真实的未加粉饰的风云人物,向他们学习,从他们那里得到灵感,并为他们的奉献与勇气而心存感激。

祝您阅读愉快!

卢卡斯·奥托

Table of Contents

目　录

Table of Contents
目　录

Table of Contents

Table of Contents

目　录

4

Table of Contents
目　录

50+1位最具影响力的风云人物

讲述风云人物如何影响社会，
改变我们的观念，
让世界变得更加美好。

9/11 Heroes,
Just Good People

Who They Are

As the eighth anniversary of the 9/11 disaster has come and gone, and the praise and memorials to all the victims have faded just a bit, we can only think of the thousands of people involved in this series of disasters as the truest of true heroes of the 21st century. Greatness has abounded throughout the world in the last 50 or 60 years, but nothing is more remarkable than the acts of self-sacrifice in an airplane or the willingness to go back into burning and falling buildings to save others.

This heroism has been recorded for posterity and as we move from that time, more books and movies will come forth to describe in graphic detail the lives and misfortunes of both victims and first-line responders. A nation will never forget the debt that it owes to so many people.

Stepping aside from the politics and the Monday morning recriminations about who should have known what, the events and people of 9/11 show the true spirit of human compassion and decency. Victims, survivors, helpers and those who cleaned up afterward are the truest of true heroes. We salute them all.

What Made Them

September 11, 2001, is one of those days on which people remember where they were and what they were doing when suddenly the world changed forever. In the midst of horrifying death and chaos, many of these people distinguished themselves and their country by risking their lives to save others.

They are all heroes in every sense of the word.

It was a perfect morning along the East Coast of the United States, but it would not last. Hijackers associated with bin Laden and the al-Qaida terrorist group had boarded four airliners and were preparing to use them as guided missiles to destroy targets on American soil. Airport security was spotty in those days; the airplanes were not fully booked and all the flights were going to California—ensuring the maximum amount of damage from full loads of airplane fuel.

Three of the planes took off at approximately the same time. Soon after they were airborne, the hijackers made their moves, overpowering the flight crews with small knives that they had smuggled on board and threatening to blow up the plane with a bomb if the passengers did not cooperate. At least one hijacker per plane had received enough flight training to fly the airliner but not to land it (which, it would turn out, would not be necessary). The hijackers turned off the planes' transponders and began seeking their targets.

American Airlines Flight 11 struck the north face of the North Tower of the World Trade Center in New York at 8:46 a.m. Eastern time. At the time, the authorities and the

"9·11"英雄:善良的人们

他们是谁

转瞬之间,"9·11"灾难8周年降临而又远去,对所有受难者的赞扬与悼念也有些许黯淡,我们只能把卷入这一系列灾难中的数千人看做21世纪英雄中的英雄。在过去的五六十年里,世界从不缺乏伟大,但在"9·11"事件中,有人在飞机上做出自我牺牲,有人自愿重返烟熏火炙、摇摇欲坠的大楼去救助他人,他们行为的伟大无可比拟。

这一英雄行为已经记录下来,留与后人。自此之后,会有更多的书籍和电影涌现出来,更加详细地展现罹难者和第一时间反应人的生活与不幸。国家不会忘记这些人的恩情。

抛开政治与"9·11"之后周一早晨关于"谁本该知道什么"的推诿责难不谈,"9·11"事件与卷入其中的人显示了人类怜悯与仁爱的真正精神。那些遇难者、幸存者、救助者以及善后清理工作的人都是真正的英雄。我们向他们致敬。

是什么成就了他们

2001年9月11日,世界突然之间改变了,人们会记得那天他们身在何处,在做什么。在恐怖的死亡与混乱之间,有很多人冒着生命危险去救助别人,这给他们自己与国家带来了莫大的荣光。

> 无论怎么看,他们都是英雄。

美国东海岸的清晨近乎完美,可好景不长。与本·拉登和基地恐怖组织有关联的劫机者已经登上了4架飞机,准备把飞机当成制导导弹来打击美国本土的目标。那时,机场安检十分松懈,机上乘客没有完全登记在案。所有4架飞机都飞往加利福尼亚,因此劫机者可以确保满载燃油的飞机给预定目标最大的创伤。

3架飞机几乎同时起飞。在升空不久,劫机者就开始行动了,他们用偷偷带上来的小刀制服了机组人员,并且威胁说,如果乘客不配合,他们就用炸弹炸掉飞机。每架飞机上至少有一名劫机者接受过驾机训练,但没有接受过着陆训练(后来证明也无必要)。劫机者关闭了飞机的应答器,开始寻找目标。

美国东部时间早上8点46分,美国航空第11次航班撞上了纽约世贸中心北塔的北面。当时,美国当局和媒体认为是意外事故。但他们的观点很快转变了,因为第2架飞机,

media thought it was an accident. That view changed when a second airliner, United Airlines Flight 175, hit the South Tower of the World Trade Center only 15 minutes later. American Airlines Flight 77 crashed into the west wall of the Pentagon in Washington, D. C., at 9:37 a.m. Finally, the fourth plane, United Flight 93, crashed into an empty field in Somerset County, Pennsylvania, at 10:03 a.m.

The planes hit the upper floors of the World Trade Center towers, effectively dooming almost everyone above the crash zone. Victims below the crash zone faced fire, heavy smoke, nonfunctioning communications and blocked stairwells when trying to escape the buildings. Many of them helped free other people and were able to locate passable stairwells.

While the victims were trying to make their way down, members of the New York City fire department, police department and Port Authority were climbing the towers to try to rescue any survivors. In many places, the victims and the rescuers passed each other on the stairwells. Many of the rescuers who survived believed they would not be able to save many victims, but were willing to risk their lives for anyone who might still be alive.

The rescuers would soon find themselves fleeing along with the victims. A halfhour from the time it was struck by the airliner, the South Tower collapsed from the damage caused by the crash. Victims and rescuers in the North Tower could hear and feel the collapse and realized they needed to escape while they still could. The rescuers were ordered to return to the ground, but several lingered trying to find any victims that could make it downstairs. Thirty minutes after the South Tower collapsed, the North Tower fell, killing or trapping anyone left in the structure, as well as heavily damaging nearby buildings. Even though some victims and rescuers were recovered by search teams who risked their lives going over the still unstable rubble, overall, 2,800 people were dead or missing, including fire fighters and police officers and everyone onboard the airliners.

At the same time rescuers, both inside and outside the damaged Pentagon, were trying to pull people out of the flames and smoke of the collapsed portion of the building. Professional firefighters took over the rescue operations, but not after many people were safely removed from the building by their co-workers. The collapsed section of the building claimed 189 lives, including all of the passengers and crew of the airliner.

Meanwhile, the final act of the tragedy was taking place in the skies over Pennsylvania. United Flight 93 would have been the fourth airliner to be guided into a target, but, due to heavy traffic, did not depart Newark International Airport until almost 45 minutes past its scheduled time. The plane was bound for San Francisco, California.

This delayed the takeover of the airliner by the hijackers to the point where news of the World Trade Center and Pentagon attacks was making its impact. Flight controllers sent out a warning to all flights to beware of cockpit intrusion. The pilot of Flight 93 tried to confirm the message when controllers suddenly heard the sounds of a fight and screams from the cockpit. After a few minutes, an Arabicsounding voice told passengers to remain calm, there was a bomb on board and they were returning to the airport. In reality, the plane was making a slow turn to the south and east to get to its intended target, believed to have been the U.S. Capitol in Washington.

Two hijackers remained at the front of the plane and herded the passengers and remaining flight crew to the back. Passengers now had an opportunity to use cell phones to call family and friends and realized what their probable fate was going to be. Several of the

即联合航空175次航班15分钟后撞上了世贸中心的南塔。美国航空77次航班在9点37分撞向了华盛顿特区五角大楼的西墙。最后,第4架飞机联合航空93次航班于10点03分在宾夕法尼亚州的萨默塞特县的旷野坠毁。

　　飞机击中了世贸中心高塔的上半部分,这就注定了身在撞击区以上区域中的人的命运。而撞击区以下的人在逃生时,则面临着大火、浓烟、通讯中断、楼梯通道堵塞等种种考验。很多人帮助解救其他人,寻找可通行的通道。

　　当受难者在逃生的时候,纽约消防局、警察局和港务局人员正爬上危楼去搜救幸存者。很多地方,受害者和救援人员在通道中迎面而过。很多幸存下来的救援人员认为他们根本救不了很多受害者,但依然愿意冒着生命危险去搜救每个可能还活着的人。

　　救援人员不久发现自己在和受害者一起逃生。在遭受第一架飞机撞击半小时后,世贸中心南塔轰然倒塌。北塔中的受害人和救援人员能够听到并感受到坍塌,他们意识到应该趁着还有机会赶快逃生。救援人员被命令回到地面,但有一些迟迟不肯撤离,他们试图寻找能够设法下楼的受害者。南塔倒塌之后30分钟,北塔也猝然倾颓,断壁残垣掩埋或困住了每一个尚在楼中的人,还严重毁坏了邻近建筑。有些搜救队冒着生命危险在尚不稳定的废墟中救出了一些受害者和救援人员,但仍然有2800人死亡或失踪,其中包括消防队员、警员和机上所有人员。

　　同时,五角大楼的坍塌部分大火熊熊、浓烟滚滚,大楼内外的救援人员尽力地把受害者从烟火中拖出来。专业消防队员承担起了救援任务,但还没有等很多人一起逃脱,灾难就发生了。五角大楼的倒塌部分夺去了189人的生命,包括机上所有乘客和机组人员。

　　与此同时,在宾夕法尼亚的上空,最后的悲剧也发生了。联合航空第93次班机本来可能作为第4件制导武器击向目标。但由于航班繁忙,比预定时间晚了45分钟才离开纽沃克国际机场,飞往加利福尼亚的洛杉矶。

　　这就延误了劫机者劫持飞机的时间,恰好世贸中心和五角大楼受到袭击的消息开始产生了影响。机场控制中心向所有的航班发出了警告,要警惕驾驶舱入侵。就在第93次航班的飞行员试图确认这一消息时,控制中心的人员突然听到驾驶舱传来打斗和喊叫声。几分钟后,有个操阿拉伯口音的男子告诉乘客保持镇静,机上有炸弹,他们正返回机场。实际上,飞机正慢慢转向南方和东部来寻找既定目标,而这一目标据信就是华盛顿的美国国会大厦。

　　两名劫机犯在飞机前部,把乘客和剩下的机组人员驱赶到后部。乘客现在有机会用手机给家人和朋友打电话,他们意识到了自己可能的命运。其中有几个开始谋划夺回飞

passengers now started making plans to attempt to retake the plane. Many of them were larger than the hijackers and were even trained in martial arts. It is believed they discussed using a serving cart as a shield and improvised weapons, including carafes of boiling water.

The passengers made their move on the hijackers, forcing the two left in the cabin to retreat into the cockpit. Later, the recovered black box voice recorder would show the hijackers discussing whether to fight back or crash the airplane. Just when it sounded like the passengers were breaking through the cockpit door, one of the hijackers yelled, "Allahu akbar"(God is Great) and the recording cuts out.

The plane dove straight into the ground, impacting at almost 600 miles per hour and creating a crater 115 feet deep. The only remains of the plane were small bits of debris scattered around the area. None of the passengers survived.

America changed forever after September 11, 2001. All planes were grounded for several days, the military was instructed to shoot down any unauthorized air flights and the economy took a hard hit. The United States would eventually strike back by overthrowing the Taliban regime (believed to have aided al-Qaida) in Afghanistan. But it should never be forgotten that the first heroes of 9/11 were ordinary men and women who rose to the occasion under extraordinary danger.

The Legacy of the 9/11 Heroes

The sacrifice of the heroes of 9/11 was an inspiration to a country in a state of shock. Their bravery showed that whether a trained professional or an average person, Americans were willing to put their lives on the line to help others in danger.

The country has expressed its debt of gratitude to the 9/11 victims, rescuers and passengers of United Flight 93. Memorials to the heroes include the Flight 93 Memorial in Shanksville, Pennsylvania, and the soon-to-be-completed Pentagon memorial.

As upsetting and devastating as the actual day of September 11th, the trauma and confusion continue more than five years after the event as the city and people of New York (as well as the rest of the country) struggle with what should be done to the site of the World Trade Center as a memorial to the victims. At the same time, the Port Authority of New York and New Jersey, which owns the land and the buildings of the entire World Trade Center complex (recall that there are more than just the two major towers), wants to replace the lost buildings with a complex that is both sensitive and economically viable.

In addition, the families of the victims (many of whom were never recovered from the rubble for proper burial) have equally strong opinions as to whether the site has been cleared of human remains. (As late as 2006, new efforts were made to recover victims.) To say the least, the tension and disagreements as to what the future will hold both for rebuilding and for a permanent memorial are fever-pitch. Everyone has a view on the matter.

The Lower Manhattan Development Corporation (LMDC) began a worldwide competition to design the World Trade Center Memorial in April of 2003. It would turn out to be one of the largest public design contests ever, generating competing ideas from all 50 states and 93 countries. By January of 2004, LMDC's selection committee had chosen the entry by Michael Arad and Peter Walker, Reflecting Absence, as the winning

机。他们很多人比劫机者更为彪悍,甚至接受过功夫训练。据信,他们讨论准备使用服务手推车作为盾牌,并讨论了应急武器,包括大瓶的开水。

乘客开始对劫机者采取了行动,迫使留在舱中的两名劫机者退到了驾驶舱中。后来,飞机黑匣子的录音表明,劫机者开始讨论是还击还是坠毁飞机。听起来的情况是这样,乘客们冲进了驾驶舱,其中的一名劫机者喊道"上帝万岁",至此,录音戛然而止。

飞机以接近600英里的时速直接俯冲到地面,撞出了一个115英尺深的巨坑。飞机仅存的残骸是散落在坠毁地带的碎片。没有乘客幸存。

2001年9月11日之后,美国永远改变了。所有飞机都停飞数天,军方被通知要击落任何未经授权的空中飞行物,而美国经济也遭受了沉重打击。美国最终开始反击,它推翻了阿富汗的塔利班政权(据信曾协助本·拉登)。但永远不要忘记,"9·11"事件的第一批英雄是普通人,是他们在危难之中挺身而出,不辱使命。

"9·11"英雄的遗产

"9·11"英雄的牺牲对处在震惊之中的美国而言是一种激励。他们的勇气表明,无论是受过训练的专业人员还是普通百姓,美国人愿意冒生命危险去救助处于危机中的人们。

国家向"9·11"事件的受难者、救援人员和第93次航班的乘客表达了感激之情。英雄纪念碑包括设在宾夕法尼亚州的山克斯威尔的93次航班纪念碑和即将落成的五角大楼纪念碑。

9月11日灾难深重,让人心痛,事件过去五年之后,人们依然怀有创伤和迷惑,纽约市和市民(还有其他美国人)一直在思考并争论在世贸中心的旧址要建造什么,作为对受难者的纪念。同时,纽约拥有世贸中心建筑和土地的纽约和新泽西港务局想用新的建筑取代毁坏的建筑,它不仅要反应敏感,而且经济上要切实可行。

另外,很多受难者(其中很多人没有从废墟中找到,无法体面地埋葬)的家属对旧址中的遗骸是否已经清除也有自己强烈的看法。(到2006年,寻找受难者工作又进行了新的努力。)关于旧址将来是否要重建还是作为永久纪念的对立与分歧已达到了白热化的程度。对此人们各持己见,莫衷一是。

2003年4月,曼哈顿开发公司开始在全球范围内展开竞赛,征集世贸中心纪念地的设计方案。这将是史上最大的公众设计竞赛,它激发了美国50个州和全球93个国家设计者的创意。到2004年1月,曼哈顿开发公司的遴选委员会选中了迈克尔·阿拉德和皮特·沃克尔的参赛作品"反省缺失"。该设计中有两个巨大而幽深的水池(就在原南北

---

bid. The design includes two large recessed pools of water (the original footprint of the twin towers); the pools will be about 30 feet below ground level. On street level will be a park with informal and formal groupings of trees.

The names of the victims in the memorial will be displayed in front of a curtain of water. Once again controversy arose as to what order the names were to be listed and how they were to be listed. An underground passageway will lead to an alcove where memorials can take place; included will be a large stone container to hold all the unidentified remains of victims. A Tribute of Light was the first, permanent feature put in place as a memorial. Not only the memorial itself but the costs associated with the project have come under a great deal of criticism—one estimate makes it as high as $1 billion, a figure rejected by the mayor of New York and others involved in raising the staggering sums needed to build the memorial.

In addition to the memorial, a series of new buildings is planned for the site—four commercial buildings and one residential building are shown in the final designs. (Assuming anything about this reconstruction project can ever be final with ongoing disputes by the public, the governor, the developer and architects on what the area should look like.) Work has begun on the first building, World Trade Center Tower 1 or, more familiarly, the Freedom Tower. The height of the building is estimated to be over 1,300 feet, although the final number is not confirmed and may not be until much later in construction. The cost of this one building alone is estimated at $2.6 billion, with the State of New York one of the largest tenants in the building, possibly occupying as much as one million square feet.

The Resources

Recent films on the events of 9/11 include *United 93* and *World Trade Center.* There have been many documentaries and made-for-television films on what happened that day, almost all available on video. You can find a variety of information by visiting *www. september11news.com.*

Many books have been written about the fateful day and the story of the heroes, including *The 9/11 Commission Report,* W.W. Norton, 2004; *The Puzzle of 9/11,* BookSurge Publishing, 2005; *The September 11 Photo Project,* Regan Books, 2002; *September 11: An Oral History,* Doubleday, 2002; and *One Nation: America Remembers September 11, 2001,* Brown, 2001.

双塔的地基),水池将低于地面30英尺。地上则会有一个公园,内植各种树木,成规则或不规则形状排列。

纪念碑上遇难者的名字将会在水幕上呈现。但围绕着名字按什么顺序排列以及如何呈现又有了不同的声音。一条地下通道会通向一个凉亭,凉亭中将安放纪念碑,届时将有一巨大石龛来盛放无法辨认的受难者的遗骨。"悼念之光"是首先到位的永久性纪念。不仅是纪念碑,而且整个与此相关的工程费用也受到了很多批评。有人估计总费用将高达10亿美元,这一数字让纽约市长和参与筹集业已滞后资金的人士不能接受。

除了纪念碑,在世贸双塔的原址计划还要建造一系列的新建筑,最终的设计包括四座商业建筑和一处居民楼。(如果关于重建工程的争论能最终尘埃落定的话,而目前公众、市长、开发商和建筑师对这些建筑以何种面貌出现还将争论不休。)第一座大楼世贸中心一号塔已经动工,而其"自由之塔"的名字更加广为人知。该塔高度虽未确认,或许不到建筑后期也无法得知,但据估计,其高度将达1300英尺。仅此一塔的建造费用就将高达26亿美元,占地面积可能高达1000 000万平方英尺,纽约州将是最大的租借方。

相关资源

关于"9·11"事件的电影有《93号航班》和《世贸中心》。关于当时发生的事情,已有很多纪录片和电视上播放的影片,而且都可以买到录像带。欲了解更多信息可访问www.september11news.com。

关于"9·11"和"9·11"英雄的书已有多部出版,如:《"9·11"任务报告》,诺顿出版社,2004;《"9·11"谜团》,书峰出版社,2005;《"9·11"图片集》,里甘出版社,2002;《"9·11":口述历史》,双日出版社,2002;以及《一个民族:美国永志"9·11"》,布朗出版社,2001。

One

Muhammad Ali, Boxer

Who He Is

In 1999, *Sports Illustrated* named Muhammad Ali Sportsman of the Century. Not Boxer of the Century. Sportsman of the Century. Not of the year. Not even of the decade. Of the century. He needs no further introduction. He is one of the greatest sports heroes in history. Period.

But it is not just because of these accolades that Ali is one of our heroes. In and out of the ring, he was our superhero: bold, confident, abrasive, opinionated, a man of conviction and a model for children and adults everywhere. There were times when we loved to hate him, but always we admired and respected him.

What Made the Man

Cassius Marcellus Clay Jr. was born on January 17, 1942, in Louisville, Kentucky to Odessa Grady Clay and Cassius Marcellus Clay Sr. His love affair with boxing began when he was 12 years old. His bicycle was stolen from in front of a department store. A very upset young Clay found a policeman, Joe Elsby Martin, Sr., coach of the Louisville city boxing program. Clay told Martin what had happened and that he wanted to whup whoever had stolen his bike. Martin was quick to respond that Clay should learn to fight if he really intended to whup someone. The 89-pound boy showed up at Louisville's Columbia Gym the very next day.

He started taking boxing lessons from Martin, who taught him the moves that would someday lead to his famous saying, "Float like a butterfly, sting like a bee."

From that fateful day in 1954, Clay approached boxing with a more determined and committed attitude than most of the other young fighters. He was victorious in 100 out of 108 matches during his amateur career, winning six Kentucky Golden Gloves championships, two National Golden Gloves championships and two National Amateur Athletic Union titles before he reached the age of 18. He also took home a light heavyweight gold medal from the 1960 Olympics in Rome, just a few months after he turned 18.

Throughout his professional boxing career, Clay never lost his sass. He was always running his mouth and was dubbed The Louisville Lip. Not only did he constantly dog his opponents, but he also spoke in front of the media, which was rare in the days when managers usually talked on behalf of their fighters. Clay's big mouth certainly threw some fighters off their game, as did his unorthodox heavyweight boxing style of relying on his reflexes and footwork rather than his hands to protect himself from getting hit in the face.

Clay's distinctive and unusual style of fighting would eventually lead him to become one

1

穆罕默德·阿里：拳击家

他是谁

1999年,《体育画报》授予穆罕默德·阿里"20世纪最伟大运动员"称号。请注意,是运动员,而不仅仅是拳击手;是整个20世纪,而不是短短10年。毋庸赘言,他当之无愧是历史上最伟大的运动英雄之一。

但是,阿里能成为我们的英雄并不仅仅是因为这些荣耀。无论拳台上下,他都是我们的超级英雄:果敢、自信、坚持己见、让人激动、信仰坚定,是孩子与成人共同的楷模。曾有一段时间,我们曾经憎恶他,但我们终究是要崇拜并尊敬他。

是什么成就了他

小凯西斯·马瑟卢斯·克雷于1942年1月17日生于肯塔基州路易斯维尔,其母为奥德萨·格雷蒂·克雷,其父为大凯西斯·马瑟卢斯·克雷。他12岁便与拳击结缘。一次,他的自行车在一家百货商店门前被偷走了。他十分伤心,找到了一个警察求助,警察名叫乔·埃尔斯比·马丁,是路易斯维尔拳击项目的教练。克雷向马丁诉说了原委,并说不管是谁偷了,他都想狠揍他一顿。马丁随即说,如果要揍人,必须先学习如何战斗。第二天,这个体重89磅的小孩子就出现在了路易斯维尔的哥伦比亚体育场。

他师从马丁学习拳击,学习攻防技巧,也因此有了他的名言:"像蝴蝶一样飞舞,像蜜蜂一样蜇人。"

从1954年那个重要的日子开始,克雷就以一种比其他大多年轻的拳击手更为坚定和虔诚的态度对待拳击。做业余选手时,他参加了108场比赛,赢了100场。18岁之前,他就6次获得肯塔基州金拳套冠军,2次获得全美金拳套冠军,2次获得全美业余运动联盟拳击冠军。他还获得过1960年在罗马举行的奥运会次重量级的金牌,而就在几个月前,他刚满18岁。

在他的整个职业拳击生涯中,他总是口无遮拦。他总是不住嘴,因此被冠以"路易斯维尔嘴巴"的绰号。他不仅让他的对手大感头疼,在媒体面前,他也总是滔滔不绝,这在当时并不多见,因为当时一般都是经纪人为拳手代言。克雷的大嘴巴也把很多人扫下了拳台,正如他出乎常规的重量级拳击风格一样:他靠习惯反应和步法而不是靠双拳来避免被对方击中面部。

克雷的拳击风格鲜明、有别传统,终于成了历史上最杰出的拳击手。他于1960年10

of the best, if not the best, heavyweight boxers of all time. He won his first professional fight on October 29, 1960, in Louisville, and, from 1960 to 1963, his record was 19-0, with 15 knockouts. In 1964, Clay was the No. 1 contender for Sonny Liston's title. He beat Liston in the seventh round and shocked the world even further by announcing the next day that he had joined the Nation of Islam and changed his name to Cassius X. Soon after, Elijah Muhammad, the leader of the Nation, gave Clay his true Islamic name: Muhammad Ali.

In 1975, Ali converted from the Nation of Islam to orthodox Sunni Islam and won what many of his fans felt should have been his last fight before retirement. He fought Joe Frazier on October 1 in Quezon City, Philippines, and won by a technical knockout after 14 rounds, when Frazier's trainer refused to let him continue fighting. The fight, coined The Thrilla in Manila, became the fifth Ali match to be named Fight of the Year by Ring Magazine.

Ali finally retired permanently after he lost a 10-round unanimous decision to Trevor Berbick on December 11, 1980, in the Bahamas. He left the world of professional boxing with a career record of 56 wins (37 by knockout) and 5 losses.

The Legacy of the Man

After Ali's retirement, he was diagnosed with Parkinson's syndrome in the early 1980s. Doctors argued about whether or not his symptoms had been caused by boxing and he was finally diagnosed with Pugilistic Parkinson's syndrome, a variation of the disease that plagues professional boxers due to receiving multiple blows to the head.

Ali has managed to accomplish much since stepping out of the boxing ring. In practicing his Islamic duty of carrying out good deeds, he has donated millions of dollars to organizations and disadvantaged people of all religious denominations. He has also been involved in work that is political and moral at the same time. He went to Iraq in 1990 to meet with Saddam Hussein and was able to negotiate the release of 15 hostages. He also asked the U.S. government and its people to come to the aid of the refugees in Rwanda. It has been estimated that Ali has helped to feed more than 22 million people who are afflicted by hunger.

On November 19, 2005, the doors of the $60 million nonprofit Muhammad Ali Center opened in downtown Louisville. The center not only showcases Ali's boxing memorabilia but also promotes the themes of peace, respect, social responsibility and personal growth. In addition, he has received the following awards:

○ Ellis Island Medal of Honor (1986)
○ United Nations Messenger of Peace Award (1998)
○ BBC Sports Personality of the Century Award (1999)
○ Living Legend Award, Library of Congress (2000)
○ Presidential Medal of Freedom (2005)

Amongst all his activities, boxing has always remained an important part of Ali's life. According to the documentary *When We Were Kings*, when asked about whether he had regrets about boxing because of the disorder he developed, Ali said that if he had not become a boxer, he would still be a painter in Louisville. But Muhammad Ali remains a boxer at heart, and he will remain in the hearts of others throughout the world long after he is gone.

月29日在路易斯维尔获得了他职业生涯的首场胜利；从1960到1963年，他的战绩是19战全胜，其中15次击倒对手。1964年，克雷成了桑尼·利斯顿金腰带的头号挑战者。他在第7回合击垮了对手。而更让世人震惊的是他第2天宣布已经加入一伊斯兰国家，并把名字改成了凯西斯·埃克斯。不久之后，穆罕默德总统给了他真正的伊斯兰名字：穆罕默德·阿里。

1975年，阿里转向了正统的逊尼派伊斯兰教，同时，他赢了一场拳赛，而这场拳赛在阿里的拥护者看来本应该是他离开拳台的谢幕之战。10月1日，阿里在菲律宾的奎松城再次与弗雷泽对决，他在14回合之后技术性击倒了弗雷泽，而弗雷泽的教练拒绝再让他打下去。这场被称作"马尼拉激战"的拳赛是阿里第5次被《拳台》杂志誉为年度大战的拳赛。

1980年12月11日，阿里在巴哈马一场10回合的较量中无争议地输给了伯比克，之后他永远退出了拳坛，其职业战绩是56胜（其中37次击倒对手）5负。

他的遗产

阿里退出拳坛后，在上世纪80年代初被检查出患有帕金森综合征。医生对他的病症是否因拳击引起争论不休。他最终被确诊上了帕金森拳击综合征。该病是帕金森综合征的一种，它常常困扰着很多职业拳手，其原因是他们的头部遭受了过多的击打。

告别拳击生涯后，阿里通过不懈的努力取得了非凡的成就。他恪守伊斯兰教义，爱善行良，向各个信仰的宗教组织和贫穷的个人捐献了几百万美元。他同时还参与了兼有政治与道义的工作。1990年他身赴伊拉克与萨达姆·侯赛因会晤，成功说服萨达姆释放了15名人质。他还要求美国政府和人民帮助卢旺达的难民。据估计，阿里已经帮助2 200万饱受饥饿困扰的人填饱过肚子。

2005年11月19日，位于路易斯维尔市中心投资高达6 000万美元的非营利性的穆罕默德·阿里中心的大门正式开放。该中心不仅展示了阿里的职业大事，同时还弘扬和平、尊重、社会责任与个人成长等主题。此外，阿里还获得了以下荣誉：

- 埃利斯岛荣誉奖章(1986)
- 联合国和平使者奖(1998)
- BBC世纪体育人物奖(1999)
- 国会图书馆"活着的传奇人物"奖(2000)
- 总统自由勋章(2005)

在阿里的所有活动中，拳击一直占有非常重要的地位。在一部名为《我们曾是王者》的纪录片中，阿里被问及他是否因现在的疾病而后悔从事拳击时，阿里说如果他没有成为拳击手，他仍然会是路易斯维尔的一个画家。但阿里内心永远把自己当成一个拳击手，在他离开之后，他依然会活在人们的心中。

Two

Lance Edward Armstrong, Cyclist

Who He Is

Lance Armstrong is an American who achieved the longest-ever string of victories in the Tour de France—a European(read French) sporting event. Further, he became a world hero not just for his athletic supremacy, but because he overcame cancer and still managed to maintain his supremacy in an enormously competitive and grueling sport.

Naturally, heroes are haunted with rumors and innuendos—in this case, about whether Armstrong ever used performance-enhancing drugs. No one, the critics said, could be this good and this successful without something on the side to help his performance. To date, nothing has been proved, but the rumors continue to dent his reputation.

However, as a cancer survivor, he is an indisputable hero, continuing to drive home the importance of early detection of cancer and the need for a cure. He is the poster child of survivors and inspires millions who are victims of the disease.

What Made the Man

He was born on September 17, 1971, in Plano, Texas, where he was raised by his mother (his father left the family soon after Lance's birth). Armstrong developed an interest in being a triathlete and developed his own training regimen by riding his bike while anchored in a pool.

By age 13, he was competing regularly in triathlons, but it soon became clear that his talent and interest centered on cycling. It was during this time that Armstrong demonstrated his single-minded devotion to succeed. His success as an amateur and his obvious talent as a cyclist led to the Junior National Cycling Team inviting Armstrong to train with them. He petitioned his high school to allow him to take 42 days off from school during the final semester of his senior year to take part in the training. The school refused, so Armstrong simply left school and started training with the team.

Armstrong continued to compete as an amateur and won the U.S. Amateur Championships in 1991 and finished fourteenth in the Olympics road race. Armstrong believed that this success indicated cycling was the sport for him, and he turned professional in 1992. He started inauspiciously by finishing last in his first pro race, the Classica San Sebastian—the only time that Armstrong would finish that far back in a professional race.

He earned his first major professional victory the next year by winning the World Cycling Championship in Oslo, Norway. The king of Norway invited Armstrong to an audience, based on his impressive performance. Armstrong would only appear if the invitation included his mother. The king quickly agreed.

After tasting his first professional victory, Armstrong turned his attention to the prestigious Tour de France. He joined Team Motorola and won stages in the 1993 and 1995 races. At this time, he also won several individual races, including the 1992 and 1996 Tour du Pont, considered the United States' premier cycling race.

2

朗斯·埃德沃德·阿姆斯特朗：
自行车手

他是谁

朗斯·阿姆斯特朗是环法自行车赛中创造连胜纪录的自行车手。他成为世人的英雄并不仅仅是因为他的运动才能，而是因为他战胜了癌症，同时又在高强度而又竞争残酷的自行车运动中维持了他的运动天赋。

英雄总被流言飞语包围着，这很自然。而关于阿姆斯特朗的流言就是他是否服用了提高比赛成绩的药物。批评者说，如果不服用兴奋剂，没有人可以这么出色，取得这么大的成功。但到目前为止，无法证明他服用了兴奋剂，但谣言却一直在侵蚀着他的声誉。

然而，作为一个癌症幸存者，他毫无疑问是个英雄，他一直强调早期发现并治疗癌症的重要性。他就是数百万癌症患者的标杆，他激励着他们去与病魔战斗。

是什么成就了他

阿姆斯特朗于 1971 年 9 月 17 日生于得克萨斯州的普莱诺，是母亲把他抚养大的（父亲在朗斯出生不久就离了这个家庭）。阿姆斯特朗对铁人三项感兴趣，并且发明了在水池中蹬自行车这种独特的强化训练方法。

13 岁时，他定期参加铁人三项赛，但不久他就发现，自己的天赋和兴趣主要是在自行车上。这段时期，阿姆斯特朗一心想要获得成功。由于他作为业余选手获得的成功与他的自行车运动天赋，全美少年自行车队邀请他一起训练。他向自己的中学申请最后学年期末请假 42 天以便能参加训练，但学校不同意，阿姆斯特朗只能退学，由此开始了随队训练。

阿姆斯特朗继续作为业余选手参赛，他获得了 1991 年美国业余自行车赛的冠军，后来获得了奥运会公路自行车赛的第 14 名。他相信，他的成功表明自行车运动正是适合自己的运动，于是次年就成了一名职业选手。但他在自己的第一场职业比赛中获得了最后一名，这似乎不是好兆头，但这是阿姆斯特朗唯一一次在职业比赛中落后这么多。

1993 年他获得了在挪威首都奥斯陆举行的世界自行车锦标赛的冠军。挪威国王因为他令人印象深刻的表现而准备接见他，而阿姆斯特朗说只有母亲同时受接见他才出席，国王很爽快地答应了。

首次尝到了职业胜利的滋味之后，阿姆斯特朗把注意力转向了著名的环法自行车赛。他加入了摩托罗拉自行车队，并获得 1993 与 1995 年多个分站赛冠军。在此期间，他还获得了其他一些比赛的胜利，包括 1992 年与 1996 年美国最重要的自行车赛事 Tour du Pont。

Armstrong briefly left the pro tour to take part in the 1996 Olympics, but was disappointed in his nonmedal performance. This perceived failure acted as an impetus, and he began training even harder with his eyes set now on the Tour de France.

However, this commitment to athletic success was shaken severely when, in October 1996, Armstrong was diagnosed with stage three testicular cancer. The cancer had metastasized and was spreading to his lungs and brain. Armstrong was given only a 40 percent chance of survival, but like his racing, he viewed his cancer as a challenge. His right testicle and a brain lesion were removed, and he received extensive chemotherapy. Armstrong recovered from the disease (his doctors would tell him later that his actual chances had been much smaller than 40 percent).

Even during his recovery, he kept his mind on racing and insisted on using a more radical form of chemotherapy that would have less long-term debilitating effects on his breathing.

Armstrong resumed training to race, but had been dropped by his team during his bout with cancer. In 1998, he joined the then-new U.S. Postal Service cycling team and quickly returned to form. He was now poised to make racing history by returning to the Tour de France. One of the more ironic side effects in Armstrong's chemotherapy is that the treatment caused some loss of muscle mass in his upper body. This proved to be a benefit to his racing, giving him more stamina in the grueling mountain portions of the Tour de France.

Armstrong won his first Tour de France in 1999. He would go on to win for the next 6 years, making him the only cyclist to win seven Tour de France races. What was even more remarkable is that in all but two of these races his lead-time was 6 minutes or more ahead of the second place finisher. In 2005, he won his last Tour de France, as a member of the Discovery Channel Pro Cycling Team.

Armstrong's seven consecutive Tour de France victories rank as one of the greatest sporting achievements in history. Many racers and cycling enthusiasts have tried to explain his success: He focused mainly on the Tour de France (some criticized him for ignoring other racing events); he trained almost all year on the same type of terrain as that offered by the Tour de France; his mental preparation and strategy planning for the race were just as intense as his physical training; his unusual aerobic stamina allowed him to maintain a higher cadence at a lower gear on his bicycle; and he improved the cooperation between his sponsors, suppliers and cycling team.

A controversial aspect of Armstrong's success is the recurring allegations that he used performance-enhancing drugs. These allegations surfaced in a book, L.A. Confidential: Les Secrets de Lance Armstrong, which quoted fellow riders saying that they and Armstrong had used such drugs. Sections of the book appeared in the British newspaper, The Sunday Times; Armstrong sued for libel and the case was settled out of court with the newspaper printing an apology.

In 2005, the French sports newspaper, L'Equipe, printed that Armstrong had been using drugs since 1999. In 2006, the French newspaper, Le Monde, reported claims that Armstrong had been using performance-enhancing drugs based on a deposition taken as part of a lawsuit that Armstrong filed against SCA Promotions. Later the same year, The

阿姆斯特朗曾短暂地离开职业赛场,参加了 1996 年的亚特兰大奥运会,但他没有斩获奖牌,这让他大失所望。这一失败成了他的动力,他于是着眼环法,更加刻苦地训练。

然而,他对运动成功的虔诚被动摇了。1996 年的 10 月份,他被检查出患有睾丸癌第三期,癌细胞已经转移并扩散到肺部和大脑。医生说他只有 40% 的生存希望,但他把病魔看成了挑战,一如他看待自行车运动一样。他的右侧睾丸和大脑病灶部分被切除了。他接受了大强度的化疗。最终,阿姆斯特朗从癌症中康复了(他的医生后来告诉他说,实际上生存概率远远不到 40%)。

即使在康复期,阿姆斯特朗也念念不忘自行车比赛。他坚持要用一种更为极端的化疗方法以减缓该病对呼吸的远期负面影响。

阿姆斯特朗又恢复了训练,但他在与癌症作斗争时被摩托罗拉车队抛弃了。1998 年,他加入了当时刚刚成立的美国邮政自行车队,很快恢复了状态。他重返环法,并即将创造历史。具有讽刺意味的是,阿姆斯特朗接受化疗的副作用之一就是他的上身肌肉堆积消失了不少,这有助于比赛,让他在环法的山地赛段有了更强的耐力。

阿姆斯特朗于 1999 年获得了首个环法自行车赛的冠军。接下来又连续 6 年获得总冠军,使他成为唯一取得环法自行车赛七连冠的车手。更不可思议的是,除了两次,他至少领先第 2 名 6 分钟或者更多的时间。2005 年,他为探索频道职业自行车队效力,并获得了他自己最后一次环法自行车赛冠军。

阿姆斯特朗的环法自行车赛七连冠成为历史上最伟大的体育成就之一。很多自行车选手和自行车迷解释了他成功的原因:他着眼环法(有些人批评他忽视其他比赛);几乎长年在跟环法自行车赛相类似的山地赛道训练;训练刻苦,心理与战术准备与体能训练都很充分;有氧运动耐力非同寻常,使他在自行车低挡时能保持更快的节奏;促进了赞助商、供应商以及自行车队之间的配合。

阿姆斯特朗的成功具有争议性的一面是关于他服用禁药的猜测。这些猜度在一本名为《阿姆斯特朗绝密:环法赛中的秘密》的书中首先浮出水面。该书援引了阿姆斯特朗队友的话说他们自己与阿姆斯特朗都服用了禁药。该书的部分章节甚至还出现在了英国的《星期日时报》上。阿姆斯特朗控告报纸诽谤,最终双方达成庭外和解,时报刊登了道歉声明。

2005 年,法国一家体育报《队报》刊登文章说阿姆斯特朗自从 1999 年开始就一直使用禁药。2006 年,法国报纸《世界报》报道基于阿姆斯特朗控告美国 SCA 保险公司时

Los Angeles Times reviewed the facts of the SCA trial and also other allegations against Armstrong.

These later reports were unimportant, because in 2005, after investigations by cycling authorities into the questionable drug-testing methodology of LNDD, the French national anti-doping laboratory, Armstrong was exonerated of illegal drug use based on the improper handling and testing of athletes' urine samples.

During this period, Armstrong and Kristin, his wife of 6 years, filed for divorce in 2005. It was revealed that Armstrong had developed a relationship with rock star Sheryl Crow in 2003. The news of their relationship was made public in 2005, but the couple split in 2006.

Armstrong retired from competitive racing after his seventh Tour de France victory in 2005. He remains active in promoting cycling, cancer awareness and physical fitness. His achievements expanded American awareness of the Tour de France and helped make the race an even more high-profile international sporting event.

The Legacy of the Man

Lance Armstrong will always be remembered as one of the greatest athletes of all time, but his reputation may always have a cloud over it because of the drug-use allegations. Armstrong continues to defend himself in public and on his Website.

Armstrong remains an advocate for cancer awareness and early treatment of the disease. He sits on the President's Anti-Cancer Panel, and founded the Lance Armstrong Foundation for fighting cancer. One of its fundraising methods was to sell rubber band Livestrong bracelets. The bracelets became very popular during the 2005 Tour de France.

There have also been rumors that Armstrong may enter politics in his native Texas. Lately, he has been making statements that sound like he might be open to eventually running for office.

The Resources

You can find almost all you want to know about Lance Armstrong, including daily postings from him, on his Website at *www.lancearmstrong.com* or from the Lance Armstrong Foundation at *www.livestrong.org.*

You can read about Armstrong in his autobiographies, *It's Not About the Bike: My Journey Back to Life,* Berkeley Trade, 2001, and *Every Second Counts,* Broadway, 2004; *Lance Armstrong's War,* Harper Press, 2006; *23 Days in France: Inside Lance Armstrong's Record-Breaking Tour de France Victory,* De Capo Press, 2005; and *No Mountain High Enough: Raising Lance Raising Me,* Broadway, 2005.

所用的证词,宣称其一直使用违禁药物。同年晚些时候,《洛杉矶时报》回顾了 SCA 一案的事实以及不利于阿姆斯特朗的种种猜测。

此后的种种猜测已无关紧要,因为 2005 年,自行车运动官员调查了受到质疑的法国国家反兴奋剂实验室的检测手段,该实验室处理与检测尿样方法不恰当,因此,阿姆斯特朗就免除了服用兴奋剂的怀疑。

2005 年,阿姆斯特朗和结婚 6 年的妻子克里斯汀离婚。原来,他在 2003 年即与摇滚歌星谢丽尔·克劳发生了恋情。两人的恋情 2005 年曝光,但两人在 2006 年旋即分道扬镳。

阿姆斯特朗于 2005 年获得第 7 次环法自行车赛总冠军之后宣布退出职业比赛。此后,他一直积极地推动自行车运动,提升对癌症的认识,宣传强健体魄。他的成就拓展了美国人对环法自行车赛的认识,让该项目成为非常著名的国际体育赛事。

阿姆斯特朗的遗产

阿姆斯特朗作为史上最伟大的运动员之一将永远被人们记住,但由于对他是否服用禁药有种种猜度,他的名声簿單上了一层阴影。他不断地在公开场合和自己的网站上为自己辩护。

阿姆斯特朗一直在宣传,号召人们认识并及早治疗癌症。他是总统预防癌症小组的成员,并成立了旨在抗击癌症的阿姆斯特朗基金会。其筹集资金的方法之一就是出售"勇敢生活"橡胶带手镯。这种手镯在 2005 年环法自行车赛中十分流行。

还有谣言说,阿姆斯特朗欲进入得克萨斯州政界。后来,他还发表了声明,听起来他似乎要参加竞选。

相关资源

在阿姆斯特朗的个人网站 www.lancearmstrong.com 或者阿姆斯特朗基金会的网站 www.livestrong.org 上,读者几乎可以找到自己感兴趣的任何关于他信息。

你可以通过阅读阿姆斯特朗的自传去了解他,他的自传有《与自行车无关:我的回生之路》,伯克利贸易出版社,2001;《生命在于每一秒》,百老汇出版社,2004;《朗斯·阿姆斯特朗的战争》,哈帕出版社,2006;《在法国的 23 天:透视阿姆斯特朗的环法七连冠》,德·凯卜出版社,2005;以及《没有无法逾越的高山》,百老汇出版社,2005。

Three

Neil Alden Armstrong, Astronaut

Who He Is

Heroes are often the stuff of firsts—to navigate around the world, to fly across the Atlantic, to climb Mt. Everest and dozens more. Certainly any individual with the courage to land on the moon with what could be described, at best, as very tentative technology and planning, has to be one of our heroes.

The wonder of Neil Armstrong is the complete lack of ego and ambition beyond his desire to be part of the NASA mission and program. Whether active or retired, he accepted the admiration of millions with the humility of a child. His right kind of stuff can hardly be underestimated, and his superior intellectual ability helped NASA with an ambitious and politically sensitive mission to the moon.

How does history understand this seemingly aloof man? Gently, kindly and with a great deal of affection and appreciation, the nation has chosen to honor a truly modest hero who seemingly does not wish to be honored or lauded.

What Made the Man

Neil Armstrong was the first man to walk on the moon, and the phrase he uttered when he first stepped foot on the surface of Tranquility Base has become part of the English folklore. What many people do not know is that Armstrong, unlike most of his fellow astronauts, was a civilian and not part of the military.

Armstrong is from America's heartland, born on August 5, 1930, in his home at Wapakoneta, Ohio. His father was an Ohio government employee and the family moved frequently during Armstrong's childhood. Popular history has Armstrong taking his first plane ride at age six, where he reportedly fell in love with aviation. By the time he was 15, he was saving his money to take flying lessons and progressed rapidly in a number of aircraft to get his pilot's license.

In 1957, Armstrong made his first flight in a rocket plane, thought at the time to be the natural transition to real spacecraft. He would end up flying the Bell X-1B and the North American X-15. He had the usual mishaps for a test pilot, but managed to walk away from all of them. Most of his fellow test pilots valued his engineering ability and one said that "he had a mind that absorbed things like a sponge". Other old-guard pilots, such as Chuck Yeager, thought that the engineers approached flying too mechanically and that they got into trouble because they did not have a real feel for flying.

As Armstrong was coming to the end of his test pilot career. The Mercury program was already sending up astronauts in solo flights and NASA was now planning the next

3

尼尔·阿尔顿·阿姆斯特朗：宇航员

他是谁

英雄通常敢为天下先,如环球航行,飞越大西洋,登上珠穆朗玛峰以及其他种种壮举。毫无疑问,以一种尝试性的技术和计划且有勇气在月球着陆的任何人都可以成为我们的英雄。

尼尔·阿姆斯特朗的不同寻常之处就是他除了想成为美国航空航天局项目的一员之外,并没有私心和野心。主动也好,内敛也罢,他以儿童般的谦卑接受了数百万人的崇拜。他的壮举不可低估,而他的出色才智帮助美国航空航天局完成了一个大胆而且十分具有政治敏感性的登月活动。

历史怎样了解这个似乎置身事外的人呢?美国人带着喜爱与欣赏,选择了去给这个谦卑的英雄以荣耀,而他本人,似乎并不希望拥有这些荣耀和光环。

是什么成就了他

尼尔·阿姆斯特朗是第一个在月球表面行走的人,他踏上月球平静的表面时说的第一句话已经成为人们耳熟能详的一句英文掌故。但不为众人所知的是,阿姆斯特朗与其他宇航员不一样,他不是军人,而是平民。

阿姆斯特朗于 1930 年 8 月 5 日生于美国中部俄亥俄州的瓦帕克尼塔市。他的父亲是俄亥俄州政府的雇员,在阿姆斯特朗的童年时期,他们经常搬家。人们所熟知的历史是阿姆斯特朗 6 岁首次坐飞机,据报道,他当时就喜欢上了航天飞行。15 岁时,他攒钱参加了飞行培训,进步迅速,并获得了飞行执照。

1957 年,阿姆斯特朗首次进行了火箭式飞机飞行,而火箭式飞机当时被认为是向真正航天器的自然过渡。他后来开始试飞贝尔 X-1B 和北美 X-15 型航天飞机。他经历了其他试飞员都会遭遇的灾祸,但他总是能化险为夷。他的同行都非常看重他的工程技术才能,其中一人说"他的大脑像海绵一样吸收知识"。有些保守的飞行员,如查克·伊格则认为工程师们对待飞行过于机械,对飞行没有真正的情感,因此容易导致麻烦。

阿姆斯特朗即将结束自己试飞员生涯的时候,美国在军备竞赛中被前苏联赶超。美国的水星计划已经在单独飞行中发送宇航员,美国航空航天局计划下一步用双子星飞船

phase with two astronauts flying on Gemini flights.

By now Gemini was almost over and the Apollo program was starting. Following orbital flights of the three-person Apollo spacecraft and two trips to the moon, NASA was ready to attempt a landing with Apollo 11. Armstrong was made commander of the spacecraft, and, after deciding Armstrong had a more matter-of-fact personality, NASA named him to be the first man to walk on the moon. Apollo 11 blasted off on July 17, 1969, with Armstrong, lunar module pilot Buzz Aldrin and command module pilot Michael Armstrong.

Apollo 11 landed on the moon on July 20. A few hours after landing, Armstrong descended the LEM ladder to the lunar surface and said, "That's one small step for a man, one giant leap for mankind." Radio static masked the "a" from the first part of the statement, although Armstrong admitted later he sometimes omitted syllables when he spoke. He said he had come up with the statement only while waiting to leave the LEM for the moon.

The Legacy of the Man

Neil Armstrong was the perfect man in the perfect place at the perfect time. His nonsense approach to life and his work stood in stark contrast to the drama of walking on the moon and made the event even more exciting. He will go down in history, along with people like Charles Lindbergh, as a man who defined an era.

把两名宇航员送往太空。

现在,双子星项目已经结束,阿波罗计划启动了。在经过搭载 3 人进行轨道飞行并 2 次抵达月球之后,美国航空航天局准备用阿波罗 11 号飞船在月球着陆。阿姆斯特朗成了飞船的指挥,考虑到他更具实事求是的个性,因此航天局指派他首次在月球行走。1969 年 7 月 17 日,阿波罗 11 号搭载着阿姆斯特朗,月球舱驾驶员巴兹·阿尔德林和指挥舱飞行员迈克尔·阿姆斯特朗呼啸升空。

阿波罗 11 号于 7 月 20 日在月球表面着陆。着陆几个小时之后,阿姆斯特朗走下登月舱着陆梯,他说道:"这是我个人的一小步,但却是人类的一大步。"无线电干扰掩盖了前半句中的不定冠词"a"(因此前半句就成了"这是人类的一小步"),他后来承认自己说话时经常省略一些音节。他说他在等待出舱登陆的时候想出了这么一句话。

他的遗产

尼尔·阿姆斯特朗是在恰当的时间合适的地点出现的合适人选。他对待生活和工作的一丝不苟的态度与他月球行走的戏剧性事件形成了强烈的对比,让事情变得更有意思。他将与查尔斯·林白等人一样,作为一个时代的标记将在历史上永远留名。

Four

Lucille Desiree Ball, Comedian

Who She Is

Imagine our hero, not as a great thinker, statesman or author, but as an absolutely zany woman with wacky ideas, putting herself and her friend, Ethel, in ridiculous situations, and having the entire nation love her for it!

What Made the Woman

Despite her public image as a screwball, Lucille Ball was a shrewd performer who knew exactly what she wanted. She was a successful producer who, along with husband Desi Arnaz, formed Desilu Productions, one of the most profitable independent production companies in Hollywood history.

However, it was a long and often frustrating journey that led to the fame and notoriety that her comic skills merited. Ball was born on August 6, 1911, in Jamestown, New York, to Henry Durrell Ball and Desiree DeDe Eve Hunt. She was always proud of her family background, which traced itself back to the earliest American colonists(through her father's side, she was related to George Washington).

Ball's father's job as a telephone lineman sent the family to live all over the country. Henry Ball died in 1915 from typhoid fever and Ball and her brother Fred were raised by her working mother and grandparents. Her grandfather loved the theater and took the family to vaudeville shows. He saw how much the girl enjoyed them and encouraged her to get into performing.

During this period, Ball developed her reputation as a hard worker, helping to support the family while still finding time to perform in plays for the local Elks Club and her high school. She even staged her own production of Charley's Aunt, Encouraged by her experiences and her grandfather, Ball, in 1926, enrolled at the John Murray Anderson American Academy of Dramatic Art in Manhattan.

> She was counseled not to continue with her acting career because of what her teachers perceived as a terminal case of shyness.

Ball persevered in her dream by returning to New York and getting intermittent work as a chorus girl and model (at one point, she was the Chesterfield cigarette girl). After suffering a series of hirings and firings on Broadway, she got an uncredited role as one of the Goldwyn girls for movie producer Samuel Goldwyn. This led to her going out to Hollywood, where her first picture was *Roman Scandals*, co-starring Eddie Cantor.

After a brief stint on Broadway and appearances in a couple of films, Ball returned to television in the successful *The Lucy Show* and later *Here's Lucy*, which ran until 1974. Despite her reputation, Ball's career went nowhere fast after she left television. A film

露西·德斯瑞·鲍尔：喜剧演员

她是谁

很难想象我们的英雄并不是一位思想家、政治家或者作家，而是一个充满了稀奇古怪点子的古灵精怪女人，她让自己和她的朋友伊塞尔处在极其滑稽的情境之中，让全美国人因此而喜爱她！

是什么成就了她

尽管鲍尔的公众形象有些许古怪，但她是一个伶俐的演员，知道自己想要什么。她还是一位成功的节目制作人，她与丈夫德西·阿纳兹一起创办了德西露制作公司，这公司成了好莱坞历史上最赚钱的独立制作公司之一。

然而，在她的喜剧才华带给她名望之前，她走过了漫长而又曲折的道路。鲍尔于 1911 年 8 月 6 日出生于纽约的詹姆斯顿，其父为亨利·杜莱尔·鲍尔，其母是德斯瑞·亨特。她一直为自己的家庭背景感到骄傲，因为她的家族可以追溯到北美殖民地时期（父亲这边与乔治·华盛顿有关系）。

鲍尔的父亲是电话架线员，因此在全美搬来搬去。他于 1915 年死于伤寒，因此鲍尔和她的胞弟由工作的母亲和外祖父母抚养长大。她的外祖父喜欢看戏，经常带全家去看杂耍表演。他发现鲍尔非常喜欢这些表演，于是就鼓励她进入表演行当。

在此期间，鲍尔逐渐成就了其勤恳工作、帮助家人的名声，她同时找时间在当地的驼鹿俱乐部和她的中学进行演出。她甚至还把她自己制作的《查雷的阿姨》搬上了舞台。鲍尔在外祖父和已取得成绩的鼓励下，于 1926 年进入了坐落于曼哈顿的约翰·穆里·安德森美国戏剧艺术学院。

有人建议她不要再继续她的表演事业，因为她的老师认为她十分害羞，难以改变。

鲍尔坚持自己的梦想，重回纽约，偶尔担当合唱团成员或者模特（有一段时间，她做了切斯特菲尔德香烟女郎）。她在百老汇经历了几次被炒的遭遇，后来获得了一个无名的小角色，成了电影制作商塞缪尔·古德温的古德温女郎之一，这让她走向了好莱坞。在好莱坞，她的第一部电影是和艾迪·坎特尔共同主演的《罗马丑闻》。

鲍尔曾在百老汇和几部电影中短暂出现，在《露西秀》和《露西来了》大获成功之后，她回归电视，而这两部电视剧也一直放映到 1974 年。尽管她名声显赫，但在她最初离开

version of the musical *Mame* was a flop, and her attempt at returning to television also ended in failure.

Ball made only a few personal appearances during her last years. She died from a ruptured aorta following open-heart surgery on April 26, 1989.

The Legacy of the Woman

During her heyday on television, Lucille Ball was called the queen of comedy, and few would dispute it. Her shows were undeniably hilarious. She proved almost single-handedly that women could be just as funny as men.

Ball also broke the gender barrier for women on the business side of Hollywood. After her divorce from Arnaz, she ran Desilu Productions, later selling it to Gulf-Western for a very healthy profit.

This success was not without its price. Her marriage to Arnaz was never smooth. Her children said she was a cold and controlling mother who had few friends in show business. However, her audience cared little about this, and her lovable screwball in *I Love Lucy* is still seen every day on some television station or cable network.

电视后事业却毫无进展。电影版的音乐剧《妈咪》实为败笔,而她重返电视的努力也以失败告终。

在她最后的岁月里,她仅仅露过几次面。1989 年 4 月 26 日,她在做打开心脏手术之后,死于动脉破裂。

她的遗产

在鲍尔电视生涯的辉煌时期,她被称作喜剧女皇,对此无人质疑。她演出的喜剧总是十分滑稽热闹。她几乎单枪匹马证明了女性也可以和男性一样滑稽可笑。

鲍尔还打破了好莱坞商业圈内的性别障碍。与阿纳兹离婚之后,她独立经营德西露制片公司,后来又卖给了伽尔夫·沃斯顿,利润不菲。

但是这些成功并非没有代价。她与阿纳兹的婚姻从不平坦。她的子女曾说她作为母亲性格冷漠、控制欲强,在演艺界没几个朋友。然而,观众并不在乎,她在《我爱露西》中扮演的可爱的怪癖人仍然在有些电视台和有线网播放。

Five

Barbara Roberts "Barbie", Toy Superstar

Who She Is

Can a toy be a hero? It can if it brings joy and entertainment to generations of girls. It can if it becomes a household name, an icon, a symbol of this, a symbol of that, a symbol of what take your pick. And a toy is certainly a hero if, instead of referring to the toy as it, you feel more comfortable saying she. And she is Barbie.

She is a hero because she is a best friend, a companion, a confidante. She can be shared with others or played with alone. But most importantly, she is always there when needed—a reflection of ourselves and our times.

What Made the Doll

The Barbie doll is one of the most popular toys in history. From her creation in the late 1950s, there have been millions of the dolls and accessories sold. The toy is still much sought after by collectors and little girls of all ages and is a $1.9 billion a year industry. Mattel, which markets the doll, says that approximately three Barbie dolls are sold every second.

Mattel had very humble beginnings before the Barbie doll helped make it one of the most successful toy companies in the world. It was founded by Ruth and Elliot Handler. The company slowly grew into a more structured business and by the mid-1950s, the Handlers found themselves with less and less input in the creative side of the company.

Handler noticed that her daughter, Barbara, did not play with baby dolls. She preferred to play with dolls that were adults. Handler realized that there was a hole in the market, a hole that could be filled with an adult doll. She was excited about what she believed was a sure-fire success and took the idea to the executives who were now running Mattel. They quickly brushed aside Handler's adult doll idea as being impractical, and too expensive to create and market.

Handler was still convinced she had a great idea, but was unsure how to proceed. Finally, during a visit to Germany with her daughter, Barbara, Handler found in a German shop window a doll called the Bild Lilli. The doll, made to look like an adult, was the type of doll that Handler had in mind, and she bought three of them (one for her daughter and two to take back to the naysayers at Mattel).

Doing her research, Handler found out the Bild Lilli doll was based on a popular character that appeared in a comic strip for the German newspaper, Die Bild-Zeitung. The character was a society girl with a head for fashion. She knew what she wanted and was not above manipulating men to get it. Ironically, the doll was originally marketed in 1955 to men and was sold in tobacco shops. It eventually caught on with children, who dressed her in outfits that were sold separately (a brilliant marketing move that vastly increased profits). The doll became very popular and was exported overseas, including the United States.

Handler finally persuaded Mattel to let her change the doll and showcase it at various

5

芭芭拉·罗伯特和"芭比娃娃"：
玩具超级巨星

她是谁

　　玩具能成为英雄吗？如果它能给一代又一代的女孩带来快乐和愉悦，它就能成为英雄。如果它已是家喻户晓，成为一种典型形象或者某种象征，它就是英雄。如果你不用"它"来称呼一个玩具，而用"她"来称呼，这让你感到更为恰当，那么这个玩具就是英雄。而"她"就是芭比娃娃。

　　她成了英雄，是因为她是挚友、是伙伴、是知己。她可以与人分享，也可为一人所有。但更重要的是，我们需要她时，她就在眼前，她反映了我们自身以及我们的时代。

是什么成就了她

　　芭比娃娃是历史上最受欢迎的玩具之一。从 20 世纪 50年代末她诞生之日起，已经有千百万芭比娃娃及其饰件被售出。时至今日，该玩具仍然受到众多收藏家和女孩们的青睐，每年产值高达 19 亿美元。负责营销芭比娃娃的迈特尔公司说，每秒大约有 3 只芭比娃娃售出。

　　迈特尔公司起步卑微，而芭比娃娃让它成了全球最成功的玩具公司之一。该公司的创始人是鲁斯和艾略特·汉德勒。公司逐渐走向拘谨，到了上个世纪 50 年代中期，汉德勒发现公司的创造性江河日下。

　　汉德勒发现自己的女儿芭芭拉并不玩儿童形的娃娃，而是更喜欢成人化的娃娃。她意识到市场存在着空白，而这个空白正可以由成人娃娃来填补。她认为这注定会成功，自己十分兴奋，于是就把这个点子提交给了当时掌管迈特尔的行政高管。他们立刻否决了她的点子，认为该点子不现实，并且开拓新市场代价高昂。

　　汉德勒仍然坚信她的创意十分绝妙，但苦于不知道如何推行。最后，在她与女儿的一次德国之旅中，她发现一家商店的橱窗里摆着一个娃娃叫比尔德·丽丽。这个娃娃更像成人，正是汉德勒脑中的那个形象，于是买了 3 只回去(一只给女儿，另外两只带给公司里该创意的否决人)。

　　作了一番研究之后，汉德勒发现丽丽娃娃是基于在德国报纸上经常出现的一个喜剧漫画中的人物。她是一个交际花，对时尚十分敏感。她知道自己想要什么，而不是通过操纵男人而去得到它。具有讽刺意味的是，该玩具最初于 1955 年在烟店里面向男性出售。它最终吸引了儿童的注意，孩子们另外买一些配套服饰让丽丽穿上(营销手段堪称绝妙，利润因此大涨)。该玩具变得十分红火并出口到海外，包括美国。

　　汉德勒最终说服了迈特尔公司让她对该娃娃进行改造，并在各个玩具展销会上亮相

toy shows to gauge its popularity. She worked with engineer Jack Ryan to revamp the concept of the doll into what is still the basic design. She gave it the all-American name of Barbie after her daughter Barbara.

Barbie made her official debut at the New York International Toy Fair on March 9, 1959 (which is listed as Barbie's official birth date). Interest was immediately strong and Mattel finally realized they had a potential blockbuster on their hands. In 1964, to cement their hold on the market, they purchased the rights to the rival Bild Lilli doll and discontinued its manufacture.

The original Barbie dolls were either blonde or brunette and wore a zebra-striped swimsuit and signature topknot ponytail. Later Barbies would feature other hairstyles and hair colors. The genius of the marketing of the doll was to feature it as a teenage fashion model so that girls could be encouraged to build up a large wardrobe of clothing and accessories. Much of the early Barbie wardrobe was designed by Mattel fashion designer Charlotte Johnson, who took her inspiration from the New York and Paris fashion runways.

During the next few years, Mattel would introduce the Ken doll as her boyfriend and Skipper, her little sister doll. Other dolls would come and go from Barbie's circle. During the 1960s, the Mattel designers gave Barbie bendable legs (making it easier for owners to change her clothes) and a redesigned face that had Barbie look straight ahead at attention. She was also given the power of speech.

In 1980, Mattel stretched the kinds
of the doll even more by creating Black Barbie and
Hispanic Barbie dolls.

Not only did Mattel make billions of dollars on sales of the actual dolls and clothing, the company also profited by the creation of Barbie cars, boats, workplaces and the famous Barbie Dream House. All these items were sold separately. Barbie also started to take on very different personas based on the type of occupation with which the individual doll was associated. Over the years, these occupations included astronaut, gymnast, soldier, doctor, paleontologist, rock star, firefighter, McDonald's employee and even a candidate for president.

Barbie, her friends, fashions and accessories quickly moved from being toys to being much-sought-after collectible items. Mattel has estimated there are over 100,000 avid collectors who buy as many as 20 Barbie dolls every year. The collectors created special terms for the merchandise they were purchasing and trading, including collector edition (designed for collectors 14 and older), customized(designed exclusively for specific retailers), limited edition(collector editions made in limited quantities), vintage and modern(dolls made before and after 1972, respectively) and OOAK(one-of-a-kind dolls that have been modified by an individual artist).

The doll has her own biography that identifies her as Barbara Millicent Roberts. She was born in Willows, Wisconsin, and attended Willows High School and Manhattan International High School in New York. Besides her friends, she has 38 known pets, including cats, dogs, horses, pandas, lion cubs and a zebra. Some of the world's top designers have created outfits for the doll. Barbie has also become a multimedia presence, featured in books, cartoon videos, music and video games.

以检验它的受欢迎程度。她和工程师杰克·瑞恩一道,把丽丽娃娃的设计理念融入了新娃娃的设计当中,时至今日,其基本设计仍然不变。汉德勒根据自己女儿芭芭拉的名字把新玩具命名为芭比娃娃。

芭比娃娃于1959年3月9日(这一天被定为芭比娃娃的生日)在纽约国际玩具展销会上正式亮相。人们对芭比娃娃立刻产生了浓厚的兴趣,迈特尔公司终于意识到他们的手上掌握了一张潜在的王牌。1964年,为了巩固对市场的主宰地位,迈特尔公司收购了其竞争对手丽丽的所有权,并终止了生产丽丽娃娃。

最初的芭比娃娃要么一头浅黑色头发,要么是棕色头发,身着斑马纹的泳装和标志性的马尾辫。后来芭比娃娃有了其他的发型和发色。营销芭比娃娃的绝妙策略就是让她成为少女时装模特,这样一来,女孩们就会去拥有一整橱的衣服和饰品。早期芭比衣柜的衣物大部分是迈特尔公司的服装设计师夏洛特·约翰森设计的,她的设计灵感来自于纽约和巴黎的时装走秀。

在接下来的几年,迈特尔推出了芭比娃娃的男朋友肯,妹妹丝吉帕。围绕着芭比娃娃有为数不少的其他娃娃出现又消失。在20世纪60年代,迈特尔公司的设计人员给芭比装上了可以弯曲的双腿(便于主人为其换衣服),并重新设计了芭比的脸庞,让她凝神望向前方。她还拥有了语音功能。

1980年,迈特尔延伸了芭比娃娃的种类,创造出了黑人芭比和拉美芭比娃娃。

迈特尔公司靠销售芭比娃娃和衣服赚了数十亿美元,而且,它还创造了芭比汽车,芭比轮船,芭比工作间以及著名的芭比梦想小屋,利润不菲。所有这些商品都是独立销售。根据与每个具体的娃娃相联系的职业不同,芭比娃娃也因此具有了不同的个性。历数下来,这些职业包括宇航员、体操运动员、法官、士兵、医生、古生物学家、摇滚歌星、消防员、麦克唐纳的雇员,甚至还有总统候选人。

芭比娃娃、她的朋友以及相关饰件很快从玩具变成了颇受欢迎的收藏品。迈特尔曾估计目前有10万痴迷的收藏者平均每年会购买芭比娃娃多达20件。收藏者为他们购买和交易的商品创造了一些专门术语,如收藏版(为14岁及以上收藏者设计)、定制版(专为特定零售商设计)、限量版(数量非常有限的收藏版)、珍藏版(1972年之前)、现代版(1972年之后)、OOAK版(每类一个,该类曾被某一艺术家修改过)。

芭比娃娃有自己的传记,传记中她的全名是芭芭拉·米丽塞特·罗伯茨。她生于威斯康星州的威劳斯市,曾在威劳斯中学和纽约曼哈顿国际中学读书。除了朋友,她还有38个为人熟知的宠物,包括猫、狗、马、熊猫、幼狮和斑马等。世界很多顶尖的时装设计师为芭比娃娃设计过服装。芭比还出现在各种媒体中,如图书、卡通录像、音乐和电子游戏等。

The Legacy of the Doll

Fans of Barbie respond to criticism of how the doll represents life to a little girl by stressing the number and variety of occupations Barbie has done over the years. The critics believe that Barbie presents a type of body image that most girls will never achieve and could possibly lead to eating disorders. In addition, Barbie is seen as an example of Western materialism and is not popular in all countries of the world(especially in the Middle East).

Besides problems with the body image the doll presents, many critics have also pointed out that there is negative stereotyping associated with the doll—talking models that can only remark about going out and shopping for clothes. Mattel continued to respond to these critics and has recently widened the doll's waist and created more ethnically diverse versions.

Of course, anything as popular as Barbie was bound to create its own types of satire and parodies. A series of real-life Barbies were released with such names as Trailer Trash Barbie. The character was the subject of the song *Barbie Girl* by the Danish pop-group, and has been lampooned on *Saturday Night Live* and *The Tonight Show*. The doll, renamed Malibu Stacy, is Lisa's favorite toy on *The Simpsons*.

Despite the critics' use of Barbie as a derogatory name for a shallow female, Barbie's future seems secure. She is now on her own, having separated from Ken in 2004 (supposedly because he would not marry her) and still occupies a special place both in the hearts of little girls and on the shelves of collectors.

The Resources

Mattel has created a variety of videos and books based on Barbie and her friends, all of which are easily available. There are a variety of Websites for Barbie fans of all ages with *www.barbiecollector.com* being a particularly popular site.

Books about Barbie include *The Ultimate Barbie Doll Book: Identification and Price Guide,* Krause Publications, 2004; *The Story of Barbie Doll,* Collector Books, 1999; *The Barbie Chronicles: A Living Doll Turns Forty,* Touchstone, 1999; and *The Collector's Encyclopedia of Barbie Dolls,* Collector Books, 1984.

她的遗产

批评的声音认为芭比娃娃代表了小女孩的生活,但其忠实粉丝进行了回应,他们强调芭比娃娃所先后拥有的职业数量和种类很多。批评者认为芭比娃娃代表的身体形象是大多女孩永远无法达到的,并且很可能导致女孩子们的饮食问题。另外,芭比被视作西方物质主义的一个例证,并不是在每一个国家都受欢迎(在中东国家尤其不受欢迎)。

除了芭比娃娃身体形象所代表的问题之外,很多批评者还指出芭比娃娃容易让人产生一个负面的固定思维:认为语音芭比娃娃只是会说出去和买衣服。迈特尔公司对这些批评做出了反应,他们最近让芭比娃娃的腰变得更粗了一点,并创造出了适合各个不同道德标准的版本。

任何如芭比娃娃一样受欢迎的东西注定会产生出自己的嘲讽和仿拟。有一些真人芭比娃娃出现了,如崔乐·特莱施·芭比。该人物是丹麦流行乐队组合的歌曲《芭比女孩》的主角,并在《周六晚直播》与《今夜好戏》中被嘲讽了一通。该玩具在《辛普森一家》中更名为麦丽布·斯德西,是丽莎的最爱。

尽管批评者经常把芭比的名字当成浅薄女性的代称,但芭比娃娃似乎前程无忧。她2004 年与男朋友肯分手,现在恢复单身了(或许是因为肯不会娶她)。今天,芭比娃娃在小女孩的心里和收藏者的收藏架上依然占有特殊的位置。

相关资源

迈特尔公司根据芭比和她的朋友创造了各种录像以及书籍,都很容易买到。芭比娃娃的各个年龄层次的粉丝建立了不少网站,其中 www.barbiecollector.com 尤其受欢迎。

关于芭比娃娃的书有《终极芭比娃娃全攻略:辨认与价格》,克劳瑟出版社,2004;《芭比娃娃的故事》,收藏家出版社,1999;《芭比大事记:小玩具 40 年》,塔奇斯通出版社,1999;《芭比娃娃收藏家宝鉴》,收藏家出版社,1984。

Six

The Beatles, Musicians

Who They Are

Not all the greatest heroes of the last 50 years come with moral or political gravitas; some are simply people whose creativity and style continue to influence each successive generation. And who could have imagined the worldwide impact of a rock band that was actually just one of countless bands who crossed the pond from Britain to the United States in the 1960s? Who could have anticipated the effect of their music on generations to follow? Who could have appreciated their style and sound in the context of a wider cultural revolution? Who could have predicted the longevity of their careers both together and individually? Absolutely no one could have thought they would be so influential for so long.

The Beatles were controversial in their time—both when they first appeared on the scene and later when they were seen as embracing a lifestyle of drugs and countercultural social and political views. But now they are so mainstream that Paul McCartney has even performed during the halftime show of the Super Bowl!

What Made the Men

Among the Fab Four, John Lennon is generally credited as being the one who formed the band and was most instrumental in its development as a group. It was Lennon who found Paul McCartney and, later, George Harrison. This core group, along with a variety of drummers and other musicians that came and went, haunted the small venues of Liverpool looking for work. The band had a variety of names—almost as many as there were drummers. The Quarrymen became Johnny and the Moondogs, which begot Long John and the Beatles, which begot the Silver Beatles which begot the Beat Brothers, which finally, thankfully, begot the Beatles!

Their first hit, Love Me Do, finally brought the Beatles to national prominence.

It took almost a year and a half before the same song became
a hit in the United States, because most record producers
and radio station managers were convinced that British
groups would not appeal to American audiences!

That first hit was followed by a succession of hits in Britain—*please, Please Me, From Me to You* and *She Loves You* just for starters. Some believe that the reason American teenagers did not embrace the Beatles for so long was...their haircuts! It just was not what real rockers looked like! In the beginning, not even Dick Clark's famous *American Bandstand* could crack American audiences' indifference to this new English band.

6

披头士乐队：
音乐家

他们是谁

　　并不是过去五十年里所有最伟大的英雄们在道德或政治立场上都很严肃庄重。有些人仅仅是因为他们的创造性和独特的风格不断影响着一代又一代人。今天，谁会想到一个摇滚乐队在世界范围内的影响有如此之大，而在 20 世纪 60 年代，他们也只不过是无数支从英国跨越大西洋来到美国的普通乐队中的一员。有谁，能预料他们的音乐对未来数代人的影响是何等巨大？有谁，在更广阔的文化变革的语境下，能够欣赏他们音乐的风格与旋律？又有谁，能够预言他们音乐生涯的长短，无论是他们组队合作或是成员独自单飞？他们持久而巨大的影响力让许多人始料不及。

　　在他们的年代里，"披头士乐队"一直备受争议。这从他们第一次登台亮相就开始了。并且后来人们发现他们既沾染毒品，又有反文化、反社会、反政治的思想观念。然而现在，他们成了主流中的主流：保罗·麦卡特尼甚至在"超级碗"比赛中场的时候现身表演！

是什么成就了他们

　　在这超级 4 人组里，约翰·列侬一直被认为是这支队的创始者，并且在乐队的发展中发挥了关键性作用。列侬慧眼识英才，先后发掘了保罗·麦卡特尼和乔治·哈里森。当时利物浦的一些不甚知名的场馆里经常需要举办音乐演出，于是这 3 位核心人物，再加上经常更换的一些鼓手和其他音乐家们，便成了那些地方的"常客"。从"采石工人"、"约尼和月亮狗"、"永远的约翰和披头士"、"银色披头士乐队"、再到"披头士兄弟"，乐队数易其名，幸运的是，乐队的名字最终被定为"披头士乐队"！

　　"披头士乐队"组建完毕，发行了第一张单曲《爱我吧》。这首歌曲也如愿以偿地使他们成为一支全英伦知名的乐队。

　　然而过了将近一年半的时间，这首歌才在美国红起来，因为大多数美国唱片制作商和电台经理们认为英国乐队对美国听众根本没什么吸引力！

　　《爱我吧》热卖之后，以《请让我愉快》，《从我到你》，《她爱你》作为先锋，"披头士乐队"在英国又接连出了好几首十分受欢迎的歌曲。有些人认为美国青年人之所以很长一段时间不接受"披头士乐队"，只因为一件事，即他们的发型！他们的发型根本不像一个真正摇滚歌手应有的发型！起初，即使迪克·克拉克主持的美国电视歌唱节目的"美国音乐台"也没能使观众们对这支新建的英国乐队敞开心扉。

It was Brian Epstein who came to the rescue; he arranged three gigs on the then-famous *Ed Sullivan Show*—a Sunday night staple that was watched by huge audiences. The show and the song *I Want to Hold Your Hand* were just the ticket—Beatlemania was on, and there would be no end to it. The song made it to No. 1 on the U.S. charts, and the Beatles never looked back.   Perhaps the best evidence of their irrefutable success came when they arrived at New York's JFK Airport to near-riotous mobs of fans.   The years 1964 and 1966 took the Beatles around the world,   going on tours throughout the United States, Australia and New Zealand, Japan and the Philippines.

The Legacy of the Men

The Beatles left not only a portfolio of some of the most creative and ingenious music from the midcentury but also a series of films—many of which were critical and financial successes. There seemed nothing that they could not do. And, yet, sometimes with success, there comes a degree of arrogance and a detachment from the people and events that propel a person to success.

Of course, all of this is clear in retrospect. On one trip to the Philippines, they snubbed the powers that be—and then had cause to regret it. The band found itself barely able to get to the airport safely. Every effort was made to threaten and harass them before leaving the country. Lennon general disregard for generally accepted beliefs and behavior, helped further estrange the group increasingly from its fan base.

So how do we think of our heroes after some 45 years? We think of them fondly, although at times with some confusion. However, we know for a fact that they remade music as we know it. What we do not know is why they could not have continued, why were the many strange sideshow activities necessary and how such mistrust could creep in. Was it because of all the money? Were the differences a matter of artistic temperament? We may never know for sure, but we will always have the music(and the movies) to comfort us.

可以说正是布莱恩·爱波斯坦改变了这种局面。他在当时著名的"苏利文剧场"安排了3场特约演出。"苏利文秀"是周日晚上一档主要的节目，有着非常多的观众。乐队的精彩表演以及那首雄踞排行榜首位的《我想握住你的手》成了"披头士乐队"在美国的"敲门砖"。从此，人们对"披头士乐队"的痴迷变得一发不可收拾。他们的成功是无可争议的，最好的证明也许就是当他们到达纽约肯尼迪国际机场的时候，狂热的歌迷们曾一度使场面近乎失控。1964年到1966年，"披头士乐队"进行了全球巡演，地点包括美国、澳大利亚、新西兰、日本和菲律宾。

他们的遗产

自上世纪中叶以来，"披头士乐队"不仅给我们带来了一些最具独创性的音乐，同时他们也拍摄了多部电影。这些电影不论在艺术上还是票房上大都取得了成功。他们似乎无所不能。然而，伴随他们成功而来的，是其他人的些许傲慢和几分漠然，以及足以使每个人都要发奋努力、收获成功的一些事件。

当然，今天我们回顾历史，一切都趋于明朗。在一次去菲律宾的旅途中，他们因冷落了某些势力集团而遭到了这帮人的报复：差一点未能安全到达机场。在离开菲律宾之前，乐队受到了形形色色的威胁与骚扰。列侬对人们普遍接受的信条和行为表示漠视，这些都导致了乐队进一步脱离了广大的歌迷。

45年后的今天，我们该如何怀念我们的英雄？我们依然深爱着他们，虽然有时候有些茫然。但是，我们清楚，他们曾经重新创造了我们今天所熟悉的音乐。我们不清楚的是，他们为什么不能继续走下去，为什么总是有这么多荒诞的小插曲，乐队内部的种种猜忌和不信任又是如何发生的。难道仅仅是金钱的原因吗？难道个人音乐风格上的差异关系到一个人的艺术气质？这些我们永远都不能确定，但是，我们总有他们的音乐(和电影)陪伴着我们，抚慰着我们的心灵。

Seven

Paul David(Bono) Hewson, Musician

Who He Is

How is it that an Irish rocker can influence presidents and popes, the rich, the powerful and the ordinary in such a profound way? Why is this man so very different from his contemporaries in music and entertainment? What has motivated this man to take a stand on one of the worst crises to hit the world in a thousand years?

If nothing else, we need more people like him; but at the very least, we should know more about him and what makes him respond with such righteous indignation to the misery and suffering in Africa.

What Made the Man

Of course, Bono is not really Bono, nor is he Bono Vox(his full nickname), but rather Paul David Hewson, born in Dublin into a mixed family (in this case, not racial, but religious—one parent was Catholic and the other Protestant). The young man was greatly influenced (as was some of his early music) by the premature death of his mother when he was 14 years old. It was in high school that the basis of his band, U2, was formed—but not until after the name went through a number of iterations, including Feedback and Hype.

U2 has continued to participate in great public works of charity through a series of live concerts, as well as maintaining a superb musical career that is both creative and well respected. They are only one of four bands ever featured on Time magazine, and Rolling Stone has continued to declare U2 to be one of the greatest bands in the history of rock and roll.

The Legacy of the Man

How do we understand this man, Bono? What makes him tick? At a time when so many celebrities spend their time and money on themselves and on small, insignificant projects that have little meaning beyond their personal interest, what makes a man like Bono respond so differently? Bono is first of all a Christian and takes that part of Christianity that says that you must take care of the children, the poor and the widowed very seriously.(He notes that Judaism and Islam also have the same charity-based tenets and that the three religions ought to make common cause for the sake of Africa.)

7

保罗·大卫·博诺·休森：
音乐家

他是谁

为什么一名爱尔兰摇滚乐手会对这么多人产生如此深刻的影响，且不论他是总统、教皇、富翁、有权势的人，还是普通民众？为什么在音乐和娱乐界，这个人会和他同时代的人有如此大的差别？当世界遭遇千年难遇的危难时，又是什么力量促使这个人为维护人类利益而奋斗？

我们需要更多像休森这样的人；至少我们应该了解他，了解是什么使他有这样的正义感去积极地帮助非洲那些受苦受难的人们。

是什么成就了他

当然，他的原名不是博诺，也不是博诺·沃克斯（这是他昵称全名），而是保罗·大卫·休森。他出生在都柏林一个"混合"家庭里面（不是种族混合，而是宗教信仰上的混合——父母一方信天主教，一方信新教）。母亲过早地离开了人世，这对年仅14岁的博诺产生了很大的影响（这可以从他早期的音乐中看出来）。上高中时，他的乐队 U2 的基础已经形成，但此前乐队的名字几经更改，如一度曾命名为"回首"和"刺激"。

U2 以一系列现场演唱会的形式继续参与到慈善公演当中。同时，他们的音乐生涯也得到了很好的发展，他们的音乐独具创新精神，得到了人们的尊敬。时至今日，仅有4支乐队登上《时代》杂志，而他们就是其中之一。而在滚石乐队的眼里，U2 永远是摇滚音乐史上最伟大的乐队之一。

他的遗产

我们怎么来评价博诺？是什么让他与众不同？当大多数名人将时间和金钱花在自己身上和一些意义甚微的事情上时，当这些事情完全出于个人兴趣而毫无意义可言时，到底是什么促使博诺这样的人有如此异于常人的举动？首先，博诺是个基督徒。基督教义说一个人必须加倍关心孩子、穷人和寡妇，博诺当然做到了。（他还说犹太教和伊斯兰教里也有同样关于慈善的信条，因此这三教应该同心协力为援助非洲做贡献。）

Eight

Warren Buffett, Businessman

Who He Is

To be among the top two or three richest people in the world invites heroic status. The amazing thing about Warren Buffett, however, is that he got rich not by being a robber baron or by founding some spectacular high-tech company to much public acclaim. Rather, he was an investor of quiet demeanor and habit (never did build that mega-mansion in Omaha) who viewed investing and business in the long term. Slowly and deliberately, he acquired company after company, which he folded into his holding organization, Berkshire Hathaway—the most expensive stock on the New York Stock Exchange.

What makes Warren Buffett a true hero is that he has given most of his money to charity. With one swipe of the pen, tens of billions of dollars went to a variety of good causes, mostly under the auspices of the Bill and Melinda Gates Foundation to be used in ways that will benefit the world.

He is our hero because he remains humble and retains a sense of humor, despite billions in wealth and enormous personal power and prestige. All would agree that this is a rare combination, considering the typical vast egos of the world's rich and famous!

What Made the Man

Buffett was born into an upper-middle-class family on August 30, 1930, in Omaha, Nebraska. His father, Howard, was a stockbroker and later would be a U.S. Congressman. Buffett had two sisters. His grandfather owned a grocery store in Omaha where both Warren and his friend Charlie Munger worked as boys. Munger would go on to be the president of Buffett's investment company, Berkshire Hathaway.

At an early age, Buffett was able to calculate columns of numbers in his head, a feat he still performs today. When he was 6 years old, he bought six-packs of Coca-Cola from his grandfather's store for 25 cents, then turned around and sold the bottles for a nickel each, giving him a profit of five cents.

Although Buffett was making good money delivering newspapers in high school and had no desire to go to college, his father urged him to attend the Wharton School at the University of Pennsylvania. After two years, Buffett was complaining that he knew more about business than his professors. His father was defeated for re-election and Buffett returned home, where he graduated from College of Business Administration at the University of Nebraska.

It was there that Buffett would meet the man who would have a major influence on his future career and success as an investor. By the 1940s, Ben Graham was considered one of the most influential investors in America. He had built his reputation on careful consideration of the market and purchasing stocks at such a low price that they presented a minimal risk. He wrote the groundbreaking book *Security Analysis*. Later, he would publish *The Intelligent Investor,* which made a huge impression on Buffett.

8

沃伦·巴菲特：
商人

他是谁

成为世界上最富有的两三个人中的一位很容易成为英雄。然而,令我们惊奇的是,沃伦·巴菲特不是靠偷盗致富的,也不是靠建立备受公众称赞的高科技公司而发家。他是位为人处世很低调的投资家(从来没有在奥马哈建豪宅),具有长远的投资和经商眼光。他以十分缓慢的速度但非常明确的目的收购了一家又一家公司,将这些公司纳入他的控股公司伯克希尔·哈撒韦公司,公司的股票是纽约证券交易所最昂贵的股票。

使沃伦·巴菲特成为一名真正的英雄的是,他将自己大部分的财产都捐给了慈善事业。只要大笔轻轻一挥,数百亿美元就被捐出去支持那些高尚的事业。这些钱大多是在"比尔及梅林达·盖茨基金会"的帮助下用以资助全世界的人们。

之所以把他当成我们的英雄,是因为虽然他有数十亿美元的个人财富以及巨大的权力和名望,但沃伦·巴菲特仍然保持着谦虚和幽默。我们都清楚沃伦·巴菲特身上这些品质都是极其难得的,特别是在那些名人和富翁们个人主义不断膨胀的今天。

是什么成就了他

1930年8月30日,巴菲特出生于内布拉斯加州奥马哈市一个中上层阶级的家庭里。他父亲霍华德是证券经纪人,后来成了国会议员。巴菲特有两个姐姐。他祖父在奥马哈拥有一家杂货店,沃伦和他的朋友查理·蒙加就在那儿打杂。后来蒙加成了巴菲特组建的伯克希尔·哈撒韦投资公司的主席。

巴菲特在很小的时候便能心算好几列数字,今天也是如此。在6岁时,巴菲特用25美分从他祖父的店里买了6瓶可口可乐,然后以每瓶5美分的价格转卖给其他人,这样自己赚了5美分。

虽然上中学时巴菲特从送报纸中获得了不错的收入,而且不想上大学,他的父亲却不断敦促他去宾夕法尼亚大学的沃顿商学院听课。上了两年的学之后,巴菲特不停地抱怨,说那儿的教授对商业的了解不如他多。当父亲在重新选举中失败之后,巴菲特便回家乡上学,后来从内布拉斯加大学工商管理学院毕业。

也就是在那儿,巴菲特遇到了一个人,他对巴菲特未来成为一名成功投资家产生了巨大影响。20世纪40年代,本·格雷厄姆被认为是美国最具有影响力的投资家之一。他的名声依赖于他对股市细致入微的考虑,所买入的低价股风险相当低。他出版了一本具有开拓性的书,《证券分析》。后来,他又出版了《做个智慧的投资人》,这本书对巴菲特产生了极大的影响。

Graham was one of Buffett's instructors at the Columbia Business College, and the young Buffett earned the only A+ Graham had ever given a student in his security analysis class. After graduation, Buffett applied for a position in the Graham & Newman investment brokerage. He was initially turned down and worked at his father's brokerage as a salesman. Graham finally hired him in 1954.

Buffett had been dating Susie Thompson in the early 1950s, and they married in 1952. They soon had a daughter, also named Susie. When Graham asked Buffett to work for him, the couple moved to suburban New York. Buffett worked tirelessly, analyzing Standard & Poor's (S&P) reports on possible investments. It was during this time that his and Graham's philosophies on investing began to diverge. Graham made his decisions solely on the basis of numbers. Buffett was more interested in how a company worked, what its business philosophy and management style were, and how it differed from the competition.

During this time, Buffett built up his own sizable funds for future investments. Graham retired from the business in 1956, and Buffett returned to Omaha to set up his own investment company. He established Buffett Associates, Ltd., and later Buffett Partnership Limited. Buffett ran all the partnerships out of his bedroom.

Buffett proved his ability by showing profits almost 50 times higher than the Dow. He soon found himself a millionaire and a father of three. Also at this time, he made an important professional decision when he hired Charlie Munger. The two shared a similar business philosophy, and Munger was instrumental in expanding Buffett Partnership.

> Buffett had purchased enough stock in an undervalued
> manufacturing company called Berkshire Hathaway that he
> was made a director. In 1967, he bought the whole company
> and made it into the largest holding company in the world.

Buffett's business philosophy was to take profits from the company and use it to acquire other businesses or buy stock in public companies.

Although Buffett's business life was thriving, his personal life was in disarray. His wife left him, but remained married to him, and set up her own apartment in San Francisco. Buffett was devastated, but he and Susie remained close, even taking annual vacations together. Eventually Susie would introduce Buffett to a waitress named Astrid Menks. She later moved in with Buffett, all with Susie's blessings.

By the 1970s, Buffett was considered one of the most talented investors in the country. During the decade of the 1980s, he started devoting more time to charitable efforts. He devised an innovative plan where each shareholder in his company would designate $2 for charitable giving from each Berkshire share. Eventually, Berkshire Hathaway was giving away millions of dollars each year, all to the shareholders' favorite causes.

The Buffett reputation for philanthropic giving reached new heights in 2006, when he announced that he would contribute 10 million Berkshire Hathaway Class B stocks to the Bill and Melinda Gates Foundation. At the time of the announcement, the stocks were worth almost $31 billion, making it the largest charitable contribution in history. At the same time, he also earmarked stock valued at almost $7 billion to the Susan Thompson Buffett Foundation(his wife had died in 2004) and foundations established by his children.

格雷厄姆是巴菲特在哥伦比亚商学院的导师之一。年轻的巴菲特是唯一一个在他的证券分析课上获得过"A+"的学生。毕业之后，巴菲特申请去"格雷厄姆·纽曼公司"任职。在一开始被拒绝之后，巴菲特便去了他父亲的交易部做股票经纪人。格雷厄姆最终在1954年雇用了他。

巴菲特和苏茜·汤姆森在20世纪50年代开始约会，两人于1952年结婚。不久，他们便有了个女儿，也叫苏茜。当格雷厄姆雇用了巴菲特之后，夫妇两人就搬到了纽约郊区。巴菲特工作起来不知疲倦，分析着"标准普尔"的报告以发掘可行的投资方案。在此期间，巴菲特和格雷厄姆的投资哲学发生了分歧。格雷厄姆的决策完全依赖于数字，而巴菲特则更感兴趣于公司的运作方式、经营哲学、管理方式及如何使公司在竞争中与众不同。

在这段时间里，巴菲特为他的未来投资积累了一大笔资金。1956年，格雷厄姆退休后，巴菲特就回到奥马哈建立了自己的投资公司。他先创建了"巴菲特有限公司"，后来又组建了"巴菲特合伙人有限公司"。巴菲特在自己的卧室里管理这些合伙关系。

巴菲特公司的利润几乎是道·琼斯的50倍。他的能力因此得到了证明。不久他便发现自己已是百万富翁，并有了3个孩子。同时在这个时候，他决定雇用查里·蒙加，这个决定十分重要，体现了专业的眼光。这两个人有着相似的经营哲学，蒙加在"巴菲特合伙人有限公司"的发展中起到了非常重要的作用。

由于购买了一家股值被低估的制造公司伯克希尔·哈撒韦公司足够多的股票，巴菲特成了这家公司的董事长。1967年，他买下了整个公司，并将其发展为世界上最大的控股公司。

巴菲特的经营哲学是，用本公司的利润收购其他企业，或购买其他上市公司的股票。

虽然巴菲特的生意很兴隆，但他的个人生活却是一团糟。虽然和妻子仍保持着婚姻关系，但他妻子早已离他而去，搬到了旧金山。尽管两人关系仍然很亲密，每年甚至一起去度假，但巴菲特依然因妻子离去而备受打击。最后，苏茜把巴菲特介绍给了一名叫阿斯特丽德·蒙克斯的女服务员。在苏茜的祝福下，她搬去和巴菲特生活在一起。

至20世纪70年代，巴菲特被认为是美国最有才华的投资家之一。在20世纪80年代的10年里，他把更多的时间花在了慈善事业上。他发明了一种很新颖的计划：公司的每位股东从"伯克希尔"股票中拿出2美元作慈善用。结果是，伯克希尔·哈撒韦公司每年捐出几百万美元为各个股东不同的慈善事业"埋单"。

2006年，巴菲特在慈善捐赠上的名声达到了新的高度。他宣布将"伯克希尔"公司1千万股B股捐给"比尔及梅林达·盖茨基金会"。在他宣布这个决定的时候，那些股票共值310亿美元，是慈善捐赠史上最大的一笔捐款。同时，他又将价值70亿美元的股票捐给了"苏珊·汤普森·巴菲特基金会"(他妻子于2004年过世)和他孩子们创办的一些基金会。

As he continues to operate the amazingly successful Berkshire Hathaway and pursue his charitable efforts, Buffett has made it clear that his children would not inherit any large amount of his estate. When asked about this, he answered in a way that summed up his business style: "I want to give my kids enough so they could feel that they could do anything, but not so much that they could do nothing."

The Legacy of the Man

Buffett's two most important legacies are his investment style and the management style he brings to companies he has acquired. As an investor he looks for companies that are in industries with good economic models. They should have upward earning trends with good and consistent margins, low debt-to-equity ratios, a high and consistent return on expenditures, a low maintenance cost of operations and retained earnings for growth, with prices that can be adjusted for inflation.

His management style keeps him from interfering in the running of the individual companies. Further, he is not involved in hiring and compensating top executives, and insists on careful capital management of the companies that make up his empire.

Buffett's public perception is of a successful man who mixes business with humor and is concerned with politics and the world around him. He can be a bit of a contradiction, supporting the Democratic Party, but also working as a financial adviser to the Republican Arnold Schwarzenegger during his successful run for California governor. His support of pro-choice groups has not sat well with antiabortion supporters. He is also a noted technophobe who does not even have an e-mail address. This lack of technical sophistication has not hurt his career, and in his middle 70s, Buffett is still considered one of the most successful investors in history.

The Resources

You can find out more about Warren Buffett and the holding company he created by visiting *www.berkshirehathaway.com*.

Books by and about Buffett include *The Warren Buffett Way*, Riley, 2004; *Buffett: The Making of an American Capitalist*, Main Street Books, 1996; and *Warren Buffett Speaks: Wit and Wisdom from the World's Greatest Investor*, Wiley, 1997.

巴菲特一面继续经营着极其成功的伯克希尔·哈撒韦公司，一面继续为慈善事业作贡献。同时，他坦言，自己的子女不会从他这儿继承到很多财产。当被问及原因时，他以总结自己经营风格的方式作了如下回答："我想留给我的孩子们足够多的东西，这样他们觉得自己可以去做任何事情，但不至于多到他们什么事情都不用去做"。

他的遗产

巴菲特两个最重要的遗产是他的投资风格和他为被他收购的公司所带来的管理方式。作为一名投资家，他在寻找行业里具有良好经济模式的公司。这些公司应该有向上盈利的趋势，保证良好而持续稳定的利润，较低的权益负债率，较高而稳定持续的投资回报，维持营运的较低成本，保持净增长收益，公司的股票价格必须能因通货膨胀做出相应的调整。

他的管理方式使他不会干扰每个子公司的运作。而且他也不参与雇用和补偿公司高层管理人员，他也不会要求构筑他商业王国的每个子公司必须谨慎小心地管理好公司的资金。

公众对巴菲特的印象是，一个将商业与幽默结合起来的成功人士，关心政治和时事。他有时候看上去可能有点矛盾。他支持民主党，但在共和党人阿诺·施瓦辛格成功竞选加州州长的过程中，他任其财务顾问。他因对主张堕胎是合法的群体表示支持而与反堕胎支持者们发生不和。他是个世人皆知的技术恐惧者，连电子邮箱都没有。对高技术知识的缺乏并没有影响他职业生涯的成功，即便在75岁左右的时候，巴菲特仍然被视为历史上最成功的投资家之一。

相关资源

你可以访问www.berkshirehathaway.com了解更多关于沃伦·巴菲特和他所创建的控股公司的信息。

巴菲特写的书和关于他本人的书主要有：《沃伦·巴菲特的方式》，瑞雷出版社，2004；《巴菲特：一个美国资本家的诞生》，主街出版社，1996；以及《沃伦·巴菲特如是说：世界上最伟大投资者的智慧》，韦利出版社，1997。

Nine

Cesar Chavez, Labor Organizer

Who He Is

In the early 1960s, based on his perceptions of the hardships borne by migrant workers, Chavez, along with fellow activist Dolores Huerta, founded the National Farm Workers Association, which eventually became the United Farm Workers (UFW). Chavez and the UFW used various means to alert Americans to the plight of the migrant farmworker. However, their most famous achievement was a series of boycotts of farm products produced by nonunion workers. These boycotts brought the UFW and Chavez national attention.

What Made the Man

Chavez was born on March 31,1927, near Yuma, Arizona. His father owned a small farm but was later swindled out of the land by unscrupulous white landowners. This, undoubtedly, gave Chavez his first taste of discrimination and exploitation. His family had little choice but to become migrant farmworkers. They eventually moved to California in 1938 and settled near San Jose. He worked alongside his family in the fields. However, this, for Chavez, was not a means to eke out a living, but, rather a way out of an endless loop of poverty; he believed that if he worked hard and saved, he could eventually send his children to college and a better life.

His exposure to discrimination did not ease when he entered the Navy in 1944, where he served for 2 years. After the war was over, and Chavez had been honorably discharged, he married Helen Fabela and settled in Delano, California. A few years after his marriage, Chavez returned to San Jose where he encountered, perhaps, the most influential person in his life: Father Donald McDonnell. Soon after, he met Fred Ross and Pete Fielding, who ran the new organization, Community Service Organization. Chavez agreed to work with Ross and Fielding and started organizing voter registration among Latinos.

Taking a page from one of his heroes, Gandhi, Chavez used only nonviolent tactics to promote the UFW agenda. Also, like Gandhi, Chavez was willing to sacrifice himself with a series of fasts designed to prompt action by farm owners. He went on water-only fasts in 1968 and 1972. His most famous fast was in the summer of 1988 and lasted for 36 days. After he broke his fast, other activists and celebrities passed the fast along, existing on only water for several days each.

Throughout all of his efforts, Chavez and the UFW received the moral and practical support of African-American activists such as Ralph Bunche and Jesse Jackson, as well as prominent American statesmen such as Robert Kennedy, who wholeheartedly approved of

9

塞萨·查韦斯: 劳工领袖

他是谁

20世纪60年代,查韦斯在对农业工人的苦难作了充分了解的基础上和另一个活动家德洛丽丝·惠尔塔建立了"全国农业工人联盟"。这个组织最后变成了"农业工人联合工会"。查韦斯和"农业工人联合工会"通过各种途径唤起人们对农业工人艰难处境的重视。不过,他们最著名的成就是为了反对非工会工人所生产的农产品而举行的一系列抵制活动。这些抵制活动使"农业工人联合工会"和查韦斯成了全国关注的对象。

是什么成就了他

1927年3月31日,查韦斯出生在亚利桑那州尤马附近。他父亲本来拥有一个小农场,但后来被奸诈的白人农场主骗走了。这件事情毫无疑问让查韦斯第一次感到被歧视和被剥削的滋味。这样一来,他的全家别无选择,不得不沦为农业工人。1938年,他们搬到了加利福尼亚州并最终在圣荷西附近安顿了下来。他和全家一起在田地里劳作。然而,这对查韦斯来说根本不是个维持生计的方法,更不能让他们跳出贫困的无底洞。他相信,只要他努力工作,多存些钱,他将来一定可以把自己的孩子送去上大学,让他们过上更美好的生活。

1944年,查韦斯参加了海军。他在那儿待了两年,但依然受到了歧视。二战结束后,查韦斯光荣退役。后来他和海伦·法贝拉成婚,两人搬到了加利福尼亚的德拉诺。结婚几年后,查韦斯重回圣荷西的时候遇见了对他一生影响最大的人:唐纳德·麦克唐纳神父。不久,他又遇到了弗雷德·罗斯和皮特·菲尔丁。他们是一个新兴的社区服务组织的负责人。查韦斯同意加入到他们中间去,并开始在拉丁美洲人中间组织投票登记。

查韦斯向他心目中的偶像之一甘地学习,只采取非暴力手段实现"农业工人联合工会"的每一项计划。而且同甘地一样,查韦斯随时随地愿意绝食以促使农场主们采取相关行动。他在1968年和1972年进行了两次绝食,只靠喝水撑着。他最著名的绝食是在1988年的夏天,前后整整持续了36天。在他开斋之后,其他积极分子和名人们继续他的绝食行动,每个人仅靠水又撑了一些时日。

查韦斯自始至终都不是在单枪匹马地战斗,无论在道义上还是在实际行动中,他和"农业工人联合工会"都得到了像拉尔夫·本奇和杰西·杰克森这些非洲裔美国积极分子的帮助,同时也赢得了像罗伯特·肯尼迪这样一些美国著名政治家们的支持。罗伯特·肯尼迪对查韦斯和"农业工人联合工会"的工作一直赞赏有加。人们认为这种毫不加掩饰的

what Chavez and the UFW were doing. It was thought this type of unabashed support helped immeasurably in the success of the UFW and Chavez.

The Legacy of the Man

Chavez took on his last cause shortly before his death. He had returned in April 1993 to help defend the UFW from a lawsuit by a large California producer of lettuce and vegetables. The producer wanted the UFW to pay millions in damages from a past boycott against him, and Chavez was there to plot the defense strategy and testify in court. He appeared in court on April 22, returned home afterward and then died sometime overnight of causes that were never fully identified. His official date of death is April 23, 1992.

Chavez's legacy as a man who bettered the lives of thousands of migrant workers was confirmed by the more than 50,000 mourners who honored him at the UFW field office in Delano, California, where Chavez had made his first and last public fasts. It was the largest funeral, to date, of any U.S. labor leader. Chavez was called a "special prophet of the world's farm workers" by Cardinal John Mahoney, who presided over the funeral.

支持极大地保证了查韦斯和"农业工人联合工会"工作的成功。

他的遗产

　　查韦斯最后一项事业尚未完成便猝然离去。1993年4月他回到加利福尼亚帮助"农业工人联合工会"和当地一个实力雄厚的莴苣蔬菜生产商打官司。该生产商要求"农业工人联合工会"赔偿他数百万美元作为过去他们在实施抵制运动时给他带来的损失。查韦斯回来设计辩护方案并上庭作证。4月22日他还出现在法庭上，但回家后，当天夜里便突然死去，死因至今尚未查明。官方公布的死亡日期是1992年4月23日。

　　查韦斯的遗产是改善了数以千计的农业工人的生活。这一点可由他死后感人的场景得到印证：超过5万名工人在加利福尼亚州德拉诺"农业工人联合工会"的办公楼前为他送别。而这儿正是查韦斯开始第一次和最后一次绝食的地方。葬礼规模空前庞大，至今没有哪个美国工人领袖的葬礼超过它。主持葬礼的红衣主教约翰·马奥尼称查韦斯是"全世界农业工人亲密的预言家"。

Ten

Winston Churchill, Prime Minister

Who He Is

Some would say that with an American mother and a British father, Churchill was the perfect wartime leader. He became one of the most enduring symbols of the Second World War, an image so linked with the survival of Britain and the rigors of wartime London, that he is forever remembered as one of the great heroes in one of the great struggles of all time.

He was highly educated, arrogant, complex and not always successful or appreciated—he was voted out of office even before World War II ended, despite his Herculean efforts on behalf of the people and the country. He was a man of a different era: He was part of, and believed in, the British aristocracy and the British Empire (especially the Raj in India), yet was absolutely committed to the efforts against fascism and world conquest. It was as if two different personalities existed in one man.

What Made the Man

Trying to discover the roots of Churchill's heroism in his childhood can be challenging. He was born into privilege as a child of English nobility. In the tradition of the British aristocracy, he spent most of his childhood in boarding schools. He was distant from his parents—although fascinated by his father's political career. He is said to have been a lonely, rather disappointing boy who did not do well in school (although he would one day receive the Nobel Prize in literature).

As a young man, he had decided on a military career. Like many from his class, he went to Sandhurst, the Royal Military Academy, famous for training the officers and gentlemen of the British colonial army. His first tour of duty was to India, where more time was spent in leisure than in military activity. Eager for action, he managed to find his way to Cuba and then to the Sudan, which region the British army was attempting to retake.

Interestingly, the young officer Churchill often acted as a war correspondent for various London papers. In fact, his first famous action occurred while working as a correspondent during the Boer War of 1899. Although eventually captured and put in a prison camp, he managed to take charge during a difficult trainwreck that threatened the lives of soldiers and passengers. He escaped from prison and made his way out of South Africa; when he returned, it was as a commissioned officer. Throughout this period of his life, he seems to have generated a bit of controversy. Historians are never quite sure of some of the facts or events as recounted by Churchill. He clearly was a young man who thought nothing of altering facts to fit the circumstances—or so some of his critics charged.

The year 1900 saw the beginning of his political career, when he was elected to Parliament as a Conservative. Throughout his early years, he would cause a great deal of dissatisfaction with his fellow Conservatives, to the extent that he changed sides and became a Liberal member. Although he would eventually rejoin the Conservatives, he

10

温斯顿·丘吉尔：英国首相

他是谁

有人说因为丘吉尔的母亲是美国人，父亲是英国人，所以他是再理想不过的战争领袖。他成了"第二次世界大战"不朽的象征之一。他的形象经常和英国的幸存者及战争中伦敦的困境联系在一起。在人们的记忆里，他永远是那段历史上最困难的战争时期中伟大的风云人物之一。

他接受了极好的教育，为人傲慢、个性复杂。他并不总是有成功相伴，或是受人尊敬；"二战"尚未结束，他便落选离职，尽管他在"二战"期间为整个国家和人民做出了巨大的贡献。他的性格与时代不符：他属于并推崇英国贵族统治和大英帝国时代(尤其是英国对印度的统治)的一类人。尽管如此，他却是全身心地投入到反法西斯和反对称霸世界的斗争中去。这两种不同的性格特征似乎融合在了他一个人身上。

是什么成就了他

要想从丘吉尔童年时期寻找他英雄气质的根源是很困难的。他出身高贵，正如英国贵族的传统一样，他童年的大部分时光是在寄宿学校里度过的。他虽然被父亲的政治生涯所深深地吸引着，但他还是远离父母一个人生活。据说他在学校里很孤独，学习成绩很令人失望(虽然他后来获得了"诺贝尔文学奖")。

长大成人之后，他决定去部队发展。他和班里许多同学一样去了桑赫斯特"皇家军事学院"。这所学校以培养英国殖民军官人才著称。他的第一个任务是去印度，在那儿，他更多的时间是花在休闲而非军事活动上。由于渴望参加军事行动，他便想办法经古巴来到了英国军队一直想重新占领的苏丹。

有趣的是，作为一名年轻的军官，丘吉尔通常为伦敦各种各样的报纸充当战地记者。事实上，他第一次著名行动就发生在他在1899年"布尔"战争中做记者的时候。虽然最后他被捕入狱，但在一次严重的火车失事危及到许多士兵和乘客的生命安全时，他沉着应付，帮大家逃过了一劫。成功越狱之后，他离开了南非；当再次回来的时候，他已经成了一名委任军官了。人们对他的一生似乎有些争议。对于丘吉尔所讲述的一些事实或是事件，历史学家们向来是将信将疑。很明显，他不是那种见风使舵的青年人，但一些丘吉尔评论家指责他就是这样的人。

1900年，他作为一名保守党成员被选入国会，开始了他的政治生涯。在他政治生涯早期，他的行为曾引起其他保守党成员的极大不满，以至于后来他改变了政治立场，加入了自由党。虽然他最终又重新加入了保守党，但他似乎总能在这两党之间做到游刃有余：

seemed able to have it both ways—working in various Cabinetlevel positions, including First Lord of the Admiralty. It was while he was First Lord that an infamous battle was planned in Turkey at Gallipoli, which turned out to be a disaster for British and Australian forces—a fiasco so serious that Churchill was forever associated with it.

It was his nature to meddle in matters in which he probably had no business being involved. As First Lord of the Admiralty, Churchill took the leadership in developing a then-unique weapon of war—the battle tank. Historians and others have questioned how the navy was expected to bear the costs for the development of the tank. Many inside and outside the government thought that this was massive misuse of departmental funds; but that, of course, did not stop Churchill.

It was the nature of Churchill and his worldview that Britain should be involved in every major(and sometimes minor) regional dispute.

The whole world by this point had recognized Gandhi as a great and good man. Churchill would have nothing to do with him; this attitude simply reinforces the view of a man who was stalled in a mid-19th century time warp.

If India could not have home rule, Ireland could and would. Churchill worked with members of the government to help create the Irish Free State in the 1920s. But his worldview became even more complicated with the advent of Mussolini and Italian-style fascism. He admired the man and his policies, fortunately, he did not take the same view of Hitler and was an early and strident alarmist over German rearmament and Hitler's worldview—a view that nevertheless held the British and their world empire in great admiration!

Almost alone in government, he opposed appeasement with Germany and Hitler. He was vocal in his denunciation of Neville Chamberlain and the Munich Agreement, which gave a good part of then Czechoslovakia to Germany on the pretext that a German minority was being abused by the Czech majority. Naturally, history and world events would prove that appeasement would not work. The Chamberlain government fell, and Churchill and a wartime coalition government took over.

Stalin referred to Churchill as an English bulldog for his stubbornness and his unwillingness to compromise. Hitler found Churchill even more difficult. With the fall of France, Britain stood alone in 1940 as the only viable opponent of the German war machine. It was in this context of defiance and uncompromising belief in the invincibility of Britain that he rallied the people with his famous blood, sweat and tears speech—one of many for which he would be famous.

If Churchill ever displayed genius, it was in his systematic courting of Franklin Roosevelt. Britain needed U.S. aid, U.S. armaments and, most importantly, needed the United States as an active ally in the war against Germany, Italy and Japan. Churchill and Roosevelt began what would be called the special relationship between the two countries. He was also the author of the Europe-first strategy as well as an early supporter of the Atlantic Charter(the beginnings of the North Atlantic Treaty Organization—NATO).

Postwar, Churchill found himself out of office until his political return in 1951. One of his most famous pronouncements was that an iron curtain was descending on Eastern

他在各种内阁里任过职,包括担任英国海军大臣。在他任海军大臣期间,一场臭名昭著的战争在土耳其的加利波利打响。这场战争对英国和澳大利亚的军队来说是个灾难,因为战争以他们的完败而结束,而丘吉尔也永远和这次战争联系在了一起。

丘吉尔天性喜欢管闲事。作为海军大臣,他领导发明了一种当时十分奇特的战争武器——战争坦克。历史学家们以及其他人士一直对海军部是如何承担得起研制这种坦克的费用保持怀疑。上至英国政府,下至人民大众,很多人都认为这是在无节制的滥用资金;但是很明显,这些并不能阻止丘吉尔。

丘吉尔生性认为英国应该介入到任何一个重大的区域冲突中去(有时也包括次要的较小的冲突),而且这就是他的世界观。

此时,全世界都认为甘地是个伟大而善良的人,而丘吉尔却不想和他有任何纠葛。他的这种态度只会让人觉得,丘吉尔依然没有摆脱19世纪中期的思维泥潭。

印度不能实现自治,爱尔兰却能做到,而且势不可挡。20世纪20年代,丘吉尔和政府其他官员一道帮助建立起了"爱尔兰自由邦"。但随着墨索里尼和意大利法西斯的出现,丘吉尔的世界观变得更加复杂起来。丘吉尔推崇墨索里尼和他的政策,所幸的是,丘吉尔和希特勒的世界观并不一样,相反,他很早就宣称要警惕德国重整军备和希特勒的世界观。然而,希特勒却十分仰慕英国和她的世界帝国。

在英国政府里,他几乎是孤身一人反对同德国和希特勒妥协。他强烈谴责尼维尔·张伯伦和《慕尼黑协定》。协定规定捷克斯洛伐克割让一大片土地给德国,理由是德军遭到捷克军队以多胜少的摧残。果不其然,历史和后来的世界范围内的一些事件证明了妥协毫无用处。张伯伦下台之后,丘吉尔组建的战时联合政府开始执政。

丘吉尔因他的顽强与决不妥协的精神被斯大林誉为英国的"牛头犬"。希特勒发现丘吉尔更难对付。随着法国的沦陷,1940年只有英国一个国家有希望同德国战争机器战斗下去。就是在这种顽强抵抗、始终坚信英国是不可战胜的情况下,丘吉尔用他著名的"热血、汗水和眼泪"将全国人民团结在了一起。这次演讲只是他很多著名讲演中的一例。

要说丘吉尔有什么禀赋过人之处,那就是他有计划、有步骤地向富兰克林·罗斯福献殷勤。英国需要美国的援助和军备,而且最重要的是,需要美国作为积极的战争同盟国和英国一起反抗德国、意大利和日本。丘吉尔和罗斯福开创了后人称之为英美两国的"特殊关系"。丘吉尔还是美国"欧洲第一"战略的设计者以及《大西洋宪章》的早期支持者(《大西洋宪章》是"北大西洋公约组织"的基础)。

战后,丘吉尔曾一度离职,直到1951年重返政坛。他最著名的演说之一就是"铁幕演

www.ahstp.net

53

Europe.

The Legacy of the Man

Churchill was a rogue, scholar, the ultimate politician, historian and a conservative. He saw no reason to change the world order or the British control of nearly half of it. At the same time, he exuded an almost greater-than-life connection with the British people—as though he truly was one of them in their hardship and suffering. Ironically, born to a wealthy family, he ended up with little money and used his writings and books to maintain a lavish lifestyle.

How could a man so seemingly out of touch with the contemporary world attract such enthusiasm and public acclaim? Was he perhaps the master of public image? Or is it perhaps that his words speak of a genius in public relations, history and international politics? If nothing else, his abiding legacy is that of a man willing to fill a huge void at a moment in history when the world was in chaos and on the brink of anarchy.

The Resources

The enduring hero worship of Winston Churchill by Americans is immortalized in the Washington, D.C.based organization called The Churchill Centre, which is designed for a broad base of readers and interested parties. Visit *www.winstonchurchill.org* for more details and a wonderful resource.

A thoroughly enjoyable site gives ample evidence of Churchill's cleverness and creativity. Readers can find dozens of quotes from Churchill by visiting *www.brainyquote. com*.

说",他说一张"铁幕"正降临东欧。

他的遗产

　　丘吉尔有些痞气,又是名学者;他是个终极的政治家、历史学家,还是个保守人士。他觉得不应该改变世界秩序,或是改变英国控制几乎半个世界的格局。同时,他表现出了和英国人民超出生命的亲密关系:让人感觉他似乎与他们生死与共。具有讽刺意味的是,丘吉尔出生于富贵之家,到头来却贫困潦倒,只能靠自己写的文章和书籍维持奢华的生活方式。

　　为什么一个与当今世界似乎毫无瓜葛的人依然能引起公众如此大的兴趣,并得到他们所的称颂呢?难道是因为他曾经备受公众关注?抑或是因为他的演讲显示出他是公共关系、历史和国际政治方面的天才?最重要的是,他给我们留下了不朽的遗产:当历史上世界曾经是一片混乱、濒于无政府状态的时候,他迅速地站了出来,并填补了这个巨大的空白。

相关资源

　　温斯顿·丘吉尔在美国人心目中是不朽的,他们对他永久的英雄崇拜可以从一个叫做"丘吉尔中心"的组织得到印证。该组织建在华盛顿特区,面向大多数读者和感兴趣的其他组织。读者可访问www.winstonchurchill.org了解更多细节信息和大量绝佳的资源。

　　一个纯粹以娱乐为主的网站提供了许多例子,表明了丘吉尔的智慧和创造力。读者们可以在www.brainyquote.com找到丘吉尔的大量语录。

Eleven

Jacques-Yves Cousteau, Marine Biologist

Who He Is

Anyone who has watched public television during the 1960s and 1970s knew Jacques Cousteau as that very entertaining and very special hero who brought undersea exploration into our living rooms. An environmentalist without peer, he showed us a world that we previously could just imagine. His heroic ventures are similar to space exploration: a combination of technology and sheer bravery bringing the suboceanic world to everyman.

He is even more our hero because he inspired generations to study and care for the sea, and to work to protect it for future generations. Some of his finest work revolved around the technology of sea exploration, but his most important effort, the reason he is our hero, is that he was a genuine environmentalist with all the world at heart.

What Made the Man

Jacques-Yves Cousteau was truly a man of the sea. His scientific breakthroughs in diving technology and his tireless fight against the pollution of the oceans made him a hero to a generation of future explorers and environmental activists. His voyages on his ship Calypso became the subject of books, television specials and even a hit song by John Denver.

Cousteau was born on June 11, 1910, in Saint-Andre-de-Cubzac, France, to Daniel and Elizabeth Cousteau. He began his lifelong love for the sea in 1930 when he was admitted to France's Ecole Navale (Naval Academy). He became a gunnery officer in the navy and began conducting diving experiments. His first innovation in underwater technology was the development of a better type of underwater goggles in 1936, thought to be the precursors of modern diving masks.

The Legacy of the Man

Jacques Cousteau will always be credited with helping open the seas to human exploration. Prior to his development of the Aqua-Lung, divers were forced to free-dive without support equipment, using hard suits and connected to an air hose on the surface or relying on unpredictable and frequently unsafe rebreathers.

雅克·伊夫·库斯托：
海洋生物学家

他是谁

从20世纪60年代到70年代，凡是看过公共电视节目的人都知道雅克·库斯托，一个风趣而又特别的英雄。是他把海底世界介绍到我们的日常生活中。作为一个无与伦比的环境学家，他向我们展示了一个从前仅仅是存在于我们想象中的世界。和空间探索相类似的是，他英雄式的冒险将技术和勇气相结合并将海底世界呈现给大众。

他之所以成为我们的英雄，不仅因为他激励了一代人去研究和关注海洋，并且还为了后代人的利益而致力保护海洋。他最杰出的成就是在海洋探索技术方面，但更为重要的是他是一个惠及全球的天才环境学家。这也是他能成为大家心目中英雄的原因。

是什么成就了他

雅克·库斯托确实是一个"海洋中人"。他在潜水技术方面取得了科学性的重大突破，并且他永不疲倦地与海洋污染进行着斗争，这使他在那些梦想进行海洋探索和参与海洋环境保护的人心目中成了英雄。他驾着自己的"卡里普索"号进行的那次航行成为书刊、电视专题甚至是约翰·丹佛的一首很红的歌的主题。

雅克·库斯托于1910年6月11日在法国的库兹克圣安德列出生，他的父母亲分别是丹尼尔和伊莉莎白·库斯托。当他在1930年进入法国的船舶学校（海军教育专业）学习时，他对海洋产生了无限眷恋，并且持续一生。他在海军部队里做了一名射击指挥官并且开始进行潜水实验。他水下技术的第一个革新是在1936年对水下护目镜的改进，这被认为是现代潜水面罩的雏形。

他的遗产

雅克·库斯托因其为人类打开海洋之门而做出的贡献而一直受到赞扬。在他发明水肺之前，潜水者不得不在没有任何安全保障设备的情况下穿着坚硬的服装，凭借通到水面的气管或者依靠不可预测的并且是经常要进行不安全的短暂呼吸的方式来潜水。

Cousteau excited a whole generation about the
beauty, dangers and fragility of the seas. Using his
Aqua-Lung, millions of people have been able to
visit Cousteau's sometimes-dangerous undersea
world as tourists, explorers or workers.

After Cousteau's death, Jean-Michel and his son, Fabien, carried on underwater explorations and created documentaries about the sea. They released a new series, *Ocean Adventures in 2006,* one episode of which, *Voyage to Kure,* inspired President George W. Bush to establish the Northwestern Hawaiian Islands National Monument, the largest marine protected zone in the world.

　　库斯托激起了一代人对于美好、危险又脆弱的海洋的幻想。他发明水肺已经使得数百万人,包括旅游者,探险者,工作人员等去参观他所描述的危险的海底世界。

　　库斯托死后, 吉恩·麦克和他的儿子费边继续进行海底探索并且制作了关于海洋的一些音像制品。他们还发行了一个新的电视系列片《2006年的海洋冒险》。其中有一期叫做《驶往库乐》,这部片子促使乔治·布什建立了西北夏威夷岛国家保护区,它成为世界上最大的海洋保护区域。

Twelve

Walter Cronkite, Anchorman

Who He Is

There was a time, not so long ago, when network news broadcasts in the evening were the most powerful on television. The men(and they were all men) who presented the news were icons to the American public. Walter Cronkite was the dean of television newsmen, reciting the day's events with grace and poise, and with a solemnity that they deserved. There was no cable, no instant messaging, no Internet, no streaming news. There was only Walter and men like him.

At the height of his career, he was the most admired and trusted man in the United States. If Walter Cronkite said it, it must be true. He is our hero because he never gave us cause to mistrust him; he never abused the faith we put in him, or became haughty or proud. He always remained the same: the good and righteous man who would interpret a complex world for us every evening.

What Made the Man

Although he was a legitimate star, Cronkite insisted he was an ordinary working journalist and used the values he learned growing up in the Midwest to temper his reporting on some of the most compelling and controversial issues of the 20th century.

Cronkite's big career break came during World War Ⅱ. He joined the reporting staff of the United Press (UP). He became part of a group of war journalists known as the Writing 69th. Cronkite showed he would do almost anything to get a story, including going ashore on D-Day, making parachute landings with the 101st Airborne and accompanying bombing missions to Germany. Cronkite raised his profile even higher when he was the UP reporter covering the postwar Nuremberg Trials of suspected Nazi war criminals. After that, he opened the first postwar UP office in Moscow, where he stayed for 2 years.

CBS rewarded Cronkite for his hard work and obvious talent on camera by making him the successor to Douglas Edwards as the anchorman of the *CBS Evening News* in 1962. At the time the show was only 15 minutes long but was expanded to 30 minutes less than a year after Cronkite took over.

Thanks to a combination of financial support of the news division by CBS and Cronkite's own experience as a wartime reporter, the *CBS Evening News* soon emerged as the leader in national news shows and gave CBS a reputation for both trustworthiness and in-depth reporting.

Ironically, one of Cronkite's first interviews in the new 30-minute format was with President John F. Kennedy. Barely 2 months later, Cronkite was the first with news of Kennedy's shooting and death. One of the most memorable moments in television broadcast history happened as a visibly shaken Cronkite seemed to choke up on camera when announcing the death of the president. He later admitted he almost did not make it through the broadcast because he was so upset.

沃尔特·克朗凯特：
新闻节目主持人

他是谁

曾几何时，新闻联播成了晚间最强大的电视节目。那些男新闻主持人(新闻主持人那时候都是男的)成了美国公众的偶像。沃尔特·克朗凯特是电视新闻主持界的泰斗，他沉着冷静而又风度翩翩，向观众们讲述着每天发生的事件，言语里还自然流露出新闻播报应有的严肃性。那时候没有有线电视、即时信息，没有因特网，也没有滚动新闻，只有沃尔特和像他这样的新闻主持人。

在职业生涯的巅峰时期，他成了美国最受人喜爱和信任的人。只要是从沃尔特·克朗凯特嘴里说出来的事情，那无疑都是千真万确的。他是我们的英雄，因为他从来不会使我们对他产生怀疑，从来不会背弃我们给予他的信任，也不会变得妄自尊大。他做人始终如一：善良正直，每天晚上为我们讲解这个纷繁复杂的世界。

是什么成就了他

虽然他完全可以说是明星，但克朗凯特却一直强调自己只是个普通的记者，用自己在中西部成长过程中所学到的价值观念去应对他所报道的20世纪最令人关注和最具争议的一些话题。

克朗凯特的职业生涯在第二次世界大战期间出现了重大转机。他加入了"合众社"的报道组。他正是那一批被称为"第69写作组"的战地记者中的一员。克朗凯特的行为表明，为了获得新闻故事，他可以不顾一切：在"进攻日"那天登陆法国，和101空降师一起用降落伞着陆，追随去德国执行爆炸任务的士兵。当他以"合众社"记者身份报道对纳粹战犯的纽伦堡审判时，他的姿态相当高调。那次报道结束之后，他在莫斯科开了第一家"合众社"办事处，并在那儿工作了两年。

克朗凯特工作勤奋，在摄像机镜头前表现出了毋庸置疑的才华。于是1962年哥伦比亚广播公司决定让他接替道格拉斯·爱德华兹主持"晚间新闻"栏目，以此作为对他的奖励。与此同时，原仅15分钟的节目在克朗凯特接手后不到一年的时间里便延长到了30分钟。

哥伦比亚广播公司新闻部提供了资金支持，再加上克朗凯特曾作为战地记者的亲身经历，这些使哥伦比亚广播公司的"晚间新闻"栏目迅速发展为国内新闻类节目的领头羊，并为哥伦比亚广播公司赢得了其新闻报道可信度高、有深度的好名声。

让人意想不到的是，在新的30分钟的节目安排里，采访约翰·肯尼迪总统是他所做的第一批采访之一。然而，不到两个月之后克朗凯特却成了第一个播报肯尼迪中枪身亡的人。电视播放史上最令人难忘的时刻之一就是当克朗凯特播报总统死讯的时候，他在摄像机前几乎说不出话来，人们甚至可以看到他浑身在颤抖着。后来他承认由于过度悲痛在播送新闻时自己差点没能把持住。

Another national tragedy that would define Cronkite's reputation was the Vietnam War. He was originally quite hawkish on the war but managed to maintain a balanced news approach. As the war dragged on and the American death toll kept rising, Cronkite became more disillusioned with Vietnam. He traveled to the country to cover the Tet Offensive and returned to editorialize on the air, expressing his belief that the war was unwinnable. President Johnson reportedly said after Cronkite's remarks, "If I've lost Walter Cronkite, I've lost the country."

Johnson dropped out of the presidential race, although no one can be certain it was directly related to Cronkite's dismissal of the war.

Cronkite was famously associated with the NASA manned space program and especially the Apollo program, barely able to hide his enthusiasm for what was being achieved in space. During the first moon landing mission of Apollo 11 in 1969, Cronkite was on the air 27 of the 30 hours it took for Apollo 11 to complete its mission. When Neil Armstrong descended the LEM ladder to the moon, all Cronkite could get out in terms of commentary were, "Wow! " and "Oh, boy! "

Under CBS's mandatory retirement system, Cronkite left the anchor chair in 1981 and was succeeded by Dan Rather. Cronkite has stayed very active in journalism, writing syndicated columns and broadcasting as a special correspondent for CBS, CNN and National Public Radio. Cronkite survived quadruple bypass surgery in 1997 and soon returned to an active life.

The Legacy of the Man

Walter Cronkite's legacy as a consummate professional journalist and influential broadcaster will, perhaps, never be surpassed, especially in an era when news is readily available from cable television and the Internet.

Besides his continuing on-air work, he helped found the Walter Cronkite School of Journalism and Mass Communication at Arizona State University.

Cronkite was not universally admired by other broadcast journalists. Many believed he did not take enough risks, relied too much on short, breaking stories rather than in-depth pieces and spent too much time center stage during the nightly news broadcasts.

To most Americans, however, Cronkite was one of the few people who could be trusted during a disturbing period in the nation's history, and the fact is that much of the country believed him when he ended each broadcast with, "And, that's the way it is...."

另一个体现克朗凯特名声的全国性悲剧是"越南战争"。起初他对这场战争持强硬态度，但在新闻报道上仍然保持了平衡的观点。随着战争的不断深入，美国士兵死亡人数不断攀升，克朗凯特对越战变得越来越失望。他身赴越南去报道"春季攻势"，回来之后将材料加以编辑然后在电视上播出。通过这个报道他传达了战争不可能获胜的信念。后来有报道称约翰逊总统在克朗凯特的战争评论后曾说"如果我失去了沃尔特·克朗凯特，那么我就失去了整个国家"。

约翰逊后来在总统竞选中落败，但没有人敢肯定他的失利和克朗凯特对战争持否定态度有着直接的关系。

克朗凯特常常被人们和美国航空和航天局的载人空间计划联系在一起，特别是"阿波罗"计划。他对美国在太空取得的成绩的热情溢于言表。在1969年"阿波罗11号"执行首次登月任务期间，"阿波罗11号"总共用了30个小时完成了登月任务，而克朗凯特竟然在电视上呆了足足27个小时。当尼尔·阿姆斯特朗走下登月舱梯到达月球表面时，克朗凯特能想到的评论只有"哇！"，"噢，这孩子！"。

按哥伦比亚广播公司所规定的退休制度，克朗凯特在1981年离开了主持人的岗位，并由丹·拉瑟接任。此后，克朗凯特依然活跃在新闻界。他作为哥伦比亚广播公司、美国有线新闻网和国内公用无线电台的特约记者，为它们撰写一些辛迪加专栏文章，并做一些新闻报道。1997年，他的身体经历接受了4个部位的旁搭桥手术，但不久他便恢复了活力。

他的遗产

作为一名造诣极深的专业记者以及颇具影响力的播音员，沃尔特·克朗凯特留给我们的遗产后人恐怕永远无法超越，特别是在有线电视和因特网使新闻变得触手可及的时代。

除了继续自己的播音工作，他还帮助亚利桑那州立大学成立了沃尔特·克朗凯特新闻与大众传媒学院。

当然，克朗凯特并没有受到所有记者的推崇。许多人认为他没有冒太多的危险，过分依赖于一些短小而且琐碎的故事，因而缺乏有深度的报道，并且在晚间新闻播报期间在舞台中央浪费了太多的时间。

尽管如此，对于大多数美国人来说，克朗凯特是国家历史上在那段十分动荡的时期可信赖的寥寥数人之一。事实上，他在每次新闻报道结束时说"事情就是这样的"，全国大部分人对此都深信不疑。

Thirteen

Charles de Gaulle, President

Who He Is

Charles de Gaulle may truly be said to be the founder of modern France. He led the nation to becoming a major player in world affairs during and after World War II. And though contemporaries and political enemies thought of him as the imperial French general and statesman whose increasing political independence alienated traditional allies, the French people nonetheless swooned with respect and delight at everything he did or said.

A French national hero almost on a par with Napoleon, de Gaulle was larger than life—a relatively obscure tank officer who became the president of the Fifth Republic. To the observer, the years of his ascent and presidency are fascinating and frustrating, marked by imperialism, arrogance and political gamesmanship as he changed French thought and France's role in the world economy and political sphere.

What Made the Man

Charles de Gaulle came from a traditionally Catholic background(born in 1890 in Lille, France). He was fascinated by everything French as a young man, so it probably came as no surprise that he took a military education, graduating from the Ecole Militaire in 1912. This was the prelude to an entire life spent in service to France and its military.

Like most young men of his generation, he served in the massive French army of World War I, during which he was wounded and captured by the Germans. Between the wars, he stayed with his military career, advancing up the ladder and spending a lot of time thinking and writing about military and political affairs. France and her politicians were obsessed with national security, and with the political and economic control of a smaller, now weaker Germany. After all, France had fought Germany(or its various versions, such as Prussia) for generations.

At the time, the great minds in France felt that fixed fortifications—
the Maginot Line—were the solution to everything. The French
built these massive fortifications with stationary guns facing
Germany. Of course, in the next war, the Germans simply went
around the fixed fortifications and were in Paris within months.

De Gaulle, ever the iconoclast, wrote regularly explaining why the Maginot was the wrong strategy and that only a mechanized and specialized army (with a strong air force) would provide real protection to France. His theories were soundly rejected by his superiors—which is probably the reason that his military career did not advance beyond

13

查尔斯·戴高乐：法国总统

他是谁

戴高乐或许可以说是现代法国的缔造者,他领导法国成为二战后世界事务的主要参加者,尽管与他同时期的政敌把他当成法兰西帝国一个不断以自治独立倾向疏远传统盟国的将军和政治家,但法兰西人民还是会因为他的所作所为以及每一句话而欣喜若狂。

作为一个几乎可以同拿破仑平起平坐的风云人物,戴高乐的人生远比自身有意义:从一个地位卑微的坦克军官成长为法兰西第五共和国的总统。在观察者眼中,戴高乐成为总统的过程既令人着迷又令人沮丧,他思想中的帝国主义倾向、傲慢的态度、政治上的制胜能力让他成功地改变了法国人民的思想观念,并使法国在世界经济和政治领域的角色发生了变化。

是什么成就了他

查尔斯·戴高乐1890年出生于法国里尔,生于一个天主教爱国主义家庭。很小的时候就着迷于法国的一切事务,所以他后来接受军事教育,1912年从圣希尔军校毕业,大概也就不足为奇了。这些仅仅是他为法国和她的军队奉献一生的序幕。

一战期间,像同时代的大多年轻人一样,戴高乐在庞大的法国军队里服兵役。他在战争中受伤并被德国士兵俘虏。在两次大战期间,戴高乐仍留在军队中,他常常花很多时间思考政治军事大事,同时把思考所得记录下来。这时,法国和她的政治家正为国家安全问题和如何在经济和军事方面控制一个暂时实力比较弱小的德国而大伤脑筋。毕竟,几个世纪前,法国曾对德国发动过数次战争(或者可以反过来,德国攻击法国,例如普鲁士入侵法兰西)。

这时候,妄自尊大的法国认为固定的防御计划即马其顿防线,就能解决一切问题。法国人建起庞大的防线用以对付德国的进攻。当然,二战开始后德国军队轻易地绕过了法国重兵设防的马其顿防线,然后占领巴黎长达数月之久。

戴高乐,一个不墨守成规的人,经常写些文章解释为什么马其顿防线是个错误的战略,他提出只有建立一支专门的机械化军队(拥有很强的空中力量)才能真正保卫法国。

that of a colonel between the wars.

Like great men and heroes of all generations, it was world events that in many ways made the man. World War II was the stage that would propel de Gaulle from obscurity to prominence. Once the German advance through Belgium and Holland was complete, it was only a matter of time until the poorly defended French capitulated. For his part, de Gaulle would have none of it. He pleaded with his superiors in the army and with politicians to flee France and set up a government in absentia in North Africa.

He worked with Churchill in England on a scheme to combine the two countries and their armies for the duration of the war. Marshall Petain, the French hero from World War I and now head of government, arranged an armistice with Germany. The pro-German Vichy government was formed and de Gaulle fled to England to lead the charge for a continued French war effort. In the eyes of many, the creation of the Free French forces was a symbol of a free and independent France.

Even at this very early stage of development, the so-called French government in exile exhibited an often-frustrating need to be or at least appear to be independent of the Allied forces during the war. Churchill generally supported de Gaulle. Roosevelt, on the other hand, found de Gaulle outrageous, difficult and arrogant—probably much as Roosevelt would be in similar circumstances.

When Algerian nationals started a civil war, they literally almost destroyed the national fabric of France. Military revolt, terrorism and political chaos resulted. Few Frenchmen wanted to give up Algeria; even fewer wanted to make the military and financial sacrifice of a prolonged civil war. The hero of the day was de Gaulle, but only if his role is taken in historical context. At the time, his decision to allow Algerian independence was considered by many as treason. Several attempts were made on his life. But in 1962, de Gaulle arranged a cease-fire with the Algerian National Liberation Front, and Algerian independence was approved in a popular referendum in France. It was widely conceded even by critics hostile to de Gaulle that he had succeeded in ending a crisis that no other French political leader had been able to resolve. Soon, all other French colonies in Africa were also granted independence.

But the hero would not stay a hero for long. In his second term as president, he faced increasing opposition for his high-handed political maneuvering. He made every effort possible to concentrate political power in himself and his supporters. If his stature at home was weakening, the enthusiasm of his allies and his enemies was increasingly hostile. De Gaulle did everything possible to separate France from American and British economic and political control. He refused to support the UK's admittance into the European Union, and was repeatedly and often at odds with Washington over matters of foreign policy. His insistence that France develop its own nuclear program was a direct effort to assert France's position in the world.

By 1968, his political capital at home had been used up. Inflation and a bad economy sent hundreds of thousands of students, farmers and radicals onto the streets of Paris to protest government policies and the economy. Attempts at reform failed and de Gaulle

但他的理论完全不被上级接受——这可能是二战爆发前他职位还不及一个陆军上校的缘故。

同各个历史时期诞生的伟人和英雄一样,是时势造就了戴高乐。二战成了把他从默默无闻推向声名显赫的大舞台。当时的情况是一旦德国攻克了比利时和荷兰,那么打败防御能力差的法国就只是个时间问题了。以戴高乐的身份来说,此事完全与他无关。但戴高乐仍劝说他的上级军官以及政治家们逃离了法国,前往北非建立了一个新的政府。

戴高乐和英国首相丘吉尔制定了战争中将两国及军队联合起来的计划。贝当元帅(一战中的英雄和现任法国领导人),正筹划和德国签订停战协定。亲德的维西傀儡政府建立后,戴高乐逃到英国领导的法国部分力量,坚持不懈,进行斗争。在很多人眼里,自由法国军队的创立是一个自由独立法国诞生的标志。

甚至在发展的最初阶段,所谓的法国政府事实上只处于流亡状态,并未起真正作用。它在战争中所展现出的面貌令人沮丧,或者至少表现出了要脱离同盟军的意愿。丘吉尔基本上支持戴高乐,而罗斯福则不然,他认为戴高乐蛮横、傲慢而且很难相处,大概罗斯福也是一样。

阿尔及利亚人发动了一场内战,他们差不多摧毁了法国的政治结构,并且导致了军队叛乱、恐怖主义泛滥和政治动荡。法国人不愿意放弃阿尔及利亚,更加不愿意为长期内战做出军事和财政牺牲。今日的英雄戴高乐必须面对现实的历史背景。当时,他允许阿尔及利亚独立的决定被很多人认定是叛国。他一生之中做过很多尝试。譬如1962年,戴高乐与阿尔及利亚国家群体停战,并将阿尔及利亚自由一事在法国进行全民公投票,最终获得批准。这件事得到了广泛认可,甚至那些对戴高乐怀有敌意的批评家也不得不承认戴高乐避免了一场危机,这不是其他任何一个领导人能够做到的。很快,非洲的其他法国殖民地也相继独立。

但是这个英雄称号持续的时间并不长。在其执政的第二届,他的高压政治手腕使他面对不断增长的反对势力。他尽其所能把政治权力集中到自己和他的支持者身上,如果他的势力被削弱,他的盟友和敌人的热情就会高涨。戴高乐想尽办法使法国摆脱美国和英国的经济和政治控制。他反对英国加入欧盟,而对外政策上,他一而再,再而三和美国总统华盛顿站在同一战线上。他坚信法国发展核能是在全球保持自身独立的直接方式。

到1968年,他在法国内部的政治资本所剩无几。通货膨胀和经济状况迫使上千名学生、农民和激进分子走上巴黎街头抗议政府政策及经济现状。经济改革尝试失败之后,戴

resigned the presidency in 1969. By 1970 he would be dead, nearly penniless—he never did manage to accumulate wealth, despite his personal and professional successes.

The Legacy of the Man

How should we view the man and his legacy to France and the world? If for no other reason, he is a national hero because of his unfailing belief in France, its culture and its people. He absolutely refused to allow France to become a second-rate country with a failing economy and little influence beyond Europe. His political views ensured that France and Europe would maintain independence from the two political extremes—the United States and the Soviet Union.

Some contemporaries and historians viewed his maverick ways with disdain, insisting that they were merely a reflection of the arrogance of the man himself. He personally was uncompromising and so were his domestic and international policies. In the end, however, many would accept that he was the founder of modern France. He stubbornly maintained a French political identity, including the importance of the European Union and French dominance of that Union.

The Resources

A number of very readable biographies have been published about de Gaulle over the years, including *The Last Great Frenchman: A Life of General de Gaulle,* Wiley, 1997.

The French embassy in the United States has some interesting information about de Gaulle. Visit *www.info-france-usa.org.*

高乐于1969年辞去总统一职。1970年,他与世长辞,死时几乎一贫如洗,因为他从来没想聚敛财富,尽管他名声显赫,事业成功。

他的遗产

我们应该如何看待他留给法国和世界的财富?如果不考虑其他原因,他对法国及其文化和人民坚定不移的信念,称得上一个国家的英雄。他使法国免于沦落为经济衰败、在欧洲影响力弱小的二流国家,他的政治观念使法国和欧洲得以在美苏两极中保持独立。

但同时期的一些人和历史学家用鄙夷的态度观察他特立独行的方式,并宣称这是对这个傲慢者的反映。戴高乐个人是不妥协的,他的国内外政策也是一样。然而最终,很多人还是肯定戴高乐是现代法国的缔造者。他固执地保持法国独立的政治身份,包括欧盟的重要性和法国在这个组织中的重要作用。

相关资源

近年来,很多有关戴高乐的可读性人物传记相继面世,包括《最伟大的法国人戴高乐将军的一生》,韦利出版社,1997。

美国一些大使馆保存很多有关戴高乐的有趣资料,您可以登录www.info-france-usa.org.网站进行查询。

Fourteen

Diana, Princess of Wales

Who She Is

Diana is our hero because she was a larger-than-life figure, both in the United States (with its history of fascination with the British monarchy)and worldwide. Even in death, which only strengthened her heroic status, this seemingly selfabsorbed woman of British nobility generated endless speculation about her thoughts, actions and desires.

She garnered great pity and compassion, despite her exalted status and seemingly charmed life. Fans worldwide could never get enough of her. The pressures to be perfect and to act like a future queen were intense—and the public knew it.

What Made the Woman

It seemed that the whole world watched the wedding of Lady Diana Spencer and Charles, the Prince of Wales. It was considered one of the fairy-tale love stories of the century. The sad reality was that the marriage was almost doomed from the start and would end in charges and countercharges of adultery, rumors of scandals, divorce and, ultimately, tragic death. Yet despite her personal problems, Princess Diana still symbolized a glamor and style that helped her in her work for several charities.

Diana Frances Spencer was born on July 1, 1961, at Park House near Sandringham, England. Her parents were members of the British aristocracy and at the time of Diana's birth were the Viscount and Viscountess Althorp. With two older sisters, Jane and Sarah, Diana was the youngest daughter in the family. A younger brother, Charles, would enter the family soon.

Her parents were considered a glamorous match (with Queen Elizabeth II attending the wedding). However, the marriage would end in divorce when Diana was only six. Many consider this traumatic experience to be one of the causes of Diana's feelings of insecurity.

Diana was sent to Riddlesworth Hall boarding school after her parents' divorce. She excelled at sports, but was not very successful in her academics. After graduation from boarding school, she headed to London to work as a nanny, as a cook and finally as an assistant at the Young England Kindergarten in Knightsbridge. By this time, her father had remarried a daughter of Barbara Cartland, the world-famous writer of romances.

Meanwhile Charles, Prince of Wales and next in line for the British throne, was under increasing pressure to marry. As the 1980s approached, Charles was nearing his mid-30s. He had been advised by male relatives to marry an innocent young woman who would place him on a pedestal. Also, in order to get his family's approval, he would have to marry someone with an aristocratic background, a Protestant and, preferably, a virgin.

Rumor has it that his future mistress and second wife Camilla, helped him find the 19-year-old Diana when she was working at Young England. Speculation spread quickly that Charles was going to marry Lady Diana and, after efforts from the palace to downplay the relationship, the engagement was officially announced on February 24, 1981.

戴安娜：
威尔士王妃

她是谁

戴安娜是我们时代的英雄，在美国(具有英国君主政体魅力的历史)以及全世界范围内，她是一位具有传奇色彩的人物。她的香消玉殒更加提升了她的英雄地位。这位热衷于自我想法的英国贵族女子对于自己的思想、行动以及渴望进行着延绵不断的思索。

尽管她地位尊贵、生活貌似幸福，但还是获得了人们极大的怜悯与同情。全世界的崇拜者们不断追逐着她的身影。面对外界的压力，她不得不力求表现完美，展现未来王后的风采。这种压力有何等沉重，公众心知肚明。

是什么成就了她

戴安娜·斯宾塞与威尔士王子查尔斯的婚礼全球瞩目，它被誉为20世纪的爱情童话故事。而可悲的现实是，这段婚姻似乎从开始就注定会以失败告终，经历了各种对不忠的指控与反诉、丑闻谣言与离婚之后，迎来的是悲剧性的终结。除了她的个人问题，戴安娜王妃仍然象征着一种魅力与风格，这对她奔走于各种慈善活动大有裨益。

戴安娜·斯宾塞于1961年7月1日出生在英国桑君汉附近的公园屋。她的父母都是英国贵族，戴安娜出生时他们是奥索普伯爵和伯爵夫人。戴安娜是家中最小的女儿，她还有两个姐姐简和莎拉，以及后来出生的弟弟查尔斯。

她的父母被认为是天造地设的一对(女王伊莎白二世曾参加他们的婚礼)。然而，在戴安娜6岁时，他们就离婚了。很多人猜测，这段创伤经历是造成戴安娜日后感情缺乏安全感的原因之一。

父母离异后，戴安娜被送往里德沃斯寄宿学校。她擅长体育，但文化课成绩平平。从寄宿学校毕业后，她到伦敦做过保姆、厨师，后来作了"年轻英格兰"幼儿园里的助理。在此期间，她的父亲再婚，娶了著名传奇小说作家芭芭拉·卡特兰的女儿。

与此同时，未来英国皇室的第一继承人威尔士王子查尔斯面临着婚姻的压力。20世纪80年代到来时，查尔斯也快35岁了。家中男性亲属建议他娶一位崇敬他的纯洁年轻的女子。并且，为了能获得家族的批准，他需要找一位信奉新教、贵族血统的处女新娘。

有传言说查尔斯后来的情妇、第2任妻子卡米拉帮助他找到在"年轻英格兰"幼儿园工作的19岁的戴安娜。查尔斯即将迎娶戴安娜的猜测不胫而走。随后，在皇室并未给予二人关系足够重视的情况下，1981年2月24日，查尔斯和戴安娜正式宣布订婚。

From the beginning there were doubts from family, friends and royal observers that this was a match made in heaven. Charles and Diana seemed to have little in common and there was a 13-year age gap between them. It came out after the marriage hit the rocks that Charles had confided in a friend that before the wedding he did not love Diana, but was sure he could in time.

The wedding, in full royal splendor, took place on July 29, 1981, in front of 3,500 invited guests. More than 600,000 people lined the route from Buckingham Palace to the cathedral. And the world watched the event on TV.

Diana quickly fell into the expected routine of visits to nurseries, schools and hospitals. The public, both in England and around the world, seemed to fall in love with the young and energetic princess. She had her first son, William, within a year of her wedding and her second son, Henry, 2 years after that.

It seemed a perfect life. However, underneath much was not going well for Diana. She suffered from postpartum depression after the birth of William. Her tendency to bulimia returned and she reportedly made a half-hearted attempt at suicide before William was born. Things worsened in the marriage through the rest of the 1980s and early 1990s with the royal couple spending more and more time apart. Diana suspected that Charles had maintained a romantic relationship with the married Camilla Parker Bowles. He later admitted an extramarital affair with Bowles.

The press was now publishing information regarding not only Charles' relationship, but also the several affairs Diana reportedly had while she was married. Throughout it all, Diana continued her efforts to assist AIDS charities (she was one of the first celebrities photographed hugging an AIDS victim) and also to promote the efforts to rid the world of unexploded landmines.

Under pressure from the queen, Charles and Diana were finally divorced on August 28, 1996. Diana told a friend it was the saddest day in her life. Because of the divorce, she lost the title Her Royal Highness and was identified now as Diana, Princess of Wales. She would never ascend to be queen.

The press was soon speculating on her apparent relationship with Dodi Fayed, the son of millionaire businessman Mohammed Al Fayed. The elder Fayed's assets included the London department store, Harrods. He continually resented what he considered to be snubs from the British upper class.

Reportedly, Diana and Dodi were deeply in love, and he was going to ask her to marry him. The couple took a brief holiday in Sardinia but were hounded constantly by the paparazzi, whom Diana had grown to resent deeply. They cut their holiday short and traveled to Paris, where the local paparazzi took up the chase.

On August 31, 1997, the couple left their hotel late at night to travel to Villa Windsor. They were driven by one of Fayed's men and were accompanied by bodyguard Trevor Rees-Jones. The paparazzi pursued the vehicle into the Pont de l'Alma road tunnel, where Diana's car, traveling at a great speed, crashed into a pillar in the tunnel. The driver and Dodi Fayed were killed instantly. Diana suffered massive internal bleeding and was taken to a hospital, where she died soon after. Only Rees-Jones survived.

从一开始,家人、朋友、观察者们就对这段看似完美的婚姻产生了质疑。查尔斯和戴安娜似乎共同点很少,年龄也相差13岁。他们的婚姻触礁后,查尔斯向朋友袒露心声,婚礼前的他并不爱戴安娜,但确信他们很快就能相爱。

这场皇室婚礼盛宴于1981年7月29日举行,有3500名贵宾受到邀请,60多万民众的队伍一直从白金汉宫排到了教堂,全世界都通过电视看到了这一盛况。

戴安娜很快就进入了王妃角色,对托儿所、学校和医院进行例行访问。英国和世界各地的人们都为这位充满活力的年轻王妃所折服。婚后第一年里,她生下了长子威廉;两年后,小儿子亨利出世。

表面上看,戴安娜的生活似乎完美无缺,然而,现实并不如人所愿。产下威廉后,她患上了产后忧郁症,易饥病的症状日趋明显。有报道称,戴安娜在威廉出生前曾半真半假地试图自杀。20世纪80年代后期,他们的婚姻状况开始恶化,到了90年代初,这对皇室夫妻一起生活的时间越来越少。戴安娜怀疑查尔斯与已婚的卡米拉·帕克·鲍尔拉维持着亲密关系。查尔斯后来也承认与鲍尔拉有婚外关系。

现在,媒体报道查尔斯的婚外恋的同时,也开始关注戴安娜的几段婚外情。在此期间,戴安娜仍一如既往地投身艾滋病慈善事业(她是最先出现在媒体照片中主动拥抱艾滋病患者的名人之一),为清除全世界还未爆炸的地雷进行着努力。

迫于女王的压力,查尔斯和戴安娜最终于1996年8月28日离婚。戴安娜告诉一位朋友,这是她一生中最难受的一天。离婚后,戴安娜失去了"殿下"封号,将被称为威尔士王妃戴安娜,并不再有权封后。

媒体很快又开始猜测她与巨富穆罕默德·阿里·法耶兹之子多迪·法耶兹有瓜葛。伦敦著名百货公司哈罗斯就是穆罕默德·法耶兹拥有的一处资产。他一直憎恨他所认为的来自英国上层社会的那些势利小人。

据报道,戴安娜和多迪深爱着对方,多迪已准备向她求婚。这对情侣去撒丁岛度假,狗仔队一路穷追不舍,戴安娜对这些狗仔队早已深恶痛绝。于是,他们缩短了行程,转去巴黎,而当地的狗仔队又开始对他们进行追踪。

1997年8月31日,他们夜间离开宾馆去温莎别墅。法耶兹的一名司机为他们开车,随同还有保镖特雷弗·里斯·琼斯。狗仔队一直追到阿尔玛隧道,戴安娜乘坐的车以最高的车速,撞上了通道立墩。司机和多迪当场身亡。戴安娜大面积内出血被送往医院,不久便宣告身亡。里斯·琼斯是唯一的幸存者。

The tragic death and funeral again captured the world's attention. Diana was laid to rest on an island in an ornamental lake on the grounds of Althorp Park, her family home.

The Legacy of the Woman

Despite her real concerns and efforts to help significant charities, Diana, Princess of Wales, will unfortunately be mostly remembered for what she was not. She was lovely, vivacious and glamorous, but she did not have the stamina to deal with the pressures of a royal marriage. She knew that her husband did not love her and found solace with other men in relationships that were destructive.

This sadness and vulnerability are doubtless part of Diana's continuing legacy, rather than any specific deeds she accomplished. It is impossible to say what her life might have been like if she had married Dodi Fayed.

As with the rest of her life, Diana's death was the cause of controversy. The elder Fayed was convinced the deaths were part of a conspiracy, although these theories were rejected by both British and French investigators. In 2006, an independent inquiry by Lord Stevens, former chief of the Metropolitan Police, reported the case was more complex than previously thought, although no details have been released.

Diana's life and death showed the world that, despite the best of intentions and well-wishings, fairy tales in real life do not always end happily ever after.

The Resources

A candid interview with Diana is available on a DVD, *NBC Presents: The Diana No One Knew,* Genius Entertainment, 2006. You can find information on Diana and other British royalty at *www.royal.gov.uk.*

Other books on Diana include *Diana: The Last Word,* St. Martin's Press, 2005; *The Murder of Princess Diana,* Kensington Publishing Corporation, 2004; *Diana: Her True Story in Her Own Words,* Pocket, 1998; and *Diana: Story of a Princess,* Atria, 2003.

这场悲剧性的死亡和葬礼受到了全世界的关注。戴安娜长眠在家乡附近阿尔索普公园人工湖中的一个小岛。

她的遗产

威尔士王妃戴安娜一生帮助并关注很多意义非凡的慈善事业,然而不幸的是,人们对她的记忆很多都并非真实的戴安娜。她是一个活泼可爱、魅力四射的女性,但她没有毅力来应对皇室婚姻的压力。她知道自己的丈夫并不爱她,所以才希望从其他男性身上寻求安慰,而这些绯闻的伤害也是毁灭性的。

这份悲伤和脆弱无疑是戴安娜留下的遗产之一。如果她嫁给多迪的话,她的生活会是怎样也很难以断言。

正如对她离婚后的岁月一样,戴安娜的死去也是争论的原因之一。穆罕默德·法耶兹确信,他们的死是一场阴谋,尽管这些理论最终被英国和法国调查人员否定。2006年的报告中写道,这个案件比预先想象的要复杂,而有关细节却没有向公众透露。

戴安娜的生与死告诉全世界,尽管人们有着美好善良的心愿,但现实生活中的童话故事并不一定都会有一个幸福的结局。

相关资源

2006年天才娱乐发行了NBC对戴安娜的个人访谈节目光盘:《鲜为人知的戴安娜》。有关戴安娜和英国皇室的其他信息请登录www.royal.gov.uk查询。

介绍戴安娜的书有:《戴安娜:遗言》,圣马丁出版社,2005;《戴安娜王妃谋杀案》,康星顿出版社,2004;《戴安娜:自述的真实故事》,口袋图书出版社,1998;以及《戴安娜王妃轶事》,阿特利亚出版社,2003。

Fifteen

Walt Disney, Animator

Who He Is

It many ways, it is not Walt Disney who is our hero, but the characters and animation that he and his early team created. Disney the creator continues to live every time Bambi or Snow White is re-released and another generation enjoys what the man created.

He is our hero because he left us with a legacy that can be enjoyed time and again, because he knew how to entertain us so well, and because he developed a process for creating animated films that survives even now. We marvel at his creativity, and we are thrilled every time we go to an amusement park that bears his name.

What Made the Man

The name Disney has become synonymous with innovative, family-oriented work in a variety of media—animation, live action films, television and theme parks.

Disney, a descendant of Irish immigrants, was born on December 5, 1901, in Chicago, Illinois. His father, Elias Disney, worked several jobs in Chicago and was one of the army of workers who constructed the World's Columbian Exposition of 1893.

The family left Chicago in 1906 for Marceline, Missouri. It was here that Disney developed his love for drawing. After his father was stricken with typhoid fever in 1909, the family moved to Kansas City, Missouri. Disney attended public school and also enrolled in weekend classes at the Kansas City Art Institute. Art school did not suit Disney; he spent more time doodling than listening to the lessons.

The family returned to Chicago and Disney attended McKinley High School as well as taking night courses at the Art Institute of Chicago. He dropped out of high school to join the Army and fight in World War I. He was rejected for the Army, but later joined the Red Cross Ambulance Corps. He never saw any combat. He was discharged from the Army in 1919 and returned to the United States.

His father would not support Disney in his dream of becoming an artist, so he struck out on his own and moved back to Kansas City. He worked on newspaper ads and tried to start his own art business, called Iwerks-Disney (Ub Iwerks was a good friend and fellow artist). The venture failed, and Disney ended up working at a company called Kansas City Film Ad—creating crude animated ads for local movie theaters. This is where Disney began expanding his horizons as an animator and experimenting with new techniques.

After a couple of years, he started another company, Laugh-O-Gram Films, Inc., producing short cartoons based on fairy tales and popular children's stories. Disney's innovation was to give the old material a modern spin. He employed animators who would go on to become great successes in Hollywood: his friend Iwerks, as well as Hugh Harman, Rudolph Ising, Carmen Maxwell and Friz Freleng. When Laugh-O-Gram went under he took a copy of *Alice in Wonderland*, a mixture of animation and live action, to California to try his luck in Hollywood.

沃特·迪斯尼：动画大师

他是谁

从某种意义上说，沃特·迪斯尼算不上我们时代的英雄，真正的英雄是他和他早期的团队创作的卡通形象和动画。小鹿班比或者白雪公主每一次重新发行，人们都会想起他们的缔造者迪斯尼。他创作的卡通人物吸引了一代又一代的人。

他是我们的英雄，因为他留给我们一笔遗产，让我们一遍又一遍地欣赏；因为他深谙娱乐大众之道；也因为他发展了一种创造动画电影的流程并流传至今。我们惊叹于他的创造力，每次走进以他名字命名的乐园我们都会万分激动。

是什么成就了他

迪斯尼这个名字被赋予了很多意义：一项创新性的家族事业、种类繁多的媒体动画、真人拍摄电影、电视，以及主题公园。

迪斯尼，一个爱尔兰移民的后代，1901年12月5日出生在伊利诺伊州的芝加哥城。他的父亲艾立亚斯·迪斯尼在芝加哥同时做了几份工作，曾经是1893年哥伦比亚世界博览会的建设者之一。

1906年，他们举家搬到密苏里州的马瑟琳农场。在那里，迪斯尼对绘画产生了兴趣。1909年，他父亲患上了伤寒症，随后，一家人又搬到了密苏里州的堪萨斯城。迪斯尼一边上公立学校，一边还报到到堪萨斯艺术学院的周末班学习。艺术学校并不适合迪斯尼，他在课堂上涂鸦的时间远远要比认真听讲的时间多得多。

后来，迪斯尼一家又搬回芝加哥，进入麦肯立高中学习，晚上，还参加了芝加哥艺术学院的晚间课程。在第一次世界大战期间，他从高中退学去参军。然而他没有被军队录取，转而加入红十字救护队。他没有亲历战争，于1919年退役回到美国。

他的父亲并不支持迪斯尼想成为艺术家的梦想，可他立志做艺术家，并搬回了堪萨斯。他从事报纸广告，想方设法创立自己的艺术公司伊沃克斯－迪斯尼公司（伊沃克斯是他的好友兼同事）。这个公司后来运行失败，迪斯尼到堪萨斯电影广告公司上班，为当地电影院制作粗糙的动画广告。这为迪斯尼今后成为一名动画大师提供了平台，让他有机会体验到了新技术。

几年后，他创立了另一家"欢笑动画公司"，根据童话故事和畅销儿童读物制作卡通短片。迪斯尼的创新令旧物换了新颜，展现了现代气息。他雇用了一些动画家，他们后来在好莱坞都取得了巨大的成功，如他的好友伊沃克斯·休·哈曼·鲁道夫·伊辛·卡门·迈克斯韦尔以及弗瑞兹·弗来龙等。欢笑动画公司破产后，他带着动画与真人拍摄相结合的《爱丽丝梦游仙境》的副本来到加利福尼亚，去好莱坞碰碰运气。

A New York distributor saw his *Alice in Wonderland* and wanted to set up a deal for more live action/animated films. Disney recruited his brother, Roy, to help with the business side of his studio. The partnership would last until Disney's death. Another employee, Lillian Bounds, caught Disney's eye and the two were married in 1925.

Disney began working with distributor Charles B. Mintz on the popular *Oswald the Lucky Rabbit* series. After Mintz refused to raise the fees for Disney's work on Oswald, Disney had to find a new character.

No matter whether it was Disney or Iwerks who came
up with the idea, it was Iwerks who directed the first
films with a new character called Mortimer, later to be
renamed Mickey Mouse by Disney's wife.

The Mickey Mouse silent cartoons could not find a distributor, but Disney reinvented animation by creating *Steamboat Willie,* the first sound animated cartoon (Disney did the vocal effects and provided the voice of Mickey until 1947). The cartoon was a smash hit.

In 1932, Disney created the *Silly Symphonies* series of animated all-music shorts. The first color *Silly Symphony* won the first Academy Award for Best Short Subject: Cartoons. Disney also received a special Academy Award in 1932 for his creation of Mickey Mouse. The series would soon spin off such immortal characters as Donald Duck, Goofy, Pluto and Minnie Mouse.

But, Disney had bigger ambitions. In 1934, he began plans for *Snow White and the Seven Dwarfs,* the first animated feature. The rest of Hollywood deemed it Disney's folly, but the end result was a triumph. Audiences flocked to the movie, and it was the highest-grossing film of 1938.

Unfortunately, later animated features such as *Pinocchio* and *Fantasia* were box office disappointments. Disney kept his head above water with a series of films that packaged together existing shorts, and resumed work on *Alice in Wonderland* and *Peter Pan.* The studio also started a series of nature films called *True-Life Adventures.*

On a trip to Chicago in the late 1940s, Disney began making drawings of his dream theme park as a way to pass the time. He would end up spending 5 years of his life developing the concept and finding suitable land to build on in Anaheim, California. He also insisted the park be surrounded by a railroad. Disneyland opened in 1955 and was an immediate success.

While still creating full-length and short animated classics, Disney Studios now started making more and more live-action films such as *20,000 Leagues Under the Sea, The Parent Trap* and *The Shaggy Dog.* The live-action films would reach their height with the 1964 production of *Mary Poppins.*

Disney then turned his attention to the rapidly growing medium of television. He created the daytime children's series *The Mickey Mouse Club,* and a weekly show called *Disneyland* evolved into *Walt Disney Presents, Walt Disney's Wonderful World of Color* and *The Wonderful World of Disney.*

Disney was now working on his grandest venture ever, The Florida Project. Disney had purchased large amounts of land near Orlando and envisioned a vastly expanded Magic Kingdom with adjacent hotels and resorts. The most compelling idea was to create a

纽约的一位发行商看到了《爱丽丝梦游仙境》，他想买下更多动画电影。迪斯尼雇用他的兄弟罗伊协助他工作室生意方面的事宜。他们的合作一直到迪斯尼去世。迪斯尼看上了雇员丽丽安·邦姿，他们俩于1925年成婚。

迪斯尼开始与发行商查尔斯·敏兹合作《幸运兔奥斯华》系列动画。当敏兹停止为《幸运兔奥斯华》提供经费后，迪斯尼不得不再创作新角色。

无论是迪斯尼还是伊沃克斯想出的点子，是由伊沃克斯执导了第一批新动画人物冒塔莫的故事。后来迪斯尼的妻子给它起了个新名字叫"米老鼠"。

没有人愿意做米老鼠无声卡通电影的发行商，迪斯尼不得已重新创作了米老鼠动画，也是第一部有声动画《蒸汽船威利号》。(迪斯尼制作了音响效果，为米老鼠配音一直到1947年。)这部卡通片风靡一时。

1932年，迪斯尼创作了动画音乐短剧《糊涂交响曲》系列。《糊涂交响曲》获得第一届奥斯卡最佳卡通短片奖。同年，迪斯尼还因为创作了米老鼠米奇获得了一项特别学院奖。很快，这一系列动画中新的形象唐老鸭、高飞狗、普罗托还有米老鼠米妮就诞生了。

然而，迪斯尼有着更大的抱负。1934年，他开始筹划第一部动画片《白雪公主和七个小矮人》。整个好莱坞都认为迪斯尼的动画片十分愚蠢，但结果却大获成功。观众蜂拥至电影院，《白雪公主和七个小矮人》也因此成了1938年盈利最高的电影。

然而好景不长，之后的动画片《皮诺曹》、《幻想曲》票房收入惨淡。迪斯尼靠一系列捆绑式短剧勉强维持，重新恢复制作《爱丽丝梦游仙境》和《小飞侠》。工作室又拍摄了系列自然电影《真实历险》。

40年代末，迪斯尼在一次前往芝加哥的旅行中为了打发时间，开始画起他梦想的主题公园。后来，他花了5年时间发展了这一理念，在加州的安纳海姆找到一块合适的土地。他坚持要在公园的周围环绕铁路。1955年，迪斯尼乐园对公众开放，并立刻引起了轰动。

迪斯尼工作室现在开始制作越来越多的真人电影，比如，《海底两万里》、《天生一对》和《长毛狗》。1964年《欢乐满人间》出品，真人电影达到了巅峰。

接着，迪斯尼又把目光投向了迅猛发展的电视媒体。他制作了白天儿童系列剧《米老鼠俱乐部》、一周一集的《迪斯尼乐园》以及由《迪斯尼乐园》发展而来的《沃特·迪斯尼呈现》、《沃特·迪斯尼的精彩色彩世界》和《迪斯尼的精彩神奇世界》。

这时的迪斯尼正在经历事业上最大的一次冒险，即"佛罗里达项目"。迪斯尼买下了奥兰多附近的一大片土地，准备开发一个融宾馆和度假胜地为一体的神奇王国。其中最

futuristic city from the ground up that was to be called the Experimental Prototype Community of Tomorrow(EPCOT).

Sadly, Disney would never see his dream fulfilled. He died of lung cancer in 1966. Roy Disney, who took over the Disney empire, insisted the Florida park be named Walt Disney World in honor of his late brother.

The Legacy of the Man

Walt Disney created an entertainment empire that, during its height, has not seen its equal. Disney was not a skilled artist, but he recognized talent in others. He had big dreams and was not afraid to fulfill them.

Disney was a hero with an edge. He was notoriously stubborn and hard to please and was always surrounded by a corps of yes-men who would carry out any order that their boss flung out.

Disney was also fiercely anti-labor, due, in part, to an animators' strike that crippled the production of *Dumbo*. He never forgave those he thought were traitors to him. He also spied for the FBI on union activity in Hollywood and engaged in illegal intimidation of labor organizers.

However, he also engaged in his philanthropic efforts, including one of his most enduring legacies, the California Institute of the Arts (CalArts), which is still sustained by Disney money. In such projects can be found evidence of a man interested in more than just business and animation.

While Disney was undoubtedly proud of the art of his animation, of the amazing technology of his theme parks and of his innovative use of television, he most likely would have wanted to be remembered for what he was: one of the greatest entertainment figures in American history.

The Resources

Most of Disney's animated and live-action films are available on VHS and DVD. There have been dozens of books published about his career, his art and the theme parks. You can find a variety of information on the man and his work at *www.disney.go.com*.

You can read more about Walt Disney in *Walt Disney: An American Original*, Disney Editions, 1994; *Inside the Dream: The Personal Story of Walt Disney*, Disney Editions, 2001; *Art of Walt Disney*, Harry N. Abrams, 1999; and *Walt Disney: Conversations*, University Press of Mississippi, 2006.

吸引人是将有一座名为"明日原型社区体验"(EPCOT)的未来城拔地而起。

遗憾的是,迪斯尼没能亲眼目睹梦想成真的时刻,于1966年死于肺癌。罗伊·迪斯尼接管了沃特的迪斯尼王国,为了纪念去世的兄弟,他坚持用"沃特·迪斯尼世界"来命名佛罗里达的公园。

他的遗产

沃特·迪斯尼缔造了一个娱乐王国,鼎盛时期无人能及。迪斯尼的艺术技法称不上娴熟,但他能慧眼识英才,胸怀伟大梦想,为了实现梦想勇往直前。

迪斯尼是一位棱角分明的英雄。他的固执远近闻名,取悦他决非易事,他的周围簇拥了只会点头称是、无条件执行老板命令的人。

一次漫画家的罢工,迫使《小飞象邓博》的出品陷于瘫痪,迪斯尼从此开始反对劳工。他没有原谅那些背叛他的人。他还为FBI密探好莱坞演员工会活动,并参与了劳工组织者对工人的非法胁迫。

然而,他又是一位热心慈善事业的人。由他资助至今的加利福尼亚艺术学院就是他不朽遗产的一部分。从这些项目中,我们可以看出,迪斯尼的兴趣投入远远不止在商业和动画上。

毋庸置疑,迪斯尼会为他的动画艺术,主题乐园的科技,对电视的创新运用而自豪。然而或许,他最希望人们铭记的是:他是美国历史上最伟大的娱乐大亨之一。

相关资源

迪斯尼的大部分动画和真人电影可以在家庭录像和DVD中找到。已有几十部有关他的职业、艺术和主题公园的书出版。读者可以登录www.disney.go.com查找有关他生活和工作的丰富信息。

读者还可以通过以下书籍了解沃特:《沃特·迪斯尼:一位美国的创意》,迪斯尼出版,1994;《走进梦想:沃特·迪斯尼的个人故事》,迪斯尼出版,2001;《沃特·迪斯尼的艺术》,哈里·恩·亚博拉姆斯,1999;以及《沃特·迪斯尼:对话》密西西比大学出版社,2006。

Sixteen

Doctors Without Borders, Humanitarian Organization

Who They Are

What can be said about men and women, professionally trained, who are willing to go to the worst places in the world—many terribly unsafe—and perform miracles for the poorest and the sickest among us? If these people are not heroes, who is?

Doctors Without Borders helps people of all countries, regardless of political considerations. And their service is not merely a form of triage, an immediate reaction to immediate events; they also try to establish long-term care programs and facilities. In the modern world, there are few humanitarians so dedicated and so heroic.

What Made the Organization

Created in France, Doctors Without Borders is also known as Médecins Sans Frontières(MSF). It has achieved worldwide fame and recognition by providing free medical services to crisis spots around the world, both as the result of political oppression and from natural disasters. For this story, the group will be referred to as MSF.

MSF is not the first group to offer food and medical aid to those in need. Prior to its organization, a charitable group called Oxfam helped—and continues to help—alleviate suffering. Also, the International Committee of the Red Cross(ICRC), established during the American Civil War, was a primary source of aid.

In the most visible area of medical assistance, MSF doctors and hygienists provide immediate care for the wounded, establish programs of vaccinations, treat victims of HIV/ AIDS, work with local hospitals to improve sanitation(especially with providing clean water) and help with establishing long-term medical care programs to those traditionally ignored. MSF also addresses the important areas of malnutrition brought on by war conditions. It does this through the establishment of Therapeutic Feeding Centres that monitor the nutrition of children and adults and provide direct help.

Besides actual treatment, MSF keeps careful statistics on humanitarian emergencies, so that information can be better communicated to the rest of the world. The activities of MSF may be greatly appreciated by the victims they serve, but they are often viewed harshly by the governments that the organization criticizes. Besides the dangers to volunteers from stray bullets, land mines or disease, MSF volunteers are sometimes killed or kidnapped for political motives.

Occasionally, a government will expel an entire MSF field mission for exposing its atrocities to the world.

The Legacy of the Organization

MSF has received praise throughout the world for its humanitarian activities and won the 1999 Nobel Peace Prize. As the group grew and gained international prominence, it established a reputation in some of the most dangerous areas of the world.

无国界医生：
人道救援组织

他们是谁

对于那些受过职业训练，且乐意去世界上最糟糕地区（那些地方往往极度不安全）的人们，那些在最贫穷的最为脆弱的地区上演着奇迹的人们，我们该对他们作何评价呢？若论英雄，舍此其谁？

无国界医生帮助全世界的人们，不顾政治因素，并且他们的服务不仅是一种医疗救助，也是对突然事件的迅速反应，他们同时也努力建立长期的护理计划和设施。在当今时代，很少有人道主义者如此专注，如此英勇。

是什么成就了该组织

无国界医生组织创建于法国，无国界医生也因该组织而闻名。她因向世界上受政治压迫或自然灾害造成危机的地区提供免费医疗服务而名誉全球。在这篇文章中，这个组织将被称为无国界医生组织(MSF)。

无国界医生组织不是第一个向那些需要食品和医疗的地区提供援助的机构。先前的机构，如牛津饥荒救济委员会也曾大施援手，持续帮助病人减轻痛苦。同时，国际红十字会建立于美国内战期间，是一个人道救助的主要渠道。

在大多数明显需要医疗援助的地区，无国界医生组织的医生和卫生学者们为受伤者提供及时护理，接种疫苗，治疗艾滋病病毒感染者，和当地医院一起来改进卫生设施（特别是提供干净的饮用水），并且在那些一直以来被忽略的地区建立长期的医疗护理项目。无国界医生组织还标明了那些因战争而发生营养不良的重要地区。他们通过建立治疗营养中心来跟踪儿童和成年人的营养状况，并且提供直接的帮助。

除了实质性的治疗，无国界医生组织一直对人道主义紧急援助进行仔细的统计，以便将有关信息与外界沟通，他们的活动得到了服务对象的高度赞赏，但是他们却经常被他们所批评的政府视为眼中钉。除了突如其来的子弹、地雷或者疾病给志愿者带来的危险，无国界医生组织的志愿者们有时还因为政治原因被杀害或绑架。

有时，一国政府可能会驱逐无国界医生组织的代表团，以防止自己的暴行为世人所知道。

该组织的遗产

无国界医生组织因为它的人道主义活动而得到世界范围内的赞扬，并且获得了1999年诺贝尔和平奖。随着该组织的成长和国际声誉的提高，她已经在世界上一些最危险的地区树立了良好的口碑。

Seventeen

Dwight David (Ike) Eisenhower, 5-Star General & President

Who He Is

I like Ike was the chant of the elections in the 1950s, and there was a reason why the world liked Ike: He was a national and international hero, the supreme commander of the Allied forces and the victor over fascism in Europe. What is not to like and admire?

There was a quiet effectiveness about this man that made him a hero. Both as a general and as a politician, he always took the high road. Even though he suffered by comparison to his highly popular and energetic successor, the tag that he did little is both misleading and historically not correct. We admired him for his determination, respected him for his integrity, and most of all revered him for seeing us through one of the most turbulent times in our history.

What Made the Man

It is often said that throughout its history, the United States has been able to find the right man at the right time. This is arguably the case with Dwight Eisenhower. He demonstrated a remarkable natural ability as a leader, helping the various Allies to work together for one common cause. During his two terms as president, he confronted the Soviet Union as part of the Cold War, ended the Korean War and began the American space program.

Eisenhower was born on October 14, 1890, in Denison Texas, son of David Jacob Eisenhower and Ida Elizabeth Stover. He was their only child. Eisenhower could trace his family roots in the United States as far back as 1741, when his Mennonite family immigrated to the American colonies. The family initially settled in the Pennsylvania Dutch community of Lancaster and then in Kansas. Two years after Eisenhower was born, his parents moved the family back to Abilene, Kansas, where his father made a living as a college-educated engineer. Eisenhower was originally named David Dwight but everybody called him Dwight.

Even though his family were pacifists by religion, Eisenhower showed an interest in the military. After graduating from Abilene High School in 1909, he applied for and was accepted into the U.S. Military Academy at West Point, New York. Eisenhower was not a top student, but he made an impression as an athlete and a leader.

His college football career ended, however,
when he injured his knee trying to tackle
the famous Jim Thorpe.

艾森豪威尔：
五星上将及美国总统

他是谁

我喜欢艾森豪威尔是因为他的名字在20世纪50年代的选举中经常被众人提起，而世界人民喜欢他的原因是：他既是一个民族英雄又是国际英雄。他是盟军最高指挥官，对欧洲法西斯作战的胜利者。谁会不喜欢、不敬仰他呢？

他有很高的效率，这使他成为英雄。不管作为将军还是政治家，他总是能找到捷径。尽管在他任职后期，他的话既令人误解，又有历史错误，但我们还是因为他的果断而敬仰他，因为他的廉洁而尊重他。我们尊重他最主要的原因是他带我们经历了历史上最动荡的时期之一。

是什么成就了他

经常有人说，纵观美国的历史，我们往往能够在适当的时间找到恰当的人。这一点可以从艾森豪威尔身上得到验证。身为领袖，他帮助同盟国为了共同的目标通力合作，展现了与生俱来的非凡才能。在两届总统任期内，他使前苏联陷入冷战，结束了朝鲜战争，开始了美国的空间计划。

艾森豪威尔于1890年10月14日生于得克萨斯州的丹尼森，父亲是戴维·雅克布·艾森豪威尔，母亲是艾达·伊斯托弗。他是家中的独子。他的祖先在美国的历史可以追溯到1741年，那时他的蒙诺纳特家族迁入北美的殖民地。他的家族最初定居在兰开斯特的宾夕法尼亚荷兰社区，后来移居堪萨斯。艾森豪威尔2岁时，他的父母把家搬回到堪萨斯的阿比林，在那里，受过大学教育的父亲干起了工程师养家糊口。艾森豪威尔开始叫戴维·德怀特，但是别人都叫他德怀特。

他的家族在宗教上信仰和平，但艾森豪威尔还是对军事感兴趣。1909年，他从阿比林高中毕业后，申请位于纽约的美国西点军校并被录取。艾森豪威尔不是尖子生，但是他作为运动员和领导者给人留下了深刻的印象。

当他试图拦截著名的吉姆·索普时膝盖受伤了，从此，他在校园打橄榄球的生涯画上了句号。

Eisenhower graduated from West Point in 1915. Supposedly, his name was officially flipped to Dwight David while he was in school. A year after graduating, he married Mamie Geneva Doud of Denver, Colorado. They had two sons: Doud Dwight Eisenhower who died tragically in childhood, and John Sheldon David Doud Eisenhower, who would go on to serve in World War II and would later become U.S. ambassador to Belgium.

Eisenhower was on the move in the years after graduation. He initially served with the infantry and was eventually promoted to third in command of the new Army tank corps during World War I (attaining the rank of lieutenant colonel). He was made a major after the war and served at Camp Meade, Maryland, until 1922. It was here that Eisenhower would become convinced of the importance of tank warfare in future combat.

In 1924, Eisenhower was transferred to the Panama Canal Zone, where he was executive officer to General Fox Conner. Conner helped Eisenhower expand his knowledge of war strategy and tactics. During the prewar years of the 1920s and 1930s, Eisenhower's career went nowhere fast. He served as an aide to General Douglas MacArthur and was demoted to lieutenant colonel in 1936. Eisenhower returned to the United States in 1939 and worked in several lackluster staff positions in Washington, D.C. A big break came when he was appointed chief of staff to the commander of the 3rd Army in Texas and was promoted to brigadier general in 1941. Eisenhower had made a name as a talented administrator, but at that point had never held an active command.

After the United States entered World War II, Eisenhower returned to the General Staff in Washington, where he helped draw battle plans against the Japanese and Germans. In 1942, he was appointed Commanding General, European Theater of Operations, based in London. He was later made Supreme Commander of the Allied forces fighting in Africa and Italy. Finally, in 1943, Eisenhower was made Supreme Allied Commander in Europe, charged with drafting a plan to invade the Continent and defeat Germany. He was promoted to general of the Army(equivalent to the rank of field marshal).

He was able to work with the egos of Omar Bradley, George Patton, Winston Churchill, Field Marshal Montgomery and Charles de Gaulle. The Allies invaded Europe on June 6, 1944, and by May 1945, had defeated the German armies and entered Berlin as triumphant victors. After the German surrender, Eisenhower was named military governor of the U.S. Occupation Zone.

Eisenhower returned to the United States and served as the chief of staff of the Army and later Supreme Commander of the North Atlantic Treaty Organization (NATO). He officially retired from active service in 1952 and was president of Columbia University until 1953.

Based on his heroic status, the Republican Party sought out Eisenhower as a candidate for president in the 1952 election. He agreed, and won the nomination. In a campaign stressing conservative domestic policies, he easily defeated Adlai Stevenson, winning re-election in 1956—again against Adlai Stevenson.

Eisenhower's foreign policy did not result in a major thaw in the Cold War. The Korean War ground to a stalemate. Even with the death of Stalin, Eisenhower could make

艾森豪威尔1915年从西点军校毕业,据称在学校时他的名字正式变成了德怀特·戴维。毕业一年后,他娶了来自科罗拉多丹佛的玛米·吉尔瓦·杜德。他们有2个儿子:德怀特·戴维·艾森豪威尔在童年时悲惨地死了,约翰·谢尔登·戴维·杜德·艾森豪威尔接着在二战中服役,后来成为了美国驻比利时的大使。

艾森豪威尔在毕业后的几年里四处奔波。他最初在步兵部队服役,在一战中指挥新坦克军团最终晋升到第三长官(获得陆军中校军衔)。战后他被任命为陆军少校,在坎普米德马里兰服役直到1922年。在那里,艾森豪威尔感受到了坦克在未来战争中的重要性。

1942年,艾森豪威尔被调到巴拿马运河地区,出任福克斯·康纳将军的主任参谋。康纳帮助艾森豪威尔提高了战略战术素养。在20世纪20年代和30年代战争的前几年,艾森豪威尔的事业陷入困难。他成了道格拉斯·麦克阿瑟将军的副官;1936年,被降职到陆军中校。1939年,艾森豪威尔回到美国,在华盛顿做一些沉闷乏味的参谋人员的工作。1941年,他迎来了事业的重大转折:他被委派为得克萨斯第三军指挥官的总参谋长,并且晋升为准将。艾森豪威尔作为有才干的行政人员,素有盛名,但是,他还从来没有亲自指挥过。

美国参加二战后,艾森豪威尔回到位于华盛顿的总参谋部,在那里他帮助制定对日本和德国的作战计划。1942年,他被任命为欧洲战区总司令。后来又被委任为驻非洲和意大利作战的盟军总指挥官,负责起草进入欧洲大陆和打败德国的计划。他被推举为陆军将军(相当于陆军元帅的级别)。

此时的他与奥马尔·布拉德利、乔治·巴顿、温斯顿·丘吉尔、菲尔德·马歇尔·蒙哥马利和戴高乐等伟人并肩作战。1944年6月6日,盟军进入欧洲,并于1945年5月打败德国军队,作为胜利者进入了柏林。德国投降后,艾森豪威尔成为美国占领区的统帅。

艾森豪威尔回到美国,任美军总参谋长一职,接着,又成为北大西洋公约组织的最高指挥官。他于1952年正式退役,任哥伦比亚大学的校长一职直到1953年。

由于他表现英勇,共和党竭力推荐他成为1952年总统选举的候选人。他同意了,并且获得了提名。在竞选中他强调保守的国内政策,因此轻而易举地打败了阿德莱·史蒂文森,并且在1956年总统选举时,他再次完胜。

艾森豪威尔的外交政策并没有对冷战起到明显的缓和作用。朝鲜战争陷入僵局,即使在斯大林死后,艾森豪威尔也没能与前苏联有所缓和。尽管他拒绝援救在越南的法国

little progress toward any detente with the Soviet Union. Although Eisenhower refused to rescue French colonial forces in Vietnam, he did support the division of the country into a south region allied with the United States and a communist north. He sent a few hundred advisers to the region to help the South Vietnamese armed forces.

The war hero and two-term president succumbed to congestive heart failure and died on March 28, 1969, at Walter Reed Army Hospital. He was buried alongside his parents in a small chapel at the Eisenhower Presidential Library in Abilene.

The Legacy of the Man

Dwight Eisenhower is considered one of the heroes of World War II, but his record as a president is more complicated. After the inauguration of the dynamic John F. Kennedy, Eisenhower seemed to be a dull symbol of the 1950s. He was labelled the do-nothing president because critics felt he had basically let the country run itself. He was also seen as a reluctant supporter of the civil rights movement.

However, Eisenhower's reputation began to rise again in the latter part of the 20th century, based on his wartime leadership, his support of the civil rights movement in Arkansas, his ability to balance the federal budget and a prolonged period of peace during his administration. Many historians now include Eisenhower in the list of top ten presidents.

Eisenhower's name is associated with the interstate highway system, and many institutions and schools are named after him. His image was on the dollar coin from 1971 to 1979, and the second Navy supercarrier was named the USS Dwight D. Eisenhower in his honor.

殖民军,但是他支持把越南分为南北两部分。南部与美国结盟,而北部建立起了社会主义社会。他派遣了数百人到南部帮助越南武装军队。

这位战争英雄和两届总统最终因充血性心脏病于1969年3月28日在沃尔特立德军医院去世。他的遗体被埋葬在阿比林艾森豪威尔总统图书馆的小教堂里,与父母葬在了一起。

他的遗产

德怀特·艾森豪威尔被公认为二战的英雄,但是他作为总统的经历更为复杂。在约翰·肯尼迪的就职典礼后,他好像是20世纪50年代一个暗淡的象征。由于批评家认为他只是让国家自我正常运转,因而被认为是一个无所事事的总统。他也被看成是公民权利运动不情愿的支持者。

然而艾森豪威尔的名望在20世纪末再次提升,由于他战时的领导才能,他对阿肯色斯公民权利运动的支持,他平衡联邦政府预算的能力,他在任期内维持了长时间的和平。很多历史学家把他列为10大杰出总统之一。

艾森豪威尔的名字和州际公路系统联系在了一起,很多公共团体和学校以他命名,而他的肖像也在1971到1979年间印在美元硬币上。为了纪念他,美国第二海军大型航空母舰便以他的名字命名。

Eighteen

Mahandas Karamchand Gandhi, Political Leader

Who He Is

While it may come as a surprise to many, Gandhi(as he is called) was neither the father of Indian nationalism nor particularly politically influential in the early days of the independence movement. On the contrary: well educated and a lawyer, he was very English in his Indian ways. And he used his time in England, a country that he considered to be the center of modern civilization at the time, to study more than the law. More, as he experimented with English ways, he also became a citizen of the world.

What Made the Man

Born in 1869 in a rural area of India untouched by foreign intervention, he was taught by his mother the Hindu doctrine of ahisma (to do good, not harm). This belief may have been the kernel around which his ideas about nonviolence grew, and was undoubtedly at the heart of his many nonviolent acts in the face of oppression. As was customary at the time, he was married at a very early age (13) to Kasturba Makhanji, and together they had four sons.

Interestingly, Gandhi was a lackluster student; he barely made it into the University of Bombay.

His university career seems also to have been uninspired, with the exception of his excitement about going to London to study for the bar-ven though it seems that he did not want to be a barrister! Nevertheless, after receiving a law degree from University College, London, he returned to India and attempted unsuccessfully to set up a law practice in Bombay. His failures continued—he was turned down for a part-time teaching position— but ultimately he was able to find a job drafting legal petitions for litigants at court. At this point in his life, no one could have guessed that he had the stuff of greatness in him. However, a great transformation was just around the corner.

In 1893, he was retained by an Indian firm with offices in Durban, South Africa, and moved to South Africa. His experiences there shaped his future. Horrified by the blatant disregard for the civil and political rights of Indians, he actively struggled against the oppression by demanding basic rights for them. He stayed in South Africa until 1914, all the while suffering personal and professional humiliation at the hands of the legal establishment and the general white community, which had complete contempt for blacks and Indians. What galvanized Gandhi the most, it seems, was an effort to deny Indians in South Africa the right to vote by the Natal Assembly. While unable to affect the end result, his and others' efforts did bring attention to the political and social plight of Indians, and in 1894 he organized the Natal Indian Congress.

Now active in the leadership of the Indian National Congress, he advocated the

18

穆罕默德·甘地：政治领袖

他是谁

早期的甘地(人们对他称呼)既不是印度民族之父,也没有在独立运动的早期有着特别突出的政治影响,这也许会让大多数人吃惊。但是,他受过良好教育,做过律师,他的印度生活方式颇具英伦色彩。他曾在英国,一个他认为是当时的文明中心的国家学习远远超出法律以外的知识。此外,由于他经历了英国式的生活方式,他也因此成为了世界的公民。

是什么成就了他

1869年,甘地出生在印度的一个没有被外国人干预的小山村,母亲教导他印度教中具有积极意义的教义(仁爱,不杀生)。这种信念或许是他非暴力观点发展的关键之所在,并且毫无疑问是他众多反抗压制行动的核心。依照当时的风俗,他13岁便早早与一名叫卡斯特布·莫罕吉的女子结了婚,并生了4个儿子。

甘地中学时平凡无奇,勉强考入孟买大学学习。

他的大学生活看起来同样了无生气,但他却对去伦敦学法律兴致颇高,即使他似乎并不热衷成为律师。尽管如此,从伦敦大学拿到法学学位后,他回印度,原打算在孟买从事律师事业,但遭受挫折。而后,他做兼职教师的机会也被拒绝。最终,他找到了一份起草法律文书的工作。那时,没有人看到他身上的伟人潜质。然而,一次伟大的蜕变即将到来。

1893年,他被印度的一家在南非德班的分公司留用,并移居南非。这次经历造就了他的未来。印度人的公民和政治权利遭到了忽视,这让甘地感到震惊。他为他们争取基本权力,与抵制活动积极斗争。他留在南非直到1914年,这段时间,蔑视黑人和印度人的法律机构和白人社会对他个人和职业万般羞辱,但最让甘地感到震惊得是议会竟然投票否决印度人在南非的人权。尽管没有能力影响最终的结果,但他们的努力让人们开始关注遭受政治和社会苦难的印度人们,并于1894年创建了印度国大党。

当时积极活动在国大党的甘地倡导了抵制英货的运动,并呼吁印度人民穿着朴素的衣服,抵制舶来品。最终他被逮捕并惨遭囚禁。在狱中,他最关心的一件事是国大党内部

boycott of British goods, urging Indians to wear homespun, rather than foreignmade cloth. Eventually arrested and jailed, one of his greatest concerns was the growing split in the Congress between Hindus and Moslems(a problem never fully resolved, though greater India was later split into the states of India and Pakistan).

As religious violence increased, he embarked upon his famous 3-week fast as an attempt to force reconciliation. The effort was a failure, despite his reputation.

Independence did not bring joy or celebration, but anxiety and utter frustration at partition and religious strife. Gandhi would not support his own Congress Party's acceptance of the conditions for independence(and partition). In fact, after independence, Gandhi again resorted to another maneuver that brought him near death when he protested the partition of the country and took a stand on the terrible religious rioting that was wracking the entire country. It was a great and terrible irony that Gandhi, a man of absolute peace and total dedication to religious principles, should be assassinated on January 30, 1948.

The Legacy of the Man

His legacy is one of peace, cooperation, charity and piety. In the years since his death, dozens of political and social movements have been based on or have otherwise adapted his principles and concepts, including the American civil rights movement of the 1960s. He is the model of human integrity amidst the chaos, violence and materialism of modern society.

印度教派和穆斯林教派之间不断加剧的分裂（尽管印度后来分裂成印度和巴基斯坦,这个问题始终未能很好解决）。

随着宗教暴力活动的增多,他试图强制调解,开始了著名的为期3周的禁食。尽管当时的甘地已声望很高,然而他的努力还是以失败告终。

独立没有带来喜悦和欢庆,带来的却是分裂和宗教冲突中的忧患和彻底沮丧。甘地不会支持党内关于独立和分裂的要求。独立后,甘地再次寻求另一途径,当他抗议国家分裂的时候,对重创整个国家的宗教冲突采取了坚定的立场,这条路却把他拉到了死亡的边缘。甘地,一个追求和平,献身宗教事业的人,竟然在1948年1月30日被杀害了,这实在是出人意料。

他的遗产

他的遗产就是和平、合作、仁爱和虔诚。在他逝去的这些年,很多政治活动和准则都基于或者采纳了他的原则与理念,包括美国20世纪60年代的民权运动。甘地就是现如今混乱、暴力的物质社会中诚实正直的典范。

Nineteen

Bill Gates,
Businessman

Who He Is

What is it like to be the richest man in the world, a man whose wealth at one point exceeded $100 billion, according to Forbes magazine? And what is it like to give a huge portion of this wealth to charities and good works the world over? Bill Gates, perhaps the capitalist's capitalist, founded a company that revolutionized every aspect of business, education, communication and entertainment, yet maintains a relatively low profile considering his personal and business success.

There are some, including the European Union and a number of state attorneys general, who would say Gates and Microsoft are monopolists and control too much of the personal computer and Internet world. Further, there are those who would complain that Gates was late coming to philanthropy—not really understanding or willing to take an active, charitable role until his wife Melinda brought him around during a trip to Africa.

However he is viewed—admired or not—he is still a hero to millions, because he made information and technology available for a relatively low price. He is a master of business acumen, inspiring tens of thousands to form their own companies and to attempt to take technology and computing to new levels of sophistication and service.

What Made the Man

This is not a rags-to-riches, but a riches-to-riches story. Bill Gates comes from a wealthy Seattle family, his father a prominent attorney and his mother a bank board member. There is one story, hard to verify, that Gates?father set up a million dollar trust fund for him the year he was born. Gates at various times has denied this story; however, he certainly cannot deny that he had the best in private education, including 3 years at Harvard.

> He never graduated, instead choosing to go into business with
> Paul Allen and others to form a company devoted to software
> development. The year 1975 was indeed a very good year.

Gates and his associates developed a BASIC software for a company called Altair; from this point on, there was no looking back. A big concern to Gates and Allen was that much of the software that was available—used by amateurs and others—was open sourced, meaning that it was produced and distributed for free. Gates objected to this and to the random pirating of his work. He called for a closed source approach to software, meaning that the work and end product were intellectual products that had monetary value. If you want his version of BASIC, you should pay for it. (This very theme continues to haunt software developers, movie producers, singing artists and publishers, and it has become increasingly easy and popular to take from the Internet or other sources rather than pay for the content.)

The real bonanza lay just ahead: a relationship with IBM. At the time, most operating software was written for a particular platform or machine. If you created a new computer,

19

比尔·盖茨：
商业巨擘

他是谁

根据福布斯的统计,比尔·盖茨某一时期财富曾经超过1000亿美元,身为全球最富有的人,不知他的感受如何?也不知道当他捐出财富中的很大一部分用于全世界的慈善事业和做善事时,他的感受又是怎样呢?比尔·盖茨,这位富豪中的富豪,成立了一家公司,从此彻底改变了商业、教育、交流和娱乐的各个方面。然而,面对个人和公司的成功,他一直很少露面,保持着低姿态。

包括欧盟和一批首席检察官在内的人都认为,盖茨和微软成了垄断者并控制了太多的个人电脑和网络市场。更有人抱怨道,盖茨踏入慈善事业太晚,认为直到他的妻子梅林达带他进行了非洲之旅后,他才真的理解并愿意积极地参与慈善活动。

不论人们如何看待他,是否敬仰他,盖茨依然是众人的英雄。因为他使人们可以以低廉的价格使用信息技术。他是一个具有商业头脑的佼佼者,激发了上万人去自主创业并将技术与计算的精密度与服务水平提到新的高度。

是什么成就了他

这不是一个穷小子变为富豪的故事,而是从富有变得更富有的故事。盖茨来自西雅图一个富裕的家庭。他的父亲是一位杰出的律师,他的母亲是一个银行的董事。不论在哪个时期,当盖茨听到他父亲在他出生的那年为他成立了一个百万美元的信托财产基金的说法时,他都予以否认。这种说法也变得难以证实。但是他不能否认,他曾受到最好的私人教育,当然也包括在哈佛的3年学习。

他没有毕业,相反的,他选择了与保罗·爱伦以及其他人一同弃学经商,成立了一个公司来实现微软的梦想。1975年是他大有作为的一年。

盖茨和他的合伙人为一个叫阿尔泰亚的公司开发出了BASIC软件。从此,他们便开始蒸蒸日上了。可这么多业余爱好者和其他人可用的软件是开放的资源,言下之意,这个软件生产后是免费使用的。这成了摆在盖茨和爱伦面前的最大问题。盖茨对此表示反对,并反对随意地非法盗版他的成果。他提倡对软件资源进行封闭,这意味着那些脑力工作的成果和最终产物将具有货币价值。如果你想要他的BASIC版本,你必须付钱。(就是这一问题让软件开发商、电影制片人、歌手和出版商伤透脑筋。而如今从网上或者其他渠道获取BASIC版本已变得越来越简单且流行,大家已不再去购买它。)

其实财源早已出现了,那便是与IBM的合作关系。在当时,多数的可操作软件是专门为一种平台或机器编写的。如果你创造出了一种新的计算机,你不得不为那种计算机编

you had to write software specifically for that machine. Using licensed software, Gates and Allen delivered to IBM an operating system for their first major microcomputer. But the real stroke of genius came when Gates realized that the IBM system would be just the first of dozens of competitors; rather than limit his business relationship to IBM, Microsoft was willing to license its MS-DOS (Microsoft Disk Operating System) to a variety of computer manufacturers—at that time and in the years that followed, there were many such manufacturers, though most did not survive.

Gates, and Microsoft's success in operating systems would be challenged by a new breed of developers who came up with the graphical user interface—a system particularly successful at Apple, which became the standard in the industry. Compared to DOS, the resulting Windows was a user's delight, although early versions were subpar when compared to Apple and others. But, as is always the case with Gates, Microsoft did not sit back, but came out with repeated improvements and, of course, all those licenses to the various manufacturers, which ensured installation in millions of computers each year.

Gates, while less and less involved in the day-to-day operations of Microsoft, continues to lead the company to new frontiers, including playstations, Internet-enabling software and plans to compete with the fabulously popular iPod from Apple.

The Legacy of the Man

How will the world remember our hero Bill Gates? Until recently, we would have thought of him as a captain of industry, ranked with Ford, Rockefeller and Carnegie. We would have thought of him as dynamic, rich and famously creative as he expanded Microsoft's reach into the worlds of computing and the Internet. But we would not have thought of him as a generous, giving man.

Much of Gates' current fame must be shared with his wife, Melinda. It is her awareness and her social concern that have prodded the man to participate fully in the modern world. Perhaps it was their combined efforts that attracted Warren Buffett to make much of his huge fortune available through the Bill and Melinda Gates Foundation.

While much is to be said for his and his foundation's efforts, there are some who point out that he lives in a fabulously expensive and expansive house outside Seattle, and that he is one of the most influential people in contemporary America. There are those who credit his wealth and influence to vicious, almost ruthless business practices (a pattern that was long ago set by Rockefeller and others, who cleaned up their reputations with huge grants of money to charity and the arts).

Certainly a great deal of praise was heaped on Gates when he created his foundation in 2000 with an initial gift of $106 million (small peanuts, many said at the time, considering the overall wealth of the man). Subsequent funding has increased rapidly, as has Gates' fame and reputation. The foundation emphasizes scholarships to minorities, AIDS prevention and efforts to eradicate such diseases as polio, diphtheria, measles and yellow fever—diseases that have been controlled in the Western world for many years.

The foundation has grown to over $26 billion and must give away at least 5 percent of its assets each year in order to continue as a charitable organization. (This amount does not include the recent announcement by Warren Buffett that he would give most of his accumulated wealth to the foundation.)

The foundation and his charitable works will ensure that Bill Gates will long be remembered for something more than his aggressive business tactics and great wealth.

写一个新的软件程序。盖茨和爱伦用经许可的软件,为他们的第一台主要的微型电子计算机编写了一个可操作的系统,然后交给了IBM。然而,当盖茨意识到IBM的系统只是许多竞争者中的第一个,这对这两个天才是真正的一击;他们没有将合作关系限定在IBM一家公司,而是准许不同的制造商们使用他的MS-DOS操作系统。当时乃至以后,这样的制造商为数不少,但多数都没有生存下来。

　　盖茨以及他的微软在处理系统方面取得的成功将受到挑战,这挑战来自于利用异常成功的绘图用户界面系统起家的苹果,苹果俨然已经成为业界的权威。尽管早期的Windows版本与苹果和其他品牌相比稍逊一筹,但与DOS相比,最终的Windows系统着实令使用者们兴奋。但盖茨就是这样的人,微软力图精益求精,并给予各类制造商使用许可,保证了每年上百万台电脑的系统安装。

　　尽管盖茨投身于微软日常运作的时间越来越少,他却依然继续引领着公司朝着游戏机、网络浏览器等新领域发展,并制定了与倍受消费者欢迎的苹果公司品牌iPod相竞争的方案。

他的遗产

　　世界如何才能记住我们的英雄比尔·盖茨呢? 直到最近,我们还会想到他是与福特、洛克菲勒和卡内基齐名的产业巨子,想起他是动感、富有、勇于创新的人,他将微软的触角伸到了电脑和网络领域。然而,我们却从未想起过,他还是个慷慨的捐赠者。

　　盖茨现在的许多名誉注定是要与他的妻子梅林达分享的。她的社会意识与社会关怀促使盖茨全身心地投入到了现代世界。也许就是他俩的共同努力吸引了沃伦·巴菲特,使他通过比尔·梅林达基金会捐赠了自己的巨额财富。

　　尽管比尔·梅林达基金会作了很多努力,还是有人指出,比尔住在西雅图郊外的一座相当奢华的豪宅里,并认为他是当代美国最有影响力的人物之一。更有人把他的财富和影响力归功于几乎无情的商业手段(手段很像很久以前洛克菲勒等人为了好名声在慈善事业和艺术领域不惜花费重金)。

　　当他以最初的1亿6百万美元成立他的基金会的时候,许多赞扬被加在盖茨头上(虽然当时许多人认为这与盖茨的全部财产相比只是一个小数目而已)。随后,基金数目飞速增长,与日俱增的,还有盖茨的名誉。这个基金会重点提供青少年奖学金、对艾滋病的预防以及对根除像小儿麻痹症、白喉病、麻疹和黄热病等疾病的资金援助。这些疾病在西方国家早已得到了很好的控制。

　　现如今,这个基金会已经增长到260亿美元,作为一个慈善组织,它每年会捐出财产中的至少5%。(这个数字并不包括最近沃伦·巴菲特宣布的将要送给基金会的毕生积累的大部分财产。)

　　比尔·盖茨将会被历史铭记,不是因为他杰出的商业策略和巨额财富,而是因为他创办的基金会以及他的慈善之举。

Twenty

John Glenn,
Astronaut & Statesman

Who He Is

He is a hero because he was a pioneer in the new field of jet airplanes and space missions. What was it about a man that he would let himself be strapped into an experimental jet airplane and test it at two or three times the speed of sound? What is the internal mechanism that drives a man to want—to fight—to be hurled from the face of Earth as part of the exploration of space?

In many ways, he is no different than earlier explorers who risked their lives and fortunes to do something that no one had ever attempted before. He is our hero because he was driven to repeat history and explore where few had gone before. He is our hero because he came back alive each time and made us feel special about what he had accomplished. And he was our hero because he gave us great pride in our country and its space endeavors.

What Made the Man

In many ways, John Herschel Glenn Jr., was the all-American man. He was born in 1921 in Cambridge, Ohio, and grew up in Cambridge and New Concord, Ohio. He wrote that his childhood was everything a boy could dream of and he flourished as a student.

After receiving a Bachelor of Science degree in engineering from Muskingum College, Glenn decided to enter the military. This was during the early years of World War II, and Glenn was attracted to military aviation. He enrolled in the Naval Aviation Program in 1942 and was later assigned to the Marines' VMO-155 group in 1944. Glenn flew bombing missions over the Marshall Islands in the Pacific later in the war, and by the time the war ended, had been promoted to captain and stationed at the Naval Air Station Patuxent River. By then he had married his childhood sweetheart, Anna Margaret Castor. He would later have two children with her.

Although he flew many significant test flights, his early claim to fame was completing the first supersonic transcontinental flight. When he flew over his hometown, the resulting sonic boom had a neighbor running to Glenn's house shouting,

"Johnny dropped a bomb on us! "

Around this time, the United States was scrambling to match the USSR in the space race. The Soviets had already orbited a satellite called Sputnik and sent animals into orbit. They would shortly send Yuri Gagarin into orbit as the first man to enter space. The new

20

约翰·格伦：
宇航员及政治家

他是谁

约翰·格伦成为英雄,那是因为他是喷射式飞机和宇宙空间计划领域的一名先锋。他可以把自己捆在实验喷射式飞机中进行两三次音速测试,这是一个什么样的人呢?而又是什么样的内在动力驱使着他向往飞行,飞离地球去探索宇宙空间呢?

从很多方面看,他无异于那些早期的探索者。他们冒着生命危险和财产损失去做一些没有人敢尝试去做的事。他是我们的英雄,因为他重复了历史,探索了那些以前很少有人去过的地方;因为他每次都能活着回来,而且使我们感觉他所完成的任务很特别;更因为他让我们为自己的国家以及国家在宇宙空间方面的努力而自豪。

是什么成就了他

在许多方面,小约翰·格伦是个地道的美国人。他于1921年出生于俄亥俄州的剑桥,在俄亥俄州的剑桥和新康科德长大。他曾经写道,他拥有每个男孩都梦想的童年生活,在学校,他是一名优等生。

在拿到穆斯静冈学院授予的工程机械学士学位之后,格伦决定参军。当时正值第二次世界大战前期,格伦喜欢上了军事飞行。1942年,他报名参加了海军飞行计划,并且在1944年被分配到海军VMO-155小组。在战争中,格伦参加了位于太平洋的马歇尔岛轰炸任务,并且在战争的最后阶段被提升为机长,并分配到帕图森特河海军航空基地。在那时,他已经和他小时候的玩伴安娜·玛格丽特·卡斯特结婚,并且后来有了两个孩子。

虽然他经历过许多重大的飞行实验,不过他早期的目标是完成一次超音速横贯大陆的飞行。当他从家乡上空飞过时,音速飞机的隆隆声使得他的一位邻居跑到格伦的家里大叫:

"约翰向我们扔炸弹啦!"

就在这个时期,美国正与苏联进行宇宙空间探索竞赛。苏联已经发射了一颗人造卫星,并且把一些动物也送到了太空轨道。他们还将加加林送到轨道上去,从而成为进入宇

National Aeronautics and Space Administration, or NASA, was desperate to catch up, and from hundreds of applicants chose seven test pilots as the Mercury astronauts. This group included John Glenn.

Glenn served with honor in the Senate and was the chief author of the 1978 Nonproliferation Act. He ran unsuccessfully for the Democratic nomination for president in 1984. However, his record was stained when he was included as part of the Keating Five after accepting a $200,000 contribution from a man partly responsible for the savings and loan collapses of the late 1980s. Glenn was exonerated and was found only to have exercised poor judgment. He repeatedly won re-election, finally retiring from politics in 1999.

The Legacy of the Man

John Glenn remains one of America's most beloved heroes. He was most famously portrayed by Ed Harris in the film *The Right Stuff.*

Besides his personal achievements, Glenn has lent his name to the NASA John H. Glenn Research Center at Lewis Field in Cleveland, Ohio. The highway running by the Wright-Patterson Air Force Base and Wright State University near Dayton, Ohio, is named the Colonel Glenn Highway.

宙空间的第一人。美国国家航空和航天局(NASA)拼命追赶,从成百上千的申请人当中选出了7个人作为水星计划的宇航员,约翰·格伦就是其中一员。

格伦光荣地参加了参议院工作,并于1978年成为核不扩散运动的领袖。1984年他在美国总统竞选的民主党内部选举中败北。然而,当他还是凯丁五人组的一员的时候,他从一个对在20世纪80年代末存贷款崩溃负有部分责任的人手中接手了一项20万美元的捐款,这在他的政治生涯留下了不光彩的一笔。最终,格伦仅被认为判断力缺失而被无罪释放。此后,他一次次赢得选举,最后于1999年退出了政坛。

他的遗产

约翰·格伦始终是美国人最喜爱的英雄之一。爱德·哈尔斯在电影《征空先锋》中最成功地塑造了格伦的形象。

除了个人取得的成就,格伦还用自己的名字命名位于俄亥俄州的克利夫兰路易斯菲尔德的NASA约翰·格伦实验中心。怀特·帕特森空军基地和俄亥俄州代顿附近的怀特州立大学之间的高速公路也被命名为格伦上校高速公路。

Twenty-one

Dame Valerie Jane Goodall,
Primatologist

Who She Is

What would cause someone to spend much of her life in the bush working for, studying and protecting chimpanzees? Surely most of us would see this as an unusually committed calling for a woman, even one who had developed a fascination with primates and with Africa.

But she is our hero precisely because she is so dogged in her pursuit of knowledge and because of her efforts to protect and study chimps in the wild. And she is our hero because she is unorthodox, stepping out of the box and using unusual methods to develop theories of chimp behavior and its relationship to human behavior.

She is and always will be the darling of animal lovers who
have put her on a pedestal for her work, her dedication
and her personal sacrifices for the good of the world.

What Made the Woman

Thanks to multiple appearances in National Geographic magazine (the most for any one person) and several television documentaries, Jane Goodall is one of the most recognizable scientists in the world.   Her research into the behavior of chimpanzees substantially changed the way people viewed the relationship between humans and primates.

Goodall was born on April 3, 1934, in London, the first child of Mortimer Herbert Morriss-Goodall and the former Margaret Myfanwe Joseph. She has one younger sister, Judy. Her parents divorced when Goodall was only eight and the two sisters stayed with their mother, moving to the seaside city of Bournemouth, England, to live closer to the children's maternal grandmother and two great aunts.

She quickly demonstrated a burning curiosity about the outdoors and the animals that inhabited her immediate area. Goodall devoured the Tarzan books by Edgar Rice Burroughs and told friends she would be a much better Jane to Tarzan than the character in the books. This fascination with the jungle led her to declare at age 11 that she intended to visit Africa and maybe even live there.

By the late 1950s, Goodall had achieved her dream to travel to Africa, but found her initial work as a secretary to be less than fulfilling. She heard that the famed anthropologist Louis Leakey and his wife, Mary, were digging near where she was residing in Zaire. As part of his fossil research linking humans to apes, Leakey had been planning a major study

21

珍妮·古德尔:
灵长类动物学家

她是谁

是什么促使一个人花费毕生的精力于荒野之中从事研究和保护黑猩猩的工作?可以肯定,大多数人会认为,这份工作对于女性来说异常艰难,即使是一位对非洲和灵长类动物深深痴迷的女性。

毫无疑问,她是我们的英雄,因为她对知识如饥似渴,因为她对黑猩猩竭力保护,努力研究,还因为她走出思维定式,以独特的方式完善关于黑猩猩习性及它与人类习性间关系的理论。

她为全世界所做的奉献及个人的牺牲使一些动物爱好者将她奉为完人。她现在是、并将一直是他们心中的楷模。

是什么成就了她

由于在《国家地理杂志》(对任何人都是莫大荣耀)和一些电视纪录片中的多次亮相,珍妮·古德尔现已成为世界上最受瞩目的科学家之一。她对黑猩猩习性的研究大大改变了人们看待人类与灵长类动物间关系的视角。

古德尔于1934年4月3日出生于伦敦,是莫蒂默·赫伯特·莫理斯·古德尔和马格里特·麦凡苇·约瑟夫的第一个孩子。她还有一个名叫朱迪的妹妹。古德尔年仅8岁时,父母离异,姐妹俩跟随母亲移居到了英国海滨城市伯恩茅斯,以离她们的外祖母和两个姨妈住得更近些。

她很快对郊野和栖息于附近地区的动物表现出了强烈的好奇心。她津津有味地读完了埃德加·赖斯·布朗夫的小说《人猿泰山》,并告诉她的朋友们她会比书中的主人公做得更好。对丛林的痴迷使她在11岁时就宣称她想去非洲旅行,甚至可能在那里居住。

20世纪50年代末期,古德尔实现了去非洲旅行的梦想,但她的第一份秘书工作并不让她十分满意。她听说著名的人类学家路易斯·利基和他的妻子玛丽正在离她居住地附近的以威峡谷进行挖掘工作,作为他联系人类和类人猿关系的化石研究的一部分,利基一直在计划一项重大的研究。见到古德尔后,他聘用她为助手,很快,古德尔的热忱、对丛

of the great apes. After meeting Goodall, he hired her to be his secretary and was quickly impressed by her enthusiasm, love of the jungle and ability to absorb information and ideas.

Goodall was frustrated in her initial attempts to get near to the chimpanzees; she was not allowed to get any closer than 50 feet. It did not help that she came down with two bouts of malaria in the course of only a few months.

She was finally accepted into a chimpanzee troop when a large male wandered into camp and started stomping his feet and screaming. Goodall realized he was interested in a banana on her camp table, and she quickly started using bananas to make contact with the chimpanzees. She also set up a banana-laden feeding station to lure the chimpanzees, but later believed this altered their natural behavior.

Goodall soon had complete access to the chimpanzees at Gombe, who would let her follow them and greeted her, as they do with each other, with a touch or kiss. Unlike other wildlife researchers, she assigned her subjects names rather than code numbers.

After a few months, Goodall realized she was seeing behavior that had never been noted before, behavior that showed chimpanzees to be highly intelligent, emotional creatures living in complicated social groups. She also discovered that, despite popular beliefs, chimpanzees could use mildly complicated tools and would eat meat, making them omnivores and not vegetarians.

By now Goodall's work was exciting enough to Leakey for him to continue funding the project and send additional supplies. She also attracted the attention of the National Geographic, which began chronicling her work in 1964. This would result in cover stories and a variety of television specials on her discoveries.

Goodall lived almost exclusively in her Gombe compound until 1975. She accumulated a wealth of data that is still being studied. She founded Jane Goodall Institutes in nine countries and lectures constantly on chimpanzee conservation and research, and on eliminating the use of chimpanzees in nonessential research.

The Legacy of the Woman

Jane Goodall will always be associated with bravery and honesty in research. When she made her first excursion to Gombe, many scientists questioned Louis Leakey's judgment in sending a young woman into what could be a dangerous situation. She proved them wrong.

Goodall's work has resulted in her being given numerous professional recognitions and awards. She was named a Dame Commander of the British Empire in 2004. In 2002, Kofi Annan, the secretary-general of the United Nations, named her a United Nations Messenger of Peace. Other awards for Goodall include the Medal of Tanzania, Japan's Kyoto Prize and the Benjamin Franklin Medal in Life Science. She is a member of the advisory board of BBC Wildlife magazines. In 2006, Goodall received the 60th Anniversary Medal of UNESCO and French Legion d'Honneur.

林的热爱、掌握信息以及吸取教训的能力给他留下了深刻的印象。

最初,古德尔接近黑猩猩的尝试连连失败,这令她十分沮丧。黑猩猩们无论如何也不让她靠近它们到50步以内的距离。即使这样,她还是在短短几个月内就染上了两次疟疾。

而当一只巨大的雄性黑猩猩走进她的营地并开始捶胸顿足嘶叫时,她终于被一个黑猩猩群所接受。古德尔意识到它对她营地里桌子上的香蕉感兴趣,于是她很快开始利用香蕉与黑猩猩建立联系。她甚至建立了一个储存了大量香蕉的黑猩猩喂养站来引诱它们,但事后她认定这将改变他们的自然习性。

很快,古德尔可以随意接触贡贝的黑猩猩了,它们也允许她跟着它们,并用抚摸和亲吻欢迎她,就像对待自己的同类一样。和其他野生动物学家不同,她给她的研究对象取名字,而不是用编码区分它们。

数月后,古德尔她看到了猩猩身上一个未曾被人注意到的习性,这一习性显示了黑猩猩是拥有高智商情感,并复杂群居的动物。她还发现,与普遍观念不同,黑猩猩在某种程度上会使用复杂工具。并且,它们吃肉,证实了它们是杂食动物而非素食动物。

到目前为止,古德尔的成果足以让利基兴奋不已,使他继续资助这个项目并给予额外补给。她还引起了《国家地理》的注意,而后者将她在1964年的工作按时间进行整理。有关她的发现的故事集和电视特辑也因此诞生。

到1975年为止,古德尔几乎一直居住在贡贝的营地中。她收集了大量正在被研究的资料。她在9个国家建立了珍妮·古德尔研究中心,进行有关黑猩猩保护和研究,并进行讲座,论述如何避免在非必要研究中使用黑猩猩。

她的遗产

在研究中,古德尔永远都是诚实而勇敢的。当她第一次去贡贝探究时,很多科学家对路易斯·利基的决定质疑:利基竟然将一个年轻的女子送往一个潜伏着危险的地方。而古德尔用事实证明,他们是错的。

众多专业认可和奖项证明了古德尔工作的成功。2004年,她被授予"大英帝国女爵士"称号。2002年,联合国秘书科菲·安南授予了她"联合国和平使者"的称号。古德尔还被授予"坦桑尼亚金质奖章",日本"京都奖"和"本杰明·富兰克林生命科学奖"等奖项。她是BBC电台《野生动物》杂志顾问委员会的一员。在2006年,古德尔获得了联合国教科文组织的"60周年纪念金牌奖"和法国"军团荣誉奖"。

Twenty-two

Jim Thorpe, Sports Heroes

Why He is Among the *50 plus one Greatest Modern Heroes*

Jim Thorpe was a natural athlete, playing baseball and football in the United States. He was also a track and field star who made history by setting fantastic records and winning gold medals in both the pentathlon and the decathlon in a single Olympics. At the closing ceremonies for the Games, King Gustav V of Sweden famously told Thorpe, "Sir, you are the greatest athlete in the world! " Suffice it to say that the king was right as Thorpe takes a seat as one of the greatest sports heroes ever.

On the Way Up

James Francis Thorpe was born on May 28, 1887 in a one-room cabin close to Prague, Oklahoma. Part Native American, his Indian name was Wa-Tho-Huk, meaning Bright Path. His father, Hiram, was a farmer and his mother, Mary James, was a Potawatomi Indian. Mary was also a descendent of the last great Sauk and Fox chief, Black Hawk, who was a famous warrior and athlete. Tragically, Thorpe's twin brother died when they were 9 years old.

Thorpe attended the Sac and Fox Indian Agency School during his high school years, and then, in 1904, he moved on to the Carlisle Industrial Indian School in Pennsylvania. The school gave American Indians the chance to acquire practical training in numerous trades and provided students the chance to work off-campus jobs at local farms, homes and industries. At Carlisle Industrial Indian School, Thorpe was an all-around talent and started playing football and running track, and competed in baseball, wrestling, boxing, lacrosse, gymnastics, swimming, hockey, handball and basketball. Coached by football legend, Glenn Pop Warner, he was chosen once as a third-team All-American and twice as a first team All–American. He won a collegiate National Championship in football. Thorpe was also an accomplished dancer and became an intercollegiate ballroom dance champion in 1912.

Also in 1912, Thorpe competed on the U.S. Track and Field Olympic team during the Games in Stockholm, Sweden. He outperformed all of his opponents in both the pentathlon and decathlon competitions, setting records that would remain unbroken for decades.He came in first in nine of the 15 events, and also finished fourth in the high jump event and seventh in the long jump.

King Gustav V presented Thorpe with his two gold medals during the closing ceremonies. The king then made his memorable greatest athlete statement, after which Thorpe reportedly replied with a simple "Thanks King".

His early career and Olympic awards include:

22

吉姆·索普：
体坛英豪

他为何入选《50+1位最具影响力的风云人物》？

吉姆·索普天生就是运动员，在美国打棒球和橄榄球。他也是田径明星，创造了令人难以想象的纪录，在同一届奥运会中赢得了5项全能和10项全能金牌。在闭幕式颁奖仪式上，瑞典国王古斯塔夫五世对索普有一句著名的评价："先生，你是世界上最伟大的运动员！"索普在万古体坛中享有一席之地，这也说明国王的评价是正确的。

成长之路

1887年5月28日，弗朗西斯·索普出生在俄克拉何马布拉格附近的一间陋室里。他有部分美国血统，印度名为瓦托胡克，意即"闪光的路"。他的父亲Hiram是个农民，母亲玛丽·詹姆斯是波塔瓦托米印第安人。玛丽也是最后一位伟大的黑鹰酋长的后代，他是著名的战士也是运动员。后来悲剧发生了，索普的双胞胎兄弟在9岁时不

高中时，索普就读于萨克·福克斯印第安代理学校，然后，在1904年，他转到了宾夕法尼亚的卡力索印第安人工业学校。这所学校向美国印第安人提供机会，让他们在众多贸易活动中得到锻炼，还向学生提供了在当地农场、家庭及工厂打工的机会。在卡力索印第安人工业学校，索普是个全能的天才运动员，他开始打橄榄球，跑长跑，参加了众多比赛，比如棒球、摔跤、拳击、长曲棍球、体操、游泳、冰球、手球和篮球。索普的教练是格伦·鲍伯·沃纳，他曾一次入选"全美第三阵容队"、两次入选"全美第一阵容队"。他赢过一次美国大学生橄榄球赛。索普还是个成功的舞者，1912年曾取得大学生舞蹈比赛冠军。

同样是在1912年，索普代表美国田径队参加了瑞典斯德哥尔摩夏季奥运会。在五项全能和田径十项全能比赛中，他横扫对手取胜，创下了几十年都没被打破的纪录。在15项赛事中的9项，他都拿了第一，跳高比赛排名第四、跳远排名第七。

在闭幕式上，国王古斯塔夫五世为他颁发了两枚金牌。国王赞扬索普是最伟大的运动员，据说索普只是简单地说了声"谢谢"。

他早期运动生涯及奥运会获奖包括：

· All American (1911-12)
· Olympic Decathlon and Pentathlon Champion (1912)

Professional Career

Thorpe received various honors for his achievements in athletics, many of them awarded to him posthumously. In 1999, both houses of Congress honored him as the Athlete of the Century, and he has been enshrined in many halls of fame, including the Indian Athletic Hall of Fame, the Helms Professional Football Hall of Fame, the Oklahoma Hall of Fame and the Pennsylvania Hall of Fame. Other awards include him being:

· College Football Hall of Fame (1951)
· Most Outstanding Athlete of the First Half of the 20th Century, Associated Press (1950)
· America's Greatest Football Player of the Half-Century, Associated Press (1950)
· Charter member, Pro Football Hall of Fame (1963)
· National Track and Field Hall of Fame (1975)
· U.S. Olympic Hall of Fame (1983)
· ABC's Wide World of Sports Athlete of the Century (1996-2001)

- 全美阵容队(1911–1912)
- 奥运会五项全能和十项全能冠军(1912)

职业生涯

索普因其出色的体育成就而获得无数功名,很多都是身后授予的。1999年,国会两院都授予他"世纪运动员"的光荣称号,他还入选了许多名人堂,包括印第安体育名人堂,赫姆斯职业橄榄球名人堂,俄克拉荷马州名人堂,宾夕法尼亚州名人堂。其他奖项包括:

- 入选大学橄榄球名人堂(1951)
- 被美联社评为"20世纪上半叶最杰出运动员"(1950)
- 被美联社评为"20世纪上半叶美国最伟大橄榄球球员" (1950)
- 职业橄榄球名人堂创始会员(1963)
- 入选国家田径名人堂(1975)
- 入选美国奥林匹克名人堂(1983)
- 被ABC评为"世纪全球体育人物"(1996~2001)

Twenty-three

James Maury Henson, Entertainer

Who He Is

Who could make us laugh so hard using an entertainment medium so old and so conventional that it was almost absurd? Who could possibly put life in the Cookie Monster or Miss Piggy so convincingly that we found them nearly human in their emotions and behavior? Who could take two names from the classic movie It's a *Wonderful Life,* and use them to such perfection: Bert and Ernie, silly and lovable.

Who could do all this? Jim Henson could. He was a creative and entertaining genius who lived his life through his puppets. He certainly was not the first to use puppets as part of a television act, but he was the first to do it so brilliantly. Through his association with *Sesame Street,* he taught our children the alphabet and how to be safe and how to enjoy learning each morning on public television.

> Like many of our heroes, he lives on through his creations—movies, books, television shows and the characters themselves.

What Made the Man

Besides creating creatures and special effects for fantasy television shows and movies, Jim Henson will always be most closely associated with the Muppets and *Sesame Street.* Such characters as Kermit the Frog, Miss Piggy, Fozzie Bear, Bert and Ernie, Elmo, Oscar the Grouch and Cookie Monster were created, operated and often voiced by Henson.

After a few months in college, Henson would create the first Muppets (the term is a combination of marionette and puppet) for a 5-minute children's show called *Sam and Friends* on WRC-TV. The show was momentous for Henson for two reasons: Jane Nebel, a performing partner on the show would become his wife in 1959 and, in 1955, a primitive version of what would become Kermit the Frog made his first on-air appearance.

Kermit would be a revolution in puppetry. Henson created the head out of softer, more malleable materials that allowed for a far greater range of expression. He perfected his techniques of using the camera frame to mask the puppet operator for a greater range of movement. Henson also created a style of movement for the puppets that involved having the operator use one hand to manipulate the upper body, head and mouth and the other hand to operate the character's arm with a wire from below. The result was something nobody had seen before.

The small local show soon drew the attention of national variety shows hungry for new forms of entertainment. Henson's brand of irreverent, often violent, slapstick and the novelty of the Muppet operation was just what they were looking for, and while in college he was bringing Kermit and company to programs like *The Tonight Show, The Steve Allen Show* and *The Ed Sullivan Show.*

詹姆斯·莫里·亨森:
演员

他是谁

谁能用如此古老如此传统几近荒唐的娱乐媒介让我们捧腹大笑？谁能如此令人信服地赋予甜饼魔鬼或者贪心小姐以生命，以至于我们发现他们的情感和行为接近人性化？谁能把经典电影《心想事成》中伯特和厄尼两个人物愚蠢和可爱的性格对比刻画得如此淋漓尽致？

所有这一切谁能做到？答案是吉姆·亨森。他是一个富有创造力和娱乐精神的天才，一生都致力于木偶的创作。他肯定不是第一个把木偶引入电视节目的人，但他绝对是第一个在这方面取得巨大成功的人。通过《芝麻街》，他教我们的孩子字母表，教他们如何确保安全，如何每天早晨在公共电视台享受学习的乐趣。

像许多英雄一样，他的生命通过他的创作得以延续。其创作包括：电影、书籍、电视节目以及其中的人物。

是什么成就了他

除了创造各色形象、荒诞电视节目和电影的特效外，吉姆·亨森总是和《提线木偶》、《芝麻街》紧密联系。亨森创造了诸如克米特青蛙、贪心小姐、弗仁熊、伯特和厄尼、埃尔默、心怀不满的奥斯卡、甜饼魔鬼等木偶形象，并亲自操作，而且常常亲自为人物配音。

进大学几个月以后，他为WRC电视台的一档5分钟儿童节目《萨姆和朋友们》发明了第一个提线木偶(牵线木偶和木偶的混合体)。这个节目对亨森的意义重大，原因有二：一是节目的表演合作伙伴简·尼贝尔在1959年和他结婚；此外在1955年，著名的克米特青蛙剧的最初蓝本第一次在电台中播出。

克米特后来成为木偶剧的一次变革。亨森用更软更具延展性的材料制作头部，因此人物的表情可以更丰富。为了使木偶活动更加自如，他完善了使用摄像机框架来隐藏木偶操作者的方法。亨森也创造了一种木偶动作风格，这种运动包括让操作者用一只手来控制上半身、头和嘴，另一只手用底下的一条电线来控制人物的胳膊。这一创新取得了前所未有的效果。

这个当地的小节目很快引起了急切寻找新娱乐形式的国家综艺节目的注意。亨森的这种反叛闹剧的特色以及提线木偶操作的独具匠心正是国家综艺节目所需要的。与此同时，在大学里他给克米特和同伴带来了一些像《今夜秀》、《斯蒂夫·爱伦节目》和《爱德华·苏利文秀》之类的节目。

Henson stretched his wings into experimental filmmaking. His short film, *Time Piece,* was nominated in 1966 for an Academy Award for Live Action Short. Even more significant during this period was Henson's involvement in a revolutionary new PBS show for children called *Sesame Street.* Henson's *Sesame Street* characters debuted in 1970.

The Legacy of the Man

By almost all accounts, everyone who knew him thought Jim Henson was a terrific man to work with. He encouraged taking chances, was always there to help one of his staff through a problem and was able to clearly communicate his vision to his collaborators.

Unlike many entertainers associated with children's television, Henson never talked down to his audience. He also recognized the importance of keeping adults entertained as well, and used sly humor, a fast pace, wacky slapstick and current references to delight audiences of all ages. Many of the catchphrases from the Muppet characters have entered the popular vernacular.

亨森把自己的领域扩展到试验性影片的制作当中。他的电影短片《时间段》在1966年被提名现场情节短片学院奖。更重要的是，在此期间，亨森参与了全新的美国公共广播公司为儿童制作的节目《芝麻街》。1970年，亨森的《芝麻街》人物第一次登场。

他的遗产

从任何角度来看，几乎每个认识亨森的人都认为他是一个很好的搭档和伙伴。他鼓励大胆尝试，总是帮助他的员工，清晰地向他的合作者传达他的观点。

与其他儿童电视的工作者不同，亨森从来没有居高临下地与观众谈话。他还强调保持成年人娱乐的重要性，采用顽皮的幽默、快节奏、滑稽可笑的闹剧以及当前时髦的语言来娱乐各年龄层的观众。许多来自木偶人物的名言已经成为当地的俗语。

Twenty-four

Steven Jobs and "The Apple Computer", Entrepreneur

Who He Is

Steve Jobs is a hero because he and his associates made personal computing a reality. Yes, he is a very rich man and yes, we tend to favor those who are successful and wealthy—but there is more to Steve Jobs than that. He is the quintessential self-made man—someone who rises above his station in life, who has insight into something new and different—and, most importantly, takes a chance.

He is our hero because he is also the ultimate entrepreneur. Starting a computer company was not enough for him; he saw the newest technology could be used in a range of applications and introduced the world to an array of visual delights.

What Made the Man

Very few people in private industry can claim that their creations changed the world, but Steve Jobs could. Jobs, along with Steve Wozniak, created the first truly personal computer in the Apple I and Apple II. The new machines made people rethink what a computer was and what it could do for them. Later, Apple would release the phenomenally successful Macintosh computer that further expanded the capabilities and ease of use of a personal computer.

Jobs was an orphan adopted by Paul and Clara Jobs of Mountain View, California, on February 24, 1955. He did not like the schools at Mountain View, and his parents decided to move to Los Altos, California, so Jobs could attend Homestead High School. He was described, at the time, as something of a loner and as a student who was always willing to take a fresh look at problem solving.

During the next few years, Jobs drifted. He took a short-term job as a video game designer at Atari in 1974, then left that to travel to India in search of spiritual enlightenment. When Jobs returned to California, he got back into contact with Wozniak, who had started the Homebrew Computer Club, which encouraged creating a computer that could be easily used by a large number of people. Unlike Wozniak, who loved creating electronic products, Jobs was more interested in the marketability of those products.

> He conceived the idea of a personal computer and persuaded Wozniak to provide the technical expertise.

The Apple I computer was initially designed in Jobs' bedroom and built in his garage. The initial reaction to the product was positive, and Jobs and Wozniak sold everything they could to raise operating capital to market the new computers. Jobs came up with the company name, Apple, because it reminded him of a happy summer he had spent as an orchard worker in Oregon.

Jobs and Wozniak began marketing the Apple I in 1976, selling it at a fairly

24

斯蒂夫·乔布斯和"苹果电脑"：
企业家

他是谁

斯蒂夫·乔布斯是一位旷世奇才,因为他和他的同事让个人电脑成为现实。他的确很富有——而我们也仰慕那些富有的成功人士——但除此之外,斯蒂夫·乔布斯还有更多的过人之处:他是自主创业的典范,怀有提高自己社会地位的宏伟抱负,并且能够敏锐地洞察到新鲜和不同的事物。然而最为重要的是,他总能抓住机遇。

他是我们的英雄,因为他也是一位伟大的企业家。对他来说创建电脑公司远远不够,他预见到这项最新的技术可以广泛地应用于各个领域,从而给世界带来希望。

是什么成就了他

几乎没有一个私营企业的员工敢断言他们的发明能够改变整个世界,但斯蒂夫·乔布斯却能。在第一代和第二代苹果电脑时期,乔布斯和斯蒂芬·沃兹尼克一道,发明了第一台真正的个人电脑,这项新创造促使人们重新思考"电脑是什么?"和"它能为我们做些什么"。不久,苹果公司就推出功能多样、容易操作的麦金塔个人电脑,取得了令人难以置信的成功。

乔布斯是个孤儿,1955年的2月24日他被加利福尼亚的保罗和克莱拉·乔布斯收养。他并不喜欢当地的学校。后来,他的养父母决定搬到加州的洛杉矶,因此乔布斯能够到荷姆斯德中学学习。在那段时间,他被认为是一个爱独处并总愿意用全新视角看待问题的学生。

接下来的几年中,乔布斯频繁地奔走各地,1974年,他在阿塔利公司做了一名短期电子游戏设计人员。不久就辞职去印度旅游,以寻求心灵启迪和感悟。当乔布斯重回加州后,他又和沃兹尼克取得了联系,这时,沃兹尼克已经开创了"家酿"电脑俱乐部,这推动了简单便利的大众化电脑的发明。而与酷爱发明电子产品的沃兹尼克所不同的是:乔布斯更对产品的可销性感兴趣。

他提出了个人电脑的构想,并说服沃兹尼克提供专门的技术。

第一代苹果电脑最初是在乔布斯的卧室中设计出,又在他的车库中被制造出来的,这项产品最初反应很好,乔布斯和沃兹尼克卖了他们所能卖的一切来增加运行资本,以便能够更好地推广新品电脑,这时乔布斯想到了企业的名字:苹果。因为苹果唤起了他对在俄勒冈果园当员工的美好夏日时光的回忆。

1976年乔布斯和沃兹尼克开始推广第一代苹果电脑,以比较合理的价格666美元出

reasonable price of $666. The Apple I was the first single-board computer with a built-in video interface and on-board ROM, allowing it to load programs from an external source. The first computer was designed primarily for computer enthusiasts.

For the general consumer, Jobs and Wozniak created the Apple II. The design varied little from the Apple I, but it quickly built up a reputation as the Volkswagen of personal computing, thanks to its ease-of-use and durability. Jobs brought in professional marketers and money from venture capitalists, and within 3 years of its creation, the Apple II had earnings of almost $140 million. The company went public in 1980 and Jobs and Wozniak found themselves instant millionaires.

Apple started facing a serious challenge from IBM's new line of personal computers and Jobs realized he would have to market computers that could be used in the business environment that IBM dominated. After stumbling with the Apple III and the Lisa (the first personal computer to be controlled with a mouse), Jobs hit pay dirt with the Macintosh in 1984. The computer used a unique interface that allowed users simply to point and click with the mouse to operate the computer, rather than having to type in MS-DOS commands. The new computer was still not compatible with IBM, so Jobs had to try to market it on its own merits. One of the most successful of those was the Macintosh's ability to do desktop design and publishing. Jobs also worked hard to portray Macintosh users as young, informal and still living a counterculture life.

Just as sales of the Macintosh were soaring, an internal revolt at Apple resulted in the board of directors stripping Jobs of most of his responsibilities. Jobs felt he had been forced out of the very company he had worked so hard to create. Soon, Jobs had no say in how the company was operated. He took his money and left.

Jobs spent some time bicycling and traveling, but felt lost. In September 1985, after meeting with Nobel laureate Paul Berg, Jobs came up with the idea of creating computers that would benefit higher education. Jobs officially resigned from Apple and took five employees with him for his new venture. Jobs created NexT to build hardware and software for object-oriented computers. The efforts failed at first, and Jobs is still struggling to create new software at NexT, concentrating on reference material.

Meanwhile, Jobs had married Laurene Powell in 1991 and had three children with her (he also has a daughter, Lisa Brennan-Jobs with Christine Brennan, whom he never married).

NexT was bought by Apple in 1996, and Jobs returned to the first company he had created. Jobs was made interim CEO and immediately canceled several Apple projects. He used the NeXTSTEP software to create the Mac OSX operating system. In 1998, Jobs introduced the iMac, an all-in-one personal computer with a unique and charming design.

Jobs would enter the entertainment industry in 1986 when he bought Lucasfilm's computer graphics division, renaming it Pixar. After a series of successful short films, Pixar released the first full-length computer-animated feature *Toy Story*, distributed by Walt Disney. The success of that film and its followers made Pixar a superstar. Disney and Pixar could not negotiate a new contract in 2003~2004, and Jobs said that Pixar would find a new partner. However, Robert Iger, the new CEO of Disney, patched up relations and bought Pixar in 2005. Jobs became the largest single shareholder in Disney with 7 percent of its stock.

售。第一代苹果电脑是最早的带内置视频界面和只读存储器的单键盘电脑。这使得它能够从其他资源处下载信息,这项发明主要是为电脑爱好者设计的。

为迎合普通消费者的需要,乔布斯和沃兹尼克创造了第二代苹果电脑,它的设计和第一代相比区别不大。由于它便于使用,并且持久耐用,第二代苹果电脑很快赢得了个人电脑中的大众汽车的声誉。乔布斯聘请专业电脑人才,投入了风险投资人的资金,因而在产品投入市场后的短短3年内,他销售的第二代苹果电脑已经赚取近1亿4千万美元的巨款。这家公司也于1980年上市,乔布斯和沃兹尼克也发现自己跻身了大富翁的行列。

IBM个人电脑新产品的出现使苹果电脑开始面临严峻的挑战,乔布斯意识到他应该推广一种电脑,把它应用到由IBM主宰的商务市场。在经过第三代苹果电脑和"丽莎"(第一个由鼠标控制的个人电脑)的跌跌撞撞之后,1894年,乔布斯历经千辛万苦研发出了麦金塔。这种新品电脑使用了一个独特的界面,它可以让使用者进行简单的鼠标点击来操作电脑,而不是按MS-DOS的指令来操作。这种新电脑和IBM产品是不兼容的,因此,乔布斯要靠这一独特优点来营销产品。其中最成功的是麦金塔电脑的台式设计和打印功能。乔布斯向麦金塔的用户展示了一种年轻、非正式和反正统文化的生活。

随着麦金塔的销售一路攀升,一场苹果电脑公司的内部斗争导致董事会剥夺了乔布斯几乎所有的决策权力,乔布斯感到他被排挤出这个他曾如此鞠躬尽瘁去开创的公司。不久,乔布斯对公司如何运转经营已毫无发言权,他只得带着他的财产离开。

有一段时间,乔布斯骑单车兜风或外出旅游,但却感到迷茫空虚。1985年的9月,在遇见诺贝尔奖获得者保尔·博格之后,乔布斯突然生出一个大胆的设想:发明一种服务于高等教育的电脑。乔布斯正式辞去了他在苹果的职务,并和5个员工一起开创属于他们的新事业。乔布斯创立了NexT公司,制作面向固定对象的电脑硬件和软件。这种努力最初失败了,但乔布斯仍艰难地坚持在NexT中创造新的软件。

在此期间,乔布斯于1991年娶了劳伦斯·鲍威尔为妻子,两人膝下有3个孩子(他还与克里斯汀·布莱楠有一个私生女丽莎·布莱楠·乔布斯,但他一生未娶克里斯汀)。

在1996年,NexT被苹果公司收购,乔布斯也重返他开创的第一个公司,并被任命为临时总裁。上任之后,他很快取消了苹果公司的几个项目,他用NeXTSTEP软件来创建Mac OSX操作系统。在1998年,乔布斯推出iMac:一种有式样独特、造型迷人的多功能个人电脑。

1986年,乔布斯进军娱乐产业,他购买了卢卡斯电影公司的电脑动画设计部,并重新命名为皮克萨动画工作室。该公司出版了一系列成功的短片之后,又发行了最早的栩栩如生的长篇电脑动画片《玩具的故事》。该片由华特·迪斯尼公司发行。该电影以及它的续集获得了巨大成功。这使得皮克萨动画工作室成为一颗耀眼的巨星。在2003至2004年期间迪斯尼和皮克萨动画工作室并没有谈成协议。乔布斯说皮克萨动画工作室将寻找新的合作伙伴。然而,迪斯尼新任总裁罗伯特·伊格弥合了他们之间的关系,并于2005年收购了皮克萨动画工作室,乔布斯成为迪斯尼最大的个人股东,拥有总资产的7%。

The Legacy of the Man

Steve Jobs will always be considered an amazingly successful entrepreneur who made money by providing a valuable product at a reasonable price. His management style was aggressive and demanding and not for everyone's taste, but it was well suited to the wild days of PC development in the 1980s.

His work with Pixar has created some of the best-loved animated features in recent history, and he is still pursuing new technologies in hardware and software for Apple and Pixar. Still only in his early 50s, it is likely Jobs will conquer other worlds before he is ready to retire.

Jobs certainly made his share of mistakes and erroneous assumptions as he developed his businesses, and his management style resulted in the burnout of many key employees, but he was still a true visionary who saw a way to substantially improve people's lives and make a lot of money doing it.

The Resources

More information on Steve Jobs, Apple and Pixar can be found at *www.apple.com* and *www.pixar.com*.

Jobs has been the subject of several unauthorized biographies and has yet to write an autobiography. Books about him include *The Second Coming of Steve Jobs,* Broadway, 2001; *Apple Confidential 2.0: The Definitive History of the World's Most Colorful Company,* No Starch Press, 2004; *Steve Jobs: The Journey Is the Reward,* Lynx Books, 1988; and *Steve Jobs and the Next Big Thing,* Scribner's, 1993.

他的遗产

斯蒂夫·乔布斯一直被视为一位通过销售物美价廉的商品而成为令人惊异的成功企业家。他的管理风格比较严厉和苛刻，并不是每个人都可以接受，但它却非常适合20世纪80年代个人电脑发展时期。

在现代史上，他在皮克萨动画公司创作了一批非常优秀而生动的动画人物，目前仍致力于为苹果和皮克斯动画公司研发硬件和软件的新技术。尽管他已年过半百，但他仍想退休之前征服电脑的其他领域。

当然，乔布斯在发展事业时也有一定的失误，作过错误的假设。同时，他的管理风格导致了许多重要员工过度劳累。但是，他仍然是一个有远见卓识的人，他预见了一条大大提高人们生活质量的途径，并从中获得了巨大的利润。

相关资源

查阅关于斯蒂夫·乔布斯，苹果和皮克斯动画工作室的更多信息可登录www.apple.com和www.pixar.com网站。

乔布斯已成为好几个未授权出版传记的对象，同时，他也写完了自传。涉及他的书籍有《斯蒂夫·乔布斯卷土重来》，百老汇出版社，2001；《苹果绝密2.0：世界最多彩公司的历史》，诺·斯达奇出版社，2004；《斯蒂夫·乔布斯：征程就是回报》，林克斯出版社，1988；以及《斯蒂夫·乔布斯与下一个伟大事物》，思科瑞布纳出版社，1993。

Twenty-five

Jackie Joyner-Kersee, Sports queen

Why She is Among the *50 plus one Greatest Modern Heroes*

Track and field Olympian Jackie Joyner-Kersee has been regarded by many as the best female athlete and the all-time greatest multi-event athlete in history. During her career, she won six Olympic medals and set both the world and Olympic records in the heptathlon. Joyner-Kersee was sometimes called the Queen of Track and Field and she definitely earned her right to sit high on her throne as a greatest sports hero.

On the Way Up

Jacqueline Joyner was born in East St. Louis, Illinois on March 3, 1962 and was named after Jacqueline Kennedy. Her parents, Mary and Alfred Joyner, had four children. Two would become track and field Olympic stars: Joyner-Kersee and her older brother, Al Joyner. Al became the Olympic triple jump champion in 1984 and later married sprinter Florence "Flo Jo" Griffith.

In 1980, Joyner-Kersee graduated in the Top 10 percent of her 350-member class at Lincoln High School. She accepted a full basketball scholarship to the University of California, Los Angeles (UCLA), where she was a 4-year Bruins forward starter and earned All-America honors. She also made a name for herself on the track and field team, leading the way in the long jump and heptathlon. She won the NCAA heptathlon in 1982 and again in 1983. She also won the USA championship in 1982. She was named UCLA's athlete of the year and was awarded the Broderick Cup for being the country's most outstanding female collegiate athlete. Joyner-Kersee graduated in 1985 with a B.A. in history.

During her successful time at UCLA, the family was stuck with tragedy. In the middle of her freshman year, Joyner-Kersee returned home after being notified that her 37-year-old mother had developed a rare form of meningitis.

Professional Career

Joyner-Kersee set a world record during the 1986 Goodwill Games in Moscow. She became the .rst woman to surpass 7,000 points in a heptathlon event, scoring 7,148 points. She would go on to break her own record three more times. Her highest score of 7,291 points, which she achieved during the 1988 Olympics, remains the world record to this day.

In 1987, The World's Greatest Female Athlete, as she has often been called, set the world record in the long jump event when she jumped 24 feet and 5 inches(7.45 meters), a score that has since been tied. She also ended up breaking or tying the American long jump record four times during her career and twice beat the American record in the 100-meter hurdle event. She holds the current records in U.S. indoor 50-meter, 55-meter and 60-meter hurdles.

25

杰西·乔伊娜·柯西：
田径皇后

她为何入选《50+1位最具影响力的风云人物》?

奥运会田径冠军杰西·乔伊娜·柯西是大家公认的史上最出色女运动员,也是史无前例的赢得众多赛事的最杰出运动员。在她的运动生涯中,共获得6枚奥运会奖牌,并创下了女子七项赛的世界、奥运会双料纪录。有时,大家称乔伊娜·柯西为田径皇后,她当之无愧地坐上体坛皇后的宝座。

成长之路

杰奎琳·乔伊娜1962年3月3日出生于伊利诺斯州东圣路易斯,取名来自于杰奎琳·肯尼迪的名字。她的母亲玛丽和父亲阿尔弗莱得·乔伊纳共有4个孩子。其中两个孩子是田径赛的奥运之星:乔伊娜·柯西和她哥哥阿尔·乔伊纳。阿尔于1984年奥运会中夺得三级跳远冠军,之后与短跑运动员佛罗伦萨·格里菲斯结婚。

1980年,乔伊娜·柯西在350人的班级以10%的尖子生成绩毕业于林肯高中。她获得了加州大学洛杉矶分校的篮球奖学金,担任了四年熊队前锋,并荣获全美最佳奖。她还在田径队为自己赢得名声,成为跳远和女子七项赛的领军人物。她赢得1982年和1983年的全国大学生体育协会女子七项赛冠军。1982年,她还在美国冠军赛中获胜。她获得了加州大学洛杉矶分校年度运动员奖,并以全国最出色女大学生运动员称号被授予Broderick杯。1985年乔伊娜·柯西大学毕业,获得历史学学士学位。

在加州大学洛杉矶分校的辉煌岁月中,她的家庭却遭遇了悲剧。乔伊娜·柯西在大一的年中返回家中,被告知37岁的母亲患有一种罕见的脑膜炎。

职业生涯

乔伊娜·柯西于1986年莫斯科友好运动会中创下了一项世界纪录。她是第一个女子七项赛中超过7000分的运动员,总分为7148分。接着,她又3次打破自己创下的纪录。她的最高分是7291分,这是在1988年奥运会上取得的,该项世界纪录至今仍然保持着。

1987年,这位世界最了不起的女运动员以24英尺5英寸(7.45米)的成绩创下了跳远赛的世界纪录,这个成绩至今只是持平。她四次打破美国跳远纪录或与之持平,并两次打破100米跨栏比赛的美国纪录。她保持着现在的美国室内50米、55米和60米跨栏纪录。

Throughout her outstanding career, the 5-foot-10, 150 pound Joyner-Kersee has won six medals at four different Olympic Games in both the long jump and heptathlon events. They include:
- Silver, Heptathlon (Los Angeles, 1984)
- Gold, Heptathlon (Seoul, 1988)
- Gold, Long Jump (Seoul, 1988)
- Gold, Heptathlon (Barcelona, 1992)
- Bronze, Long Jump (Barcelona, 1992)
- Bronze, Long Jump (Atlanta, 1996)

About the Woman Herself

Jackie Joyner-Kersee appeared on a *Sports Illustrated* cover in 1987 after winning the first of two heptathlon and long jump world titles at the World Championships in Rome. The title on the cover read simply, Super Woman. The magazine was referring to Joyner-Kersee's heroic athletic abilities, but the term can also be expanded to encompass her traits as a strong African American woman.

Besides her love of sports, Joyner-Kersee also has a permanent place in her heart for giving back to the community. In 1988, she created the Jackie Joyner-Kersee Foundation as a grant-making organization that supported her gold medal scholarship program. The idea for the foundation was spurred by one of her visits home to East St. Louis when she learned that the Mary Brown Community Center, open since 1968, had closed. The center had been a major support system for youth development in the community, and had helped Joyner-Kersee personally to build the basis for her successes in sports, academics and life.

在整个出色的运动生涯中,身高5尺10寸、体重150磅的乔伊娜·柯西在四次奥运会的跳远和女子七项赛中分别获得六枚奖牌,包括:

· 女子七项赛,银牌 (洛杉矶, 1984)
· 女子七项赛,金牌 (首尔, 1988)
· 跳远,金牌 (首尔, 1988)
· 女子七项赛,金牌 (巴塞罗那, 1992)
· 跳远,铜牌 (巴塞罗那, 1992)
· 跳远,铜牌 (亚特兰大, 1996)

关于此人

在罗马世界冠军赛中的女子七项赛和跳远赛事第一次大获全胜后,杰西·乔伊娜·柯西上了1987年《体育画报》封面。封面上的标题极其简单:女超人。该杂志描述了乔伊娜·柯西这为巾帼英雄的运动才能,这个称呼当然也包含了她作为美国黑人妇女所拥有的品质。

乔伊娜·柯西除了热爱体育,她内心总有个愿望,希望回馈社会。1988年,她创立了杰西·乔伊娜·柯西基金会,以此支持她的金牌奖学金工程。建立基金会是因为有一次回东圣路易斯老家时,她得知1968年成立的玛丽·布朗社团中心关闭了。这曾是支持社区青少年发展的主要中心,也为乔伊娜·柯西个人在体育、学业及生活中取得成就提供过帮助。

Twenty-six

Michael Jordan, Athlete

Who He Is

There is something about this great athlete that simply overwhelms people, to the extent that they want to be like Mike. Surely Michael Jordan, a man who captured the attention of sports fans everywhere, is the sports hero of the 20th century.

Who else could have done what Jordan did? Who else could have brought a so-so team like the Chicago Bulls to national prominence with championships year after year? What was it about him that caused us to flock to stores to buy shoes named after him? Why was—why is—his presence so appealing all over the world?

What Made the Man

Jordan is considered by most to be the greatest player in the history of the game. During his career, he was named an All-Star 14 times and led his team to two separate National Basketball Association (NBA) championship three-peats. He has also been credited with gaining global recognition for the league.

Michael Jeffrey Jordan was born on February 17, 1963, in Brooklyn, New York, the third son of James and Delores Jordan. He grew up in Wilmington, North Carolina. As a child, his greatest love was baseball, a passion that he shared with his father. However, Jordan started playing one-on-one pickup games against his older brother, Larry, and basketball soon moved into the No. 1 spot in his heart.

Jordan attended Emsley A. Laney High School. He was suspended various times during his freshman year. He was cut from varsity basketball the following season due to an underdeveloped 5-foot-11-inch physique. However, he eventually became an excellent student and a star on the baseball, basketball and football teams. He finally made the varsity basketball team, averaging 25 points per game in both his junior and senior seasons. As a senior, Jordan was selected for the McDonald's All-American team and became the only high school player in history to average a triple-double with averages of 29.2 points, 11.6 rebounds and 10.1 assists.

He was named the College Player of the Year by The Sporting News in 1983 and 1984, and received the Naismith and Wooden awards in 1984. The summer after his junior year, Jordan led the U.S. Men's Basketball Team, coached by Bobby Knight, to an Olympic gold medal in Los Angeles. Then, in the 1984 NBA draft, he was selected as the third overall pick by the Chicago Bulls. He left school after that, but eventually graduated from North Carolina with a Bachelor of Arts degree in 1986.

Jordan married Juanita Vanoy in September of 1989. The couple live in the Chicago area with their daughter and two sons.

The Legacy of the Man

Jordan carried the Bulls into the playoffs every year, but the team did not make it all the way to the NBA finals until the 1990~1991 season. The year before, the Bulls faced the Detroit Pistons in the Eastern Conference Finals and the Pistons employed what had

---

124

迈克尔·乔丹：
运动员

他是谁

这位伟大的运动员身上有着某种神奇的魔力，他完全征服了人们，使我们都想成为像迈克尔一样的人。很显然，迈克尔·乔丹征服了世界各地忠实的球迷，他是20世纪体育界的英雄。

还有谁能取得像乔丹那样的成绩？还有谁能使一支像芝加哥公牛队这样的一般球队连续几年获得NBA总冠军，并成为一支全国知名的球队？他身上到底有着什么样的东西会使我们挤到鞋店去购买以他命名的球鞋？为什么他在世界上有如此大的吸引力，过去如此，而今天也同样如此？

是什么成就了他

乔丹被认为是篮球史上最伟大的球员。在他的职业生涯里，他14次入选全明星队，两次带领全队实现NBA总冠军的3连冠。人们一直认为正是乔丹让NBA在全球声名远播。

1963年2月17日，迈克尔·杰弗里·乔丹出生在纽约的布鲁克林区。他在北卡罗来纳州的威尔明顿长大，是詹姆斯和迪洛瑞斯·乔丹的第3个儿子。和他父亲一样，他从小就热爱棒球。然而，乔丹后来开始和哥哥玩篮球一对一斗牛，这样篮球很快就在乔丹心中占据了第一位。

乔丹就读于兰尼中学，一年级时就被停学好几次。由于他发育尚未完全，只有5英尺11英寸的身高，因此第2个赛季他就被学校篮球队裁掉了。但最后他不仅成为了一名优秀的学生，还成了棒球、篮球以及橄榄球里的明星。他最终又被选入学校篮球队，并在三年级和四年级的赛季里场均得到25分。作为一名四年级学生，乔丹被选入"麦当劳全美国队"并成了历史上唯一一位场均得到"三双"的中学球员：29.2分，11.6个篮板和10.1次助攻。

1983年他被《体育新闻》选为"年度最佳大学球员"，并在1984年获得"奈史密斯奖和伍登奖"。大学三年级结束后的那个夏天，乔丹带领美国国家男子篮球队，在教练鲍比·耐森的指导下，获得了洛杉矶奥运会的金牌。在随后1984年NBA选秀大会上，他被芝加哥公牛队以第3顺位选中。之后他便离开了大学，但他最终于1986年获得了北卡罗来纳大学的文学士学位。

乔丹和胡安妮塔·范妮在1989年9月结婚。两人和他们的女儿以及两个儿子住在芝加哥。

他的遗产

乔丹每年都将公牛队带入季后赛，但他们直到1990~1991赛季才闯入NBA总决赛。在前一年，公牛队在东部赛区决赛中碰到了底特律活塞队。活塞队采用了他们和乔丹比赛的一贯方案："乔丹规则"。方案主要是，乔丹一拿到球，他们就进行2人或3人包夹，使他

become their usual game plan against Jordan's team: the Jordan Rules. Basically, they tried to force Jordan out of commission by double-and triple-teaming him every time he got the ball, stopping him from going to the baseline and hacking him whenever he drove to the basket. Jordan agreed to an offensive change by Coach Phil Jackson and Assistant Coach Tex Winter.

The Bulls began playing with a triangle offense and finished in first place for the first time in 16 years, reaching a franchise-record 61 wins in a single regular season. Jordan and his team went on to win their first NBA championship ever in 1991 against Magic Johnson and the Los Angeles Lakers. The Bulls went on to defeat Clyde Drexler and the Portland Trailblazers in 1992 and Charles Barkley and the Phoenix Suns in 1993.

In 1992, Jordan went to the summer Olympics again,
this time as a member of the original Dream Team,
which was the first Olympic team to include NBA players
on its roster. Jordan averaged 12.7 points per game in
Barcelona and won his second Olympic gold medal as the
team swept through with a 6-0 record.

In October of 1993, Jordan announced he was going to retire. It was speculated that there were two main reasons for his early first retirement. One was that his father had been tragically killed by armed robbers in July of that same year. The other was that the NBA had started an investigation into allegations that Jordan had illegally bet on league games, though all accusations against him were later cleared.

Even though the Bulls had retired his number, 23, he announced his return to the team on March 18, 1995, with probably the shortest ever press release, which stated simply, "I'm back." The very next day, he put on his new jersey number, 45, to finish out the rest of the regular season with the Bulls. They eventually lost to the Orlando Magic in that year's Eastern Conference semifinals.

Jordan retired from the NBA for a second time on January 13, 1999. He became president of Basketball Operations and part owner of the Washington Wizards. After the team won a measly 19 games in the 2000~2001 season, a disappointed yet motivated Jordan started training again, eventually signing a 2-year contract with the Wizards. After the devastating attacks of September 11, he announced that he would donate his entire season's salary to victims and their families. Jordan retired for a third and final time after his last game on April 16, 2003.

The Legacy of the Man

Jordan has become one of the most marketed and widely recognized athletes in history. His face first popped up on a cereal box in 1988, and he has worked as an influential spokesperson for such companies as Nike, Gatorade, Nestlé, McDonald's, Ball Park Franks, MCI and Rayovac. Nike developed a shoe in his honor, called the Air Jordan.

Jordan has also done his fair share of charity work. He remains an advocate of The Boys and Girls Clubs of America. Jordan, along with the Bulls franchise, built the James R. Jordan Boys and Girls Club and Family Life Center in 1996 to honor the memory of his father and to serve Chicago's West Side community. He also established the Jordan Family Institute at the University of North Carolina, and has been involved with America's Promise, the United Negro College Fund, the Make-A-Wish Foundation and the Special Olympics.

不能发挥作用,不让他走底线,他一靠近篮筐就造成他犯规。后来乔丹同意主教练菲尔·杰克逊和助理教练泰克斯·温特在球队进攻上做出调整。

公牛队开始打"三角进攻",并16年来首次获得第一名,并且61胜的成绩也创下球队常规赛单赛季获胜的新纪录。1991年乔丹率领全队击败了由"魔术师"约翰逊带领的洛杉矶湖人队,赢得了球队历史上首个总冠军。公牛队在1992年和1993年分别击败了克雷德·德雷克斯勒带领的波特兰开拓者队和查尔斯·巴克利带领的菲尼克斯太阳队。

1992年乔丹作为"梦之队"成员再次参加夏季奥运会。这届奥运会首次允许NBA球员参加比赛。在巴塞罗那,乔丹场均得到12.7分,并以6战全胜的战绩横扫所有对手获得他的第2枚奥运金牌。

1993年10月,乔丹宣布退役。人们猜测他第一次退役主要有两个原因:一个是那年7月份他父亲遭持枪劫匪残忍地杀害;另一个是乔丹被指控涉嫌非法赌球,NBA官方也开始着手调查此事,尽管后来所有针对他的指控都被一一澄清。

虽然公牛队已经将他23号球衣"退役",但1995年3月18日乔丹宣布复出。复出的新闻发布会可能是历史上最短的,只有一句话"我回来了"。回来后的第2天他便披上45号球衣,随公牛队打完了常规赛余下的一些比赛。在当年东部半决赛中,他们最终输给了奥兰多魔术队。

1999年1月13日,乔丹第2次从NBA退役。退役后他成了"篮球运营"的主席,并成了华盛顿奇才队的股东。2000~2001赛季球队仅赢了可怜的19场比赛,乔丹非常失望,开始重新投入到训练中去。最后他与奇才队签订了两年的合同。在可怕的"9·11"袭击发生后,他决定将他整个赛季的薪水捐给受难者和他们的家属。2003年4月16日,在结束他最后一场比赛之后,乔丹第3次宣布退役,永远退出了篮球赛场。

他的遗产

乔丹是历史上被商业市场宣传最多、最受人们欢迎和喜爱的运动员之一。1998年,他的形象首次出现在麦片的包装盒上。他是许多公司非常有影响力的代言人,如耐克、佳得乐、雀巢、麦当劳、弗兰克斯热狗、MCI电信,还有雷诺威电池。耐克推出了一款以他名字命名的鞋,叫"飞人乔丹"鞋。

乔丹也在做自己应做的慈善工作。他一直是"美国儿童群益会"的支持者。1996年,乔丹和他的公牛队队员建立了"詹姆斯·乔丹儿童群益会"和家庭生活中心,以纪念他的父亲并同时为芝加哥"西城"服务。他还在北卡罗来纳大学建立了"乔丹家庭学院"。与此同时,他积极参加"美国的诺言"、"联合黑人大学基金会","许愿基金会"以及残奥会的活动。

Twenty-seven

Martin Luther King, Jr., Civil Rights Activist

Who He Is

Entire generations have seen, and future generations will continue to see, the famous speech delivered in Washington during the height of the civil rights movement, *I Have a Dream*. Here stands the inspiring image of a man who had devoted his entire life to improving the rights of African-Americans, not only in the South but also the segregated cities of the North.

First and foremost a pastor and a religious leader, he gained prominence as a persistent, nonviolent revolutionary whose sole mission in life was to change society's understanding of what was right and legal and reasonable. How, he asked, could an entire segment of the United States be relegated to second- or third-class status? How was it possible, 100 years after the Civil War, that blacks had less freedom and equality? Why was it that the religious and political leaders in the United States did not do something about this? Well, it was his mission to do something about it, regardless of the cost or sacrifices.

What Made the Man

Martin Luther King Jr. was born a preacher's son in Atlanta, Georgia, in January of 1929. He would follow his father's footsteps, first taking a degree at Morehouse College, a traditionally all-black school, and then ultimately a Ph.D. from Boston University. Interestingly, historians and others have looked back at King's writing and a great deal of concern has been expressed about plagiarism in King's dissertation work. The controversy was so great that the university did an analysis of the dissertation and concluded that a substantial portion was taken from other students' efforts. Perhaps greatness—in this case a Nobel Peace Prize—allows for another standard: Boston University decided not to revoke the degree even though there was ample evidence for them to do so.

King began his formal tenure as a Baptist pastor in 1953 in Montgomery, Alabama, and used the church and its pulpit to launch his formal entry into the existing civil rights movement.(King did not start the movement; rather, attempts to get blacks equality with whites had been going on since the end of the Civil War.)

The essential elements of King's leadership style surfaced very early: nonviolence(as practiced by Gandhi and A. J. Muste) and the power and influence of the media. King intuitively understood that using force against the existing political and social structure would be futile and only inflame the situation. He understood the importance of image, as presented by the media. If blacks, striving for their rights, were the aggressors, they would gain little sympathy from the rest of America. Further, he knew that the image of innocent and passive people, abused and beaten by the police in full view of the cameras, would have a tremendous psychological effect.

马丁·路德·金：人权活动家

他是谁

几代人已看到，未来的人也将继续看到，民权运动高峰时期在华盛顿发表的演说——《我有一个梦想》。这儿屹立着一个伟人，他把整个生命奉献到了改善美国黑人权益的运动中，而这并不仅仅在南部，也在一些实行种族隔离的北方城市。

他首先是一个牧师和严谨的领导者，更因其坚持不懈、主张非暴力的彻底革命者的领导能力而获得了极高的声望。他生命的唯一使命是就改变社会对什么是权利、合法以及合理的理解。为此，他问道：如何才能使整个美国真正属于二等或三等公民？为什么内战结束100年后的今天，黑人反而获得了更少的平等和自由？为什么美国宗教和政治的领袖都没有为此做出实际行动？然而为此做出贡献就是他的使命，哪怕是以生命为代价。

是什么成就了他

1929年1月马丁·路德·金出生于佐治亚州亚特兰大市的一个牧师家庭。他跟随父亲的脚步首先获得了传统黑人学校摩尔豪斯学院的学位，然后获得波士顿大学的博士学位。有意思的是，历史学家和其他工作者经过研究金的作品等一系列线索，发现他的作品有抄袭的现象。对于这件事有很大争议，学校对他的学位论文做了分析，并得出结论，这其中确实有一部分存在抄袭现象。也许金注定会是个伟大人物，尽管波士顿大学有足够的证据，但他们对这位未来的诺贝尔和平奖得主采取另一种评判标准，他们决定不取消金的学位。

1953年，在阿拉巴马州的蒙哥马利郡，金正式开始了作为一个施洗者牧师的职业生涯，并利用教堂和教堂的讲坛正式加入到已经开展的民权运动中（金并不是这个运动的开创者，确切地说，试图使黑人与白人平等的运动始于内战后期）。

金最主要的领导风格很早就显露出来了：非暴力（曾被圣雄甘地和穆斯特实践过）、依靠政治和传媒的力量。金的直觉告诉他，用暴力来反抗现存的政治和社会结构是无用的，并且只会使之气焰更甚。他知道传媒塑造的形象是多么的重要。如果黑人是以一个侵略者的形象为自己的权益而奋斗，那么他们几乎不可能得到其他美国人的同情。他还知道那些单纯顺从的公民被警察暴打虐待的景象出现在摄像机中时，会产生多么巨大的心理影响！

It is a testament to King and the civil rights movement
that it provoked even the U.S. Supreme Court into action
when it outlawed segregation on public transportation.
This was the first of many court decisions on civil rights that
changed the face of American society forever.

Two particularly noteworthy campaigns are the marches led by King to Washington and Chicago. The demonstration in Washington was controversial before it began. President Kennedy and others used their influence to tone down the demonstration—basically to make it less critical of the role of the federal government in the civil rights movement. No matter the original intent, the demonstration was ultimately a huge success, culminating in the famous speech, I *Have a Dream*.

A fascinating relationship between King and the FBI(and its leader, J. Edgar Hoover) began in 1961-62. In an ever-growing effort to discredit King in any way possible, the FBI used a variety of tactics—accusing him of having extramarital affairs—to peel away his credibility and his moral authority. There are some who say that King's death at the hand of James Earl Ray in Memphis in 1968 was actually contrived by the FBI. However, the fact remains that he was killed by an assassin and that his work would remain unfinished—or at least that it would remain for others to complete.

The Legacy of the Man

How do we understand this man? He won a Nobel Prize and a national holiday is named for him. He was a religious man with an almost obsessive compulsion to see changes on the local and national levels in terms of race relations and greater openness for African-Americans throughout society. He had a quiet, deliberate and highly motivating personality, capable of using the media and few words to make a highly effective impression on his people and on the country at large. He was ranked in recent polls as one of the top three greatest Americans ever.

Martin Luther King Jr. gave his life for his cause. He inspired, he challenged, he acted and he led in a way that few men or women the 20th century did. He inspired a new generation of leaders not only to be active in the movement but also to join the established order and make continuous improvements. Most importantly, his legacy is reflected in the fact that the Civil Rights Act of 1964 was passed and became law.

民权运动甚至刺激美国最高法院采取实际行动,它宣布在公共交通工具上进行种族隔离为非法,这是对民权运动的最好证明。这是法院第一次就民权问题作出决议,而之后还有许多,它们永远地改变了美国的社会面貌。

金领导的尤为引人注目的两场运动是在华盛顿和芝加哥的游行。华盛顿示威在开始前就备受争议,肯尼迪总统和其他人用他们的影响力来缓和这次示威活动,希望以此来减轻对联邦政府在民权运动中所处地位的冲击。随着《我有一个梦想》这个著名的演讲的完成,无论这次游行最初的目的是什么,它都是一个巨大的成功。

金与美国联邦调查局FBI(以及其领导者J.埃德加·胡佛)之间扑朔迷离的关系始于1961~1962年,FBI用了各种手段,尽最大可能来破坏金的道德影响力和可信度,比如污蔑金有婚外情。1968年金在孟菲斯城被詹姆斯·厄尔·雷刺杀,有些人猜测这一切都是由FBI谋划的。然而争论归争论,金是确实死于谋杀;金的事业尚未完成,至少留给了其他人来完成。

他的遗产

我们如何理解他?金赢得了诺贝尔奖,美国的一个国假也是以他的名字命名的。他是一个宗教人物,而同时又有着近乎痴迷的强烈愿望,他期待看到地方乃至全国在种族关系和对美国黑人的开放程度方面作出改善。他个性冷静、从容不迫,积极性高;他才能卓越,他通过传媒寥寥数语就在他的人民甚至在整个国家中都留下了深刻的印象。金在最近的评选中被评选为最伟大的三个美国人之一。

马丁·路德·金把他的一生都献给了他的事业,他激励大家、挑战权威、亲力亲为、领导众人,其方式在20世纪几乎无人做到。他鼓舞了一代新的领导人积极参与运动,而且要加入现有秩序并进行不断完善。最重要的是,他给后人留下了一笔遗产:1964年民权法案得到通过并成为正式法律。

Twenty-eight

Bruce Jun Fan Lee, Martial Arts Star

Who He Is

Like Superman, Bruce Lee is our hero because he represents what we think a real hero ought to be—strong, quick, athletic and always the good guy. This is Bruce Lee to the millions who watched his exploits in movies and television. He is, of course, one of our many fantasy heroes, thrilling and entertaining us with amazing physical feats and always triumphing against the bad guys.

He was innovative in that he made the martial arts into a national craze. And he was a tragic hero, dying tragically young, never fulfilling his extraordinary potential. He paved the way for others to fulfill their dreams as a martial arts specialist in mainstream culture. Finally, he always was fun, letting us forget our troubles for an hour or two.

What Made the Man

Bruce Lee brought martial arts films to the mainstream American audience. He championed new styles of martial arts based on his personal philosophy and demonstrated how to develop a strong body.

Lee was Chinese-American, born in San Francisco in 1940 to a Chinese father and Chinese-German mother. They were both performers in the Cantonese Opera Company. He and his family returned to their home in Kowloon, China, when Bruce was only 1 year old.

Lee attended St. Frances Xavier's College from 1957 to 1959. During that time, he got into a fight with a local gangster's son. His father feared for his safety and sent him back to the United States to live with a family friend in San Francisco. Lee would later find his way to Seattle, where he received a diploma from the Edison Technical School. He enrolled at the University of Washington as a philosophy major and met his future wife Linda Emery.

In 1964, Lee and Emery married and had two children, Brandon and Shannon. Lee was restless at school and was eager to develop his own form of martial arts and an accompanying philosophy. He combined several types of martial arts, including Tai Chi Chuan, Hung Gar and Wing Chun (which he learned mostly while living in China) into a new type of martial art called Jun Fan Gung Fu.

The technique relied heavily on Wing Chun, combined with elements of Westernstyle boxing and fencing. Two of the showiest elements of Lee's martial arts were his two-finger pushups and the one-inch punch. The two-finger pushups used only the thumb and forefinger. The one-inch punch was much more impressive. According to observers, Lee would hold his hand outstretched to about one inch from the chest of his opponent. He would then thrust forward with enough power to send the other fighter flying backward. The technique would often be used in his films.

Lee gained notoriety in the martial arts community when he opened his first schools in Seattle, Oakland and Los Angeles in the early 1960s. After showing his techniques in a

李小龙：
功夫明星

他是谁

布鲁斯·李像"超人"一样成为我们的英雄，因为他代表了我们心目中真正英雄应有的形象：强壮、反应敏捷、运动型而且永远是正派人物。这就是布鲁斯·李，数百万人曾在电影或电视上欣赏到他的英勇无敌。当然，他只是我们想象中的众多英雄人物之一，但他精湛绝伦的武艺，总能制服恶棍，这些让我们感到既激动又兴奋。

他独具创新精神，曾使武术风靡全国。同时，他又是个悲剧英雄，因为他在盛年盛名之时突然死去，再也不能实现自己异于常人的潜质。他为其他人实现成为主流文化里武术专家的梦想铺平了道路。而且，他十分风趣幽默，总能让我们在一两小时里抛却烦恼。

是什么成就了他

布鲁斯·李将功夫电影带给了美国主流观众。他推崇基于个人哲学之上的新式武术，并且向人们展示了如何塑造强壮的体格。

布鲁斯是华裔美国人，1940年出生于旧金山。他父亲是中国人，母亲是中德混血儿。他的父母都是粤剧团里的演员。布鲁斯一岁的时候，他们全家搬回了他们的家乡，即中国九龙。

1957年到1959年，布鲁斯在"圣芳希书院"读书。在那段时间里，他曾和当地一个恶霸的儿子打过一架。他父亲由于担心他的安全，把他送回了美国，让他和旧金山的一位朋友住在一起。后来，李去了西雅图，并在当地的"爱迪生技术学院"毕业。后来他考取了华盛顿大学哲学专业，并在那儿遇见了自己未来的妻子琳达·埃莫瑞。

1964年，李和埃莫瑞结婚，并生下两个孩子，李国豪和李香凝。李小龙在学校里可不安分，他希望发明一种属于自己的武术形式和武术哲学。他将好几种武术流派结合起来，包括"太极拳"、"洪拳"、还有"咏春拳"（这些大都是他住在中国时学的），并发明了一种新的武术，名为"振藩功夫"。

这套功夫主要依赖于"咏春拳"，并结合了西式拳击和击剑的一些元素。李的武打功夫里面最精彩的两个部分是两个手指俯卧撑和寸截拳。两个手指俯卧撑是指他只用拇指和食指做俯卧撑。寸截拳则更加精彩。据有些观察者称，李将一只手伸到离对手胸前一英寸远，然后他只要用足够大的力量往前一推就可以将对手击出去很远。这项功夫经常出现在他的电影里面。

20世纪60年代初，李在西雅图、奥克兰和洛杉矶开办了自己的第一批武术学校，但这让他在武术圈里声名狼藉。在一系列武术表演和功夫挑战之后，李开始发现自己的"振藩功夫"和其他武术流派一样：约束性太大。于是他发明了一种新颖的更加自由的武术形

series of demonstrations and staged fights, Lee started to believe that his Jun Fan Gung Fu, as well as other martial arts, were too restrictive. He developed a new free-form system called Jeet Kune Do (The Way of the Intercepting Fist), which he taught and was to use in his films.

While Lee made more television and movie appearances, real stardom eluded him. He created the character Caine and the television series, *Kung Fu,* intending to play the title role himself. Instead, producers hired David Carradine for the role.

Lee was very bitter at what he perceived as a snub of his talents and turned his attention to films co-produced by Hong Kong and American producers.

He would make just five films, but each became more and more popular. He started in 1971 with *Fists of Fury,* which was a big hit, and followed it with *The Chinese Connection* in 1972(a play on the American hit *The French Connection), Return of the Dragon* in 1972, *Enter the Dragon,* released after his death in 1973, and *Game of Death,* also released posthumously in1979. Chuck Norris, a friend of Lee's and soon to be a martial arts star in his own right, played one of the villains in *Return of the Dragon.*

It appeared that Lee was well on his way to movie superstardom as well as great fame as a martial arts innovator when tragedy struck. In 1973, Lee was in Hong Kong discussing the making of the movie *Game of Death,* when he suddenly complained of a headache. His hostess gave him a prescription analgesic known as equagesic. When Lee did not show up after taking a nap, his host found him unconscious. Lee was transported to the Queen Elizabeth Hospital, where he was declared dead on arrival. Doctors found that Lee's brain had swelled and attributed his death to a cerebral edema. They later ascertained that Lee was allergic to equagesic. Death by misadventure was the final verdict.

Bruce Lee, a model of strength, discipline and physical fitness was only 32.

The Legacy of the Man

More than anyone, Bruce Lee contributed to America's fascination with martial arts in the 1960s and 1970s. His combination of good looks and unbelievable fighting moves had never been seen before. Most performers who have succeeded in martial arts movies in the United States credit their success to the early fame of Lee.

Lee's unexpected death has been the subject of much controversy. Some fans believe he was murdered by triads or was killed by jealous martial arts teachers or film producers. Despite these conspiracy theories, there has been no hard evidence that Lee died of anything other than unfortunate natural causes.

The cloud of tragedy that hung over Bruce Lee extended to his son Brandon. Brandon was beginning a promising career in the movies when he appeared in *The Crow.* He was killed by a faulty blank bullet during filming. Ironically, Lee's character Chen in *Fists of Fury* was killed in a similar way.

式，叫做"截拳道"（即拦截拳头的技巧）。他自己亲自教授这套功夫，并将它用到了自己的电影里面。

然而，尽管李频频在电视剧和电影中露面，他并未真正出名。后来他创造了"凯恩"这个人物，并打算在电视剧《功夫》中自己出演主角。但制片商却让大卫·卡拉丹出演了这个角色。

李认为别人在故意轻视他的才华，为此他非常生气，于是便把注意力投向了由香港和美国制片商共同投资的电影。

他本来只想拍5部电影，但他的电影一部比一部成功。1971年他首次拍摄了《精武门》，此片大受欢迎。紧接着1972年他又拍摄了《唐山大兄》（改编于在美国很受欢迎的电影《法国兄弟》），还有《猛龙过江》。1973年死后又发行了《龙争虎斗》。《死亡游戏》也是在他死后1979年发行的。查克·诺里斯是李的一位朋友，不久之后也成了一名当之无愧的功夫明星。他在《猛龙过江》里扮演了一个反派角色。

当李在成长为一名电影超级巨星的路上一帆风顺的时候，当他因发明了新的武术风格而声名远扬的时候，悲剧突然降临了。1973年，当李在香港商讨如何拍摄电影《死亡游戏》的时候，他突然抱怨说头痛得厉害，于是他的女侍就给了他一片止痛药。然而休息片刻之后，李还是没有出现，这时男侍发现他已经不省人事了。随后李被送到了伊丽莎白医院抢救，但刚到医院他就被宣布已经死亡。医生发现李的大脑出现了浮肿，有可能是因为脑部肿瘤致死。他们后来才肯定李对服用的止痛片过敏。李人生最后的判决是意外致死。

布鲁斯·李的力量、纪律和身体素质堪称大众的典范。然而，这位英雄在32岁时就过早地离开了人世。

他的遗产

布鲁斯·李使美国人在20世纪60、70年代疯狂地迷上了武术，这点无人能及。他集英俊的相貌和令人难以置信的武打动作于一身，可谓前无古人。今天在美国，大多数在功夫电影上取得成功的演员都将自己的成就归功于李小龙早期的名声。

李的突然离去让人始料未及，这成了人们一直以来争辩的话题。有些影迷说他是被黑社会谋杀了，或者是被那些嫉妒眼红的武术教头和电影制片商给害死的。尽管有种种阴谋理论，人们至今尚未发现一丝证据证明李不是意外死亡，而是另有他因。

发生在布鲁斯·李身上的那片悲剧阴云也落到了他的儿子李国豪身上。在李国豪拍摄电影《乌鸦》时，他是电影界一颗冉冉升起的新星。然而，在拍摄过程中他被一颗搞错的空弹打死。具有讽刺意味的是，李的电影《精武门》中有个姓陈的角色就是被相似的方式杀死的。

Twenty-nine

Charles Lindbergh, Aviator

Who He Is

Greatness and heroism are often a matter of firsts—first black player in baseball, first great inventor, the first person with a new discovery. Charles Lindbergh was the first to fly nonstop across the Atlantic Ocean in a single-prop airplane.

What Made the Man

Lindbergh was born on February 4, 1902, in Detroit. He grew up on a small farm near Little Falls, Minnesota. His father, Charles August Lindbergh, was a lawyer and also a U.S. Congressman from 1907 to 1917. His mother was Evangeline Lodge Land, a chemistry teacher.

From childhood, Lindbergh demonstrated extraordinary mechanical ability and enrolled at the University of Wisconsin at the age of 18 to study engineering. However, Lindbergh's real interest was not college, but the rapidly growing field of aviation. In 1922, he left school and joined a mechanics and pilot training program with Nebraska Aircraft.

After this training, Lindbergh purchased his own plane, a World War I era Curtiss J-N4(or Jenny) and joined the ranks of barnstorming stunt pilots. These pilots(many former combat pilots) attempted to maintain and build interest in aviation by flying around the country and performing risky aerial maneuvers. They also offered airplane rides to the rural spectators. Lindbergh followed his barnstorming years by training with the U.S. Army as an Army Service Reserve Pilot and then becoming a mail pilot. He quickly gained a reputation as being able to deliver the mail in any type of weather.

Lindbergh became interested in pursuing the Orteig Prize. The $25,000 prize would go to any pilot who could fly nonstop from New York to Paris. Eight years after its creation, it still had not been claimed, although some pilots were getting close to winning it.

Lindbergh used his knowledge of mechanics and flying to persuade a group of St. Louis businessmen to finance his quest for the Orteig Prize. His backers gave him the funds to design and manufacture a special plane, made by the Ryan Aeronautical Company of San Diego. He called his new plane the Spirit of St. Louis and tested it in early May 1927 by flying from San Diego to New York City with one overnight stop in St. Louis. This flight set a transcontinental record.

He was now ready to take on the challenge of winning the Orteig Prize. Lindbergh took off from the Roosevelt Airfield, Long Island, on May 20, 1927. His flight took a little over 33 hours and led to him landing successfully at Le Bourget Field, near Paris, on May 21 at 10:21 p.m. He was awarded the French Legion of Honor and the U.S. Army's

查尔斯·林白：飞行员

他是谁

伟大和英勇向来是先驱者的品质，如第一个黑人棒球运动员，第一个伟大的发明家，第一个有新发现的人，而查尔斯·林白就是利用一架单人飞机横跨大西洋的第一人。

是什么成就了他

1902年2月4日，林白出生在底特律。他在隶属明尼苏达州小瀑布附近的一个农场长大。他的父亲查尔斯·奥格斯特·林白是一名律师，同时又是1907~1917年美国的国会议员；他的母亲伊万杰琳·洛琳是一位化学教师。

从孩童时代开始，林白就表现出了非凡的机械动手能力。他18岁时就进了威斯康星州大学学习工程学。然而，他的真正兴趣并不是大学，而是迅速发展起来的航空业。1922年，他离开了学校转而加入了内布拉斯加飞行学校一个兼机械和飞行员培训的项目。

在接受训练之后，林白买了一架一战时期的Curtiss J-N4飞机，一架真正属于他自己的飞机，并加入了特技飞行表演队。那些飞行员(许多从前参战的飞行员)通过环美飞行和进行特技表演来保持和提高人们对飞行的兴趣。他们也让农村的观众乘坐他们的飞机。接着几年，林白在美国军队中度过了他不平凡的生活。他作为一名储备飞行员在美国军队中受训，后来成了一名邮递飞行员。随着他驾驶技术的日益娴熟，他能在任何天气状况下传递邮件，因此他名声大噪。

林白渐渐想竞逐奥提格奖。任何从纽约直接飞达巴黎的飞行员便可获得25000美元奖金。但自该奖金设立8年多来，虽然有一些飞行员离成功只有一步之遥，但仍无人问鼎。

林白利用他的机械学知识飞往圣露易斯，请求那里的商人资助他夺冠。他的资助者给了他大量的资金去设计并制造了一种特殊的飞机，该飞机由圣地亚哥莱恩航空公司制造的。他把新式飞机命名为圣路易斯精神号。他在1927年5月的上旬从圣地亚哥飞到纽约，其间只在圣路易斯停留了一晚，因此完成了飞机的测试。此次飞行刷新了横跨北美大陆的飞行纪录。

他已经准备好了去尝试这次挑战，并赢得奖金。1927年5月20日，他从长岛的罗斯福机场起飞，最后于5月21日晚上10点21分在巴黎附近的一个机场Le Bourget Field成功

Distinguished Flying Cross, and was celebrated in a ticker tape parade down Fifth Avenue in New York City. At this time, he gained his two nicknames: Lucky Lindy and the Lone Eagle.

Following World War II , Lindbergh essentially withdrew from the public spotlight. He served for a time as a consultant to the U.S. Air Force when Dwight Eisenhower was president. Eisenhower restored Lindbergh's commission and made him a brigadier general in the Air Force in 1954. Lindbergh later worked with Pan American World Airways and helped design the Boeing 747 jet. One of his last public appearances was to give his regards to the crew of Apollo 8, the first spacecraft to ever leave Earth orbit in 1968.

Lindbergh developed an interest in conservation and traveled the world to look at how technology and the ecology could work in harmony. He eventually settled in Maui, Hawaii, where he died of cancer in 1974. He was buried on the grounds of the Palapala Ho'omau Church in Maui with this marker inscription: If I take the wings of the morning, and dwell in the uttermost parts of the sea.

The Legacy of the Man

Lindbergh's political controversies unfortunately took attention away from the very real contributions he made to aviation. Based on his flights (often with his wife), Lindbergh developed methods of charting polar air routes, flying at high altitudes and increasing fuel-consumption rates. After his historic flight, he designed a watch for Longines to make navigation easier for pilots. The watch is still being used.

Motivated by the debilitating heart condition of his sister-in-law,
Lindbergh helped design an artificial heart.
The device was still many years from being perfected, but at
the time it worked amazingly well.

着陆，耗时33个多小时。他被授予法国荣誉骑士和美军飞行十字勋章。之后，人们在纽约第五大道为他举行了欢庆游行。同时，他还赢得了两个绰号："幸运鬼林白"与"独鹰"。

二战后，林白完全从公众的视线中消失了。当艾森豪威尔总统在位时，他曾担任美国空军顾问。艾森豪威尔恢复了林白的职务。1954年，林白被任命为空军旅长。林白后来与泛美世界航空公司合作，帮助设计了波音747客机。他后来很少公开露面，其中一次是1968年，他向阿波罗8号的机组人员慰问，而阿波罗8号是首架驶出地球轨道的人造航天器。

林白对自然保护产生了浓厚的兴趣，并开始环游世界，目的是探索科技和生态如何和谐共处。他最终定居于夏威夷的毛利岛，于1974年死于癌症。他被葬在毛利岛帕拉罕默教堂的墓地里，墓碑上刻着："假如我乘上晨曦的翅膀，定当起居最辽远宽阔的海洋。"

他的遗产

不幸的是，林白的政治言论把公众的注意力从他为航空做出的贡献上转移开来。根据自己的飞行（经常同妻子一起），林白发明了绘制极地气流图的方法、进行高空飞行以及提高燃油利用率等方法。在他具有历史意义的飞行之后，他设计了一种手表，它能让飞行变得更为简单。这种表迄今仍然在使用。

林白的弟妹心脏逐渐衰竭，受此激发，他帮助设计了一种人造心脏。这种设计虽然远非完美，但在当时使用情况却非常好。

Thirty

Nelson Mandela, Civil Rights Leader

Who He Is

Some people are heroes; others fall in the very special category of superheroes. Nelson Mandela is one of our superheroes! Imagine spending 27 years of your life in prison, most of them in one of the most brutal and horrible places in South Africa. People have survived and will continue to survive long years of confinement, but to do so with your values, dignity and principles intact is another story.

What Made the Man

Mandela was born Rolihlahla Mandela on July 18, 1918, to the family in the village of Mvezo in South Africa's Mththa district. Mandela's father was active in local politics and helped Jongintaba Dalindyebo ascend to the Thembu throne. Mandela became the first member of his family to attend a formal school when he enrolled in a Methodist-run elementary school.

One of the teachers gave Mandela the name Nelson in
honor of the British Admiral Horatio Nelson.

When Mandela was nine, his father died of tuberculosis and he was informally adopted by Jongintaba. Mandela continued his education and attended a Wesleyan mission school near the regent's palace and the Clarksbury Boarding Institute, where he studied extensively in Western culture. He received his certificate a year earlier than his peers and attended Healdtown, a Wesleyan college in Fort Beaufort. He then started to study for a B.A. at Fort Hare University where he met Oliver Tambo. The two were destined to be friends and colleagues throughout their tumultuous lives.

Mandela began his political activism with the African National Congress(ANC) shortly after the 1948 election of the pro-apartheid National Party. Apartheid was legal racial segregation, with blacks having little or no rights in a government totally dominated by white South Africans. Mandela was prominent in developing the ANC's Defiance Campaign and the 1955 Congress of the People. The adoption of the Freedom Charter at this congress provided the fundamental blueprint for a nonapartheid country.

Espousing a philosophy of nonviolence, Mandela was arrested and released several times in the 1950s. At the same time, his and Oliver Tambo's positions as leaders of the ANC were being challenged. They tried to bolster their positions by alliances with minority political parties, but these efforts were not well regarded.

After spending some time on the run, Mandela was arrested in 1962. He was finally sentenced to prison in 1964 for advocating sabotage and crimes against the government. He would spend the next 27 years in prison, 18 of them in a brutal facility on Robben Island.

尼尔森·曼德拉：
人权领袖

他是谁

有些人是英雄；还有的归属于超级英雄那一类。尼尔森·曼德拉就属于后者。他在监狱里度过人生的27年，而在这27年中，大部分时间待在南非最凶残恐怖之处，试想一下，换作是你会怎样？或许，对于漫漫牢狱之苦，有人已艰难度过，有人将继续受折磨，但在此种境遇下，若要保持节操不易，信仰不改，原则不变，那又是另一回事了。

是什么成就了他

1918年7月18日，曼德拉出生在南非曼斯萨区摩威优乡的一个家庭，那时候叫罗里拉拉·曼德拉。曼德拉的父亲在当地政坛活跃，他曾助永吉塔博·达灵德保登上坦布的宝座。曼德拉在一所教会小学注册登记后，他成了家庭里第一位到正规学校上学的成员。

曼德拉的一位老师给他取名为尼尔森，以纪念英国海军上将豪拉提奥·尼尔森。

曼德拉9岁时，他的父亲因结核病去世，他被永吉塔博非正式地收养了。曼德拉并没放弃他的学业，他上了一所靠近王宫的卫斯理教会学校以及克拉克斯博里寄宿学院，在那里，他广泛涉猎西方文化。他比同年级的学生早一年拿到了毕业证书，之后进入海德顿卫斯理学院。后来进入了福德·海亚大学攻读学士学位。在那里，他遇到了奥列佛·塔姆博。他们俩注定在他们跌宕起伏的一生中成为朋友和战友。

1948年，支持种族隔离的民族党当选不久，曼德拉开始积极参与非洲民族议会。当时，种族隔离制是合法的，并且，对于一个完全由南非白人操纵的政府，黑人在政府中很少或者几乎没有发言权。曼德拉引领非洲民族议会的反抗运动以及1955年的人民议会，其作用不可或缺，在这次国会上，自由宪章的采用为建立一个无种族隔离制的国家提供了基本蓝图。

曼德拉崇尚非暴力主义，他在50年代遭到多次拘捕。就在此时，他和塔姆博在非洲民族议会的领导地位受到了挑战。他们试图通过与少数派政党结盟来改善他们的地位，但这些努力并没有得到相应的回报。

之后，曼德拉流亡了一段时间，最终于1962年被捕。1964年，他被冠以鼓动总工和反政府的罪名而被判入狱。此后他将在监狱中度过27个春秋，而其中有18年是在罗宾岛上一个极其糟糕严酷的地方。

Mandela refused an offer of conditional release in 1985 in return for his denouncing the violence and armed movement of the ANC. He remained in prison until 1990 when overwhelming South African and international pressure led to his release. At the same time, the ban on the ANC was lifted by then President de Klerk.

In 1994, South Africa held its first election in which both blacks and whites could participate. To little surprise, the ANC won the majority and Mandela was installed as the country's first black state president. Frederik de Klerk would serve as deputy president. Mandela was president until 1999, and helped the torn country start to reconcile its racial differences and end the lingering results of apartheid.

Mandela retired from the presidency in 1999 and entered a new phase of his life as an advocate for several social causes while the world stood in line to heap honors on him. He was diagnosed with prostate cancer and underwent radiation treatment.

Due to declining health and a desire to spend more time with his family, Mandela announced his retirement from public life in 2004 at the age of 85. He still continues to write and occasionally speak on issues important to him, his country and the world at large.

The Legacy of the Man

Nelson Mandela will always be a symbol of courage and forbearance under difficult conditions. He saw an unfair system and tried to help stop it in the face of incredible odds. He was able to use his intelligence and education to articulate strong positions, make logical arguments against the very nature of apartheid and attract the loyalty and devotion of not only a small number of supporters in the ANC, but in his country and the entire world.

It is almost impossible to imagine staying imprisoned for almost three decades and still being able to inspire followers into staying the course. However, this is what Mandela did, and his ultimate reward was his release and the presidency of the country. It was an amazing change of fortune.

Mandela's main legacy as president of South Africa is the progress that was made in peaceful relations between the blacks and the Afrikaner-dominated apartheid parties. Instead of calling for reprisals against the white minority, he worked hard with former President F.W. de Klerk to bring the two races together for the common good. This would prove to be a daunting task that is still being struggled with today.

After Mandela's retirement, he was showered with accolades and awards, the highlight being the Nobel Peace Prize in 1993. Other honors he received during this time included the Order of Merit and Order of St. John from British Queen Elizabeth II, the Presidential Medal of Freedom from President George W. Bush and honorary citizenship from Canada (the only living foreigner to be given this).

Mandela has emerged as a hero, but no hero is perfect. By any standard, however, he showed the courage and perseverance to inspire his people and change his nation forever.

1985年,当局以曼德拉谴责非洲民族议会的暴力和武装运动为条件,愿意释放他,但是却遭到了曼德拉的拒绝。他在监狱里一直待到1990年,此时,国内和国际上无可抗拒的强大压力迫使当局释放了曼德拉。与此同时,当时的南非总统克拉克也撤销了对非洲民族议会的禁令。

1994年,南非举行了该国历史上首次由黑人和白人共同参与的选举。不难预料,非洲民族议会赢得了大多数席位,曼德拉随后正式就职,从而成为南非有史以来第一位黑人总统。弗莱德里奇·克拉克克成为副总统。曼德拉担任南非总统一直到1999年,在这期间,他帮助这个受尽创伤的国家弥合种族的分歧,消除残存的种族隔离的后遗症。

曼德拉于1999年卸任总统职位,之后进入了他人生的新阶段,他成为几项社会事业的支持者,与此同时,世人一致授予他荣誉。他被诊断出前列腺癌,之后接受了化疗。

由于健康状况恶化,以及出于更多地陪伴家人的渴望,曼德拉于2004年,宣布从政坛引退,时年85岁。他仍然坚持写作,偶尔对关系到他、他的祖国以及整个世界的大事发表评论。

他的遗产

尼尔森·曼德拉将永远被看做在艰难困苦下英勇、隐忍与宽容的象征。他目睹了一个不公平的体制,在备受怀疑的境遇下,仍竭尽全力要终结它。他能够用他的智慧和学识去表达强有说服力的观点和看法,通过合乎逻辑的辩论来反驳被认为是理所当然的种族隔离。他能够凝结支持者们的忠诚和奉献,不仅仅是非洲民族议会的一小部分支持者,而且还包括他的国家和全世界支持者。

曼德拉被监禁了将近30年,但他依然能够昂扬地激励追随者推进他们的事业,这让人难以想象。但这就是曼德拉所做的,而他的最终奖赏就是获得了自由和总统宝座。其命运之转变着实让人唏嘘慨叹。

作为南非总统,曼德拉的主要遗产是,他推动了黑人与白人种族隔离间和平关系的进程。不是煽动广大黑人向小部分白人报复,而是和前总统一起努力使这两个种族为了共同的利益而团结在一起。至今,这还是一件棘手但需要为之奋斗的事业。

曼德拉引退后,各种荣誉奖赏接踵而至,最光辉的顶点在1993年,他获得诺贝尔和平奖。在此期间,他还获得了其他荣誉,包括来自英国女王伊丽莎白的功勋奖章和圣约翰奖章、来自乔治·布什的总统自由勋章、加拿大荣誉公民(唯一获此殊荣的尚健在的外国人)。

曼德拉被视为英雄,但英雄并非完人。无论从哪方面看,他在南非人民面前展现了勇气和毅力,激励他们去不断改造自己的祖国。

Thirty-one

United States 1996 Olympic, Women's Soccer Team

Why the Team is Among the *50 plus one Greatest Modern Heroes*

The U.S. Olympic Women's soccer team of Hamm, Chastain, Fawcett, Foudy and Akers stood up and made fans take notice. The Americans defeated China, 2-1, to win the gold medal in the first Olympics to include women's soccer. The historic match was witnessed by a record women's soccer crowd of 76,481 at Sanford Stadium with a universal audience that saw nonstop action. The U.S. Women's Soccer team inspired many new fans and brought respect to women's soccer. A superb team effort and a hard-fought game entitle each member of the women's team to be named one of the greatest athletes of all times.

About the Team

Coach Tony DiCicco
Born: August 5, 1948
· Third head coach in the history of U.S. Women's National Team program.
· Lost just eight times as a head coach of the U.S. Women's National Team with a record of 108-8-8 establishing a winning percentage of 0.899 the best ever in U.S. Soccer history.
· Led team to five, first place finishes in the U.S. Women's Cup (1995-99).

Mia Hamm-Garciaparra
Born: March 17, 1972
Position: Forward
Three-time Olympian (1996, 2000, 2004)
· Named U.S. Soccer's Chevrolet Female Athlete of the Year 5 years in a row(1994~1998).
· Ended 1999 as the world's all-time leading scorer (114 goals, 93 assists for 321 points).
· Broke the all-time international scoring record for men or women, with her 108th career goal May 16, 1999 vs. Brazil.

Kristine Lilly
Born: July 22, 1971
Position: Midfielder
Three-time Olympian(1996, 2000, 2004)

美国1996年奥运会：女子足球队

这支队伍为何入选《50+1位最具影响力的风云人物》?

美国奥运女子足球队的哈姆、蔡斯顿、福塞特、福迪和埃克斯的成长赢得了大量球迷的注意。美国队在第一届有女子足球比赛的奥运会上以2-1打败中国队,赢得金牌,这场历史性的比赛在桑福得体育场见证了拥有76481名来自全球各地的观众观看一场没有停歇的比赛纪录。美国女子足球队受到了许多新球迷的鼓舞,也为女子足球运动赢得了尊重。一支优秀团队的努力加上一场艰辛却取得胜利的比赛让队中每个成员成为美国历史上永久的伟大球员之一。

关于该队

教练托尼迪塞科

出生日期:1948年8月5日

美国国家女子足球队的第3号总教练。

曾经以108-8-8的纪录建立89.9%的美国足球历史最好获胜几率而丧失了8次成为美国国家女子足球队的总教练机会。

带领球队从女子足球世界杯排名第5成为世界第1(1995~1999)。

米亚哈姆–贾西亚帕拉

出生日期:1972年3月17日

位置:前锋

3次参加奥运会(1996年,2000年,2004年)

被命名为5年内(1994年~1998年)雪佛兰杯美国足球年度最佳女运动员。

到1999年为止,是世界空前的得分手(114个得分,其中93次助攻,321个直接得分)。

1999年5月16日在对巴西的比赛中随着她职业生涯中第108个进球,打破了之前所有男女国际比赛的得分纪录。

克里斯汀·莉莉

出生日期:1971年7月22日

位置:中场

3次参加奥运会(1996年,2000年,2004年)

· Will become the first player, man or woman, to achieve 200 career caps.

· The U.S. Women's National Team all-time appearance leader and its third all-time leading scorer.

· Preserved the tie in the 1999 Women's World Cup Finals, later won by the U.S., by clearing a Chinese header off the goal line in sudden death overtime.

· Scored 20 goals in 1999, becoming only the fourth player in history to do so.

Shannon MacMillan

Born: Oct. 7, 1974

Position: Midfielder

Two-time Olympian(1996, 2000)

· Scored the game-winning goal against Norway in overtime of the semifinals at the 1996 Games.

· Won the 1995 Soccer American Player of the Year and Bill Hayward Award as OregoN's top female amateur athlete.

· Assistant Women's soccer coach for the University of Oregon, Portland.

The Resources

To learn more about the Women's Olympic Soccer teams visit:
www.soccerhall.org/history/OlympicFootballTournaments.htm or
www.ussoccerplayers.com/women%5Fplayers/michelle%5Fakers/.

将成为无论女子还是男子中第一个实现职业生涯200个盖帽的选手
美国国家女子足球队形象领袖和排名第3得分手
在1999年女子世界杯总决赛上帮助美国队保持紧密配合，在最后的点球比赛中赢中国队
在1999年比赛中进20个球，成为历史上第4个有如此成绩的选手。

香农·麦克米兰

出生日期：1974年10月7日
位置：中场(1996年，2000年)
2次参加奥运会
1996年对挪威的半决赛中，在加时赛时踢入制胜球
1995年美国足球年度最佳球员，比尔·海沃德为她颁发俄勒冈州最佳业余女运动员。
俄勒冈大学女子业余足球队教练。

参考资料

想更多了解美国奥运女子足球队，可以进入下列网站www.soccerhall.org/history/OlympicFootballTournaments.htm 或 www.ussoccerplayers.com/women% 5Fplayers/michelle%5Fakers/.

Thirty-two

Sandra Day O'Connor, Supreme Court Justice

Who She Is

She is our hero not just because she was the first woman to sit on the Supreme Court, but as much for her fairness, personal integrity and preoccupation for the preservation of the Constitution and the laws of the land.

She is a living standard of what most people expect from the judiciary: A judge who used her power and influence for the good. A woman with high standards, she resisted political pressure in her efforts to build a coalition on the Supreme Court that was both moderate and politically neutral. She remains a symbol of what a judge and scholar should be.

What Made the Woman

Appointed by President Ronald Reagan in 1981 and serving until her retirement in 2005, Sandra Day O'Connor was the first woman to serve as a justice on the U.S. Supreme Court. She participated in some landmark decisions during her tenure on the court, and quickly built a reputation as an intelligent and open-minded justice.

O'Connor was born on March 26, 1930, to Harry A. Day and Ada Mae Wilkey Day. Although she frequently refers to herself as a Texan, she grew up on the familyowned Lazy B Ranch, near the town of Duncan in southeastern Arizona. The Lazy B took up almost 200,000 acres and ranched more than 2,000 head of cattle. O'Connor helped tend the ranch and referred later to these experiences as helping her to develop a work ethic that led to later success.

She spent almost 8 years by herself on this lonely and remote ranch. Her early childhood companions were her parents, the ranch hands, a pet bobcat and some javelina hogs. She had to learn to entertain herself and did so by burying herself in books. Her mother kept up her informal early education by reading the Wall Street Journal, Los Angeles Times, New Yorker and Saturday Evening Post. O'Connor also learned how to mend fences, keep up when riding with the ranch's cowboys, fire a 22 rifle and drive the ranch truck.

O'Connor would say later that her grandmother's strong will and high expectations were a big influence on her life.

O'Connor, a gifted student, graduated from high school when she was only 16. She entered Stanford University in 1946 and received a degree in economics, in 1950. At this

桑德拉·戴·奥康纳：
美国联邦最高法院大法官

她是谁

她是我们的英雄并不仅仅因为她是第一位在联邦政府最高法庭占有席位的女性，更是因为她具有公正高尚的情操，以及维护国家宪法和法律的持久恒心。

对于那些对司法有所期待的人们，她就是一个活生生的例子，一个运用权力和影响力维护正义的法官。她是一个有着高标准的女性，为建立一个结合温和与政治中立的最高法院，她抵抗着来自各方的政治压力。然而，她同样树立了一个优秀法官和严谨学者的典范。

是什么成就了她

自从1981年被里根总统钦定任命直到2005年她决定卸任退休，桑德拉·戴·奥康纳是首位任职于美联邦最高法院的首席大法官。在她任职于最高法院期间，她参与并制定了一系列具有里程碑意义的决策，并迅速地树立起一位聪慧开明的法官形象。

1930年3月26日，奥康纳出生于得克萨斯州，父亲是哈里·A.戴，母亲是阿达·梅·威尔凯·戴。尽管她常说自己是得克萨斯州人，她事实上成长于一个名叫"Lazy B"的家庭牧场。"Lazy B"坐落在亚利桑那州东南部邓肯镇，是一个占地20万英亩的牧场，牧场里饲养了2000多头牲畜。奥康纳帮助家里照料牧场，后来她称这段经历帮助了她形成了一套把她引向成功的工作准则。

奥康纳独自在这个孤寂遥远的牧场待了近8年的时光。童年陪伴她的只有父母、牧场工人、宠物山猫和几只野猪。她学会了用埋头读书的方式自我消遣。她的母亲对她进行了早期教育，教她朗读《华尔街日报》、《洛杉矶时报》、《纽约客》、《星期六晚报》等报刊。她还学会了修补栅栏、与牧场牛仔赛马、使用22式步枪，以及驾驶大卡车。

奥康纳后来回忆，祖母的坚强意志和殷切期望对她而言有着不可磨灭的巨大影响。

奥康纳天资聪慧，16岁高中毕业后，于1946年顺利考入斯坦福大学，并在1950年以最优异的成绩获得经济学学位。与此同时，女性正开始打开通向律师界的大门。奥康纳决

time, women were just starting to make inroads into being attorneys. O'Connor decided to pursue the law and entered Stanford Law School. She worked on the Stanford Law Review and won membership in the prestigious Order of the Coif legal honor society. She graduated third in her class in 1952. The same year, O'Connor married John Jay O'Connor III, whom she had met while working on the law review.

Postgraduation, O'Connor found it difficult to obtain a position with a private law firm. The only job offered to her was as a legal secretary. She decided to try to work in the public sector and was hired as a deputy county attorney in San Mateo, California. She found she enjoyed working in public service and later said this first job had a profound influence on her life and career.

O'Connor won a hard-fought battle to become a state judge on the Maricopa County Superior Court in 1974. She was appointed by the governor to the Arizona Court of Appeals 5 years later. Within 2 years, in 1981, President Reagan nominated her to the U. S. Supreme Court, fulfilling a campaign promise to appoint a woman to the high court. She won Senate confirmation 99-0 and was sworn in on September 26, 1981.

The Legacy of the Woman

Sandra Day O'Connor's most visible legacy was in her groundbreaking role as the first woman to sit on the U.S. Supreme Court(she would be followed by Ruth Bader Ginsburg).

O'Connor's law clerks describe her as very much in control and an intense perfectionist. However, they also say she was warm, down-to-earth (as fits her ranch background) and always upbeat. She often eased the long hours in her office with popcorn, Mexican food or outings to the Smithsonian.

定继续学习法律,于是她又到斯坦福大学法学院学习法律,还成为"优等生协会"的成员。1952年,桑德拉从法学院毕业,成绩名列第3,同年,她与在法律评论工作时遇见的约翰·杰·奥康纳结婚。

毕业后,奥康纳发现除了做法律秘书外,很难在私人法律公司中谋得像样的职位。她决定尝试在公共部门里工作,并被任命为加利福尼亚州圣马特奥县的副检察长。她很享受自己在公共部门的工作,并说这第一份工作对她今后的事业和人生都有着深远的影响。

1974年,桑德拉在亚利桑那高等法院法官选举中艰难胜出。5年后,受州长任命,她开始在亚利桑那联邦上诉法院工作。两年内,在1981年,里根总统提名她为美国最高法院工作,实现了任命一名女性任职最高法院的竞选承诺。她以99票通过赢得了参议院的批准,于1981年9月26日宣誓。

她的遗产

桑德拉·戴·奥康纳取得的最为显然易见的遗产就是,她成为在联邦政府最高法庭占有席位的首位女性(在她之后又有另一位女法官金斯伯格被任命)。

奥康纳的法律同事们描述她是一个理智、认真的完美主义者,而且不失温和、实际(这点与她在牧场的背景有关),而且乐观。她常常在长时间的工作中用爆米花、墨西哥菜缓解压力,或者去史密斯松宁博物馆散心。

Thirty-three

Rosa Parks, Civil Rights Activist

Who She Is

Rosa Parks was no one special—just a hard-working woman who simply was tired and refused to go to the back of the bus. She had had enough of the Jim Crow nonsense and she said so, quietly and defiantly.

She used her moral authority, sense of righteousness and her moral outrage to change a system of social interaction that had been oh-so-carefully maintained for nearly 100 years. What she did was simply say no to the face of authority and power. She spoke volumes with a single action.

She is our hero specifically for saying no, for taking a small stand and showing by example that change could come and the whole Southern system of segregation could be challenged.

What Made the Woman

Rosa Parks was born on February 14, 1913, in Tuskegee, Alabama. After her parents separated when Parks was a young child, she stayed with her mother and moved with her to Montgomery, Alabama. Parks grew up as part of an extended family that included her maternal grandparents and her younger brother.

At an early age, Parks was exposed to the overt racism of the Deep South in the 1920s and 1930s. In those days, the South practiced almost total segregation of African-Americans from whites. These segregationist policies were commonly referred to as Jim Crow laws. There were separate schools(usually of inferior quality) for African-Americans, special sections in restaurants for African-Americans (some restaurants served African-Americans from the kitchen door or simply refused any service at all), separate restrooms and even separate drinking fountains.

One aspect of segregation that would later make Parks a nationally known figure was separate seating—at the back, naturally—for African-Americans on the city's public buses.

Despite all these injustices, Parks, with encouragement from her mother, grew up to be a young, proud woman. She married a barber named Raymond Parks when she was 20. They both worked and led a fairly comfortable life. At this time, Parks started to become active in the local chapter of the National Association for the Advancement of Colored People(NAACP) as well as the Montgomery Voters League, a group that helped African-Americans pass the tests that were required at the time to register to vote. Parks began to show her disdain for segregated facilities.

At the time, for Parks and many African-Americans in Montgomery, the most visible and onerous example of segregation was the city's public bus system. Under the system at

---

152   www.ahstp.net

罗莎·帕克斯：美国"人权运动之母"

她是谁

罗莎·帕克斯并不是什么特殊的人物,她只是一位辛勤劳动的妇女,因为觉得疲倦而拒绝坐到公车的后面去。她在受够了白人对黑人的歧视之后,平静地在大庭广众之下说出了自己的抗议。

她以道德上的威信、正义感以及道义上的不满改变了那个被如此小心翼翼维护了将近100年的社会体系,而她所做的也仅是在当局和权力面前说出不。她只用一个简单的行动就充分表明了自己的立场。

她之所以被我们称为英雄,尤其在于她敢于提出抗议,有自己微小但却坚定的立场并以身作则地说出来。她让人们相信,改变总会到来,对黑人的不公待遇和整个南方的种族隔离制度是应该被质疑的。

是什么成就了她

罗莎·帕克斯1913年2月14日出生于亚拉巴马州塔斯基吉市,小时候父母离异后她便和母亲一起搬到亚拉巴马州的蒙哥马利市居住。她在一个既有外祖母又有小弟弟的大家庭中长大。

早年,罗莎·帕克斯置身于南方20世纪20到30年代公开的种族歧视环境中。那个时候,南方几乎实施了黑白人种的全部隔离,而那些种族隔离政策通常被称为黑人条例。有单独的学校(通常质量很低)供黑人上学,餐馆也为黑人分出单独的就餐区,而且不少餐馆通常将黑人安置在厨房门口或者完全拒绝提供某些服务,还有分开的休息室甚至连饮水池也是分开使用的。

而种族隔离政策中有关公车上的"黑白隔离"的那一部分,是要求黑人在城市公共汽车上坐到后面的规定。正是因这一规定而起,后来罗莎·帕克斯成为了一名享誉全国的人物。

尽管存在着所有这些不公平,罗莎·帕克斯还是在母亲的鼓励下成长为一名年轻而高傲的女性,并在20岁时和一名叫雷蒙德·帕克斯的理发师结了婚。他们各自都有自己的工作,因而生活还算舒适。那个时候罗莎·帕克斯在全国有色人种协会和蒙哥马利选举联合会中开始变得积极活跃,而蒙哥马利选举联合会是一个帮助黑人通过当时必须要参加的测试以登记为选民的组织。罗莎·帕克斯开始对实行种族隔离政策的设施表现出鄙弃态度。

在当时,对帕克斯和许多蒙哥马利市的黑人来说,城市的公交车制度是实行种族隔离政策最明显和最令人焦虑的例子。在当时那些体制之下,黑人乘客们被要求从前门上

the time, African-American customers were required to use the front door to enter the bus, pay their fares, then exit back out the front door and re-enter at the rear door.

The first four rows of the bus were designated for whites only. Behind these seats was a middle section African-Americans could use. However, if so much as one white person sat there, all the African-Americans had to leave those seats. Finally, there were the rows in the back exclusively for African-Americans. Despite the fact that African-Americans constituted the vast majority of bus riders, it was not unusual to see them having to stand when there were plenty of empty seats in the whites-only rows or middle section. Understandably, this caused a lot of anger and frustration among the African-American riders.

In 1955, Parks was employed as a seamstress at the Montgomery Fair Department Store. On December 1, she had what she described as a particularly hard day. When she finally got on a bus to go home, all the seats for African-Americans were full and she ended up sitting in the middle section of the bus. When a white customer entered the bus a few stops later, he demanded a seat in the middle section. The driver told Parks and three other African-American riders to move. Parks was the only one to refuse. The driver threatened to call the police. Parks told him to go ahead.

The driver made good on his threat and Parks was arrested, fingerprinted and jailed. Black leaders in Montgomery saw this as an opportunity to challenge the restrictive bus regulations and perhaps deal a fatal blow to the other segregated facilities. Parks agreed to go to court to challenge the law that led to her arrest.

In the meantime, Montgomery African-American activists decided to boycott the entire bus system as of December 5. African-Americans walked, participated in car pools or rode bicycles to get around during the boycott. The city dug in its heels and the boycott ended up lasting 381 days, until a long-standing lawsuit by the NAACP challenging the bus segregation laws finally made it through the courts. Ending up in the U.S. Supreme Court, the justices found for the plaintiffs and outlawed racial segregation on buses, deeming it unconstitutional. The court order went into effect on December 20, 1956, and African-Americans began riding the buses the next day.

The boycott took its toll on Parks and her family. Both she and her husband, Raymond, lost their jobs and the continual harassment she received ended up causing him to suffer a nervous breakdown. In 1957, Parks, Raymond and her mother moved to Detroit, where she worked for a while as a secretary. She was still sought after as a symbol of the developing civil rights movement.

As her reputation grew, Parks was awarded several honorary degrees and eventually worked on the staff of Detroit Congressman John Conyers. Even after she officially retired, she was still a much sought-after speaker. She founded the Rosa and Raymond Parks Institute in Detroit, which offers career training for 12-to-18-year-olds.

After suffering for a year with progressive dementia, Parks died in her apartment in Detroit on October 24, 2005. In her honor, the bus systems of Detroit and Montgomery placed black ribbons in the first four rows of their buses to reserve them for Rosa Parks until her funeral. Her memorial in Montgomery was heavily attended, and her remains were later moved to the U.S. Capitol rotunda, where she lay in state on October 31, making her the first woman and only the second African-American to receive this honor. Parks was buried alongside her husband and mother in Detroit's Woodlawn Cemetery. Per her instructions, her headstone reads only Rosa L. Parks, wife, 1913~2005.

车付费后再从前门下来,只能从后门上车乘坐。

车的前4排是指定为白人准备的;紧挨其后的中间区,黑人是可以坐的,但却只是在没有任何一个白人坐那儿的情况下;最后剩下的后面一小部分位子才轮到黑人的专座。尽管黑人占乘坐公交者的绝大多数,但如果你看到车上白人专座区或中间区有足够的空位时黑人却要站着的情形,却大可不必感到稀奇。很自然的,这一规定让黑人们既愤怒又失望沮丧。

1955年,罗莎·帕克斯在蒙哥马利大百货商店做裁缝。12月1日,她度过了正如她后来所描述的极其困难的一天,当她最终坐上回家的巴士时,后排的黑人座位都已全部坐满了,她最终只能坐在中区。车过了几站之后,上来一名白人乘客,他要求坐在中间区,于是司机让帕克斯和她的3名同伴让座,她的3个同伴让了,但她还是继续坐着。司机恐吓她,要是她再不让座,就要叫来警察,帕克斯说:"你可以这么做。"

司机叫来警察将帕克斯逮捕,取了指纹后将她监禁起来。蒙哥马利市的黑人领袖将此次事件视为向那些具有限制性的巴士法规挑战的机会,并希望以此给其他有关种族隔离设施以致命的一击。罗莎·帕克斯同意出庭,向此条导致她被捕的法律宣战。

与此同时,在蒙哥马利市的黑人政治活动积极分子们决定,从12月5日起联合抵制整个公交系统。黑人们在这场抵制运动中,加入车队或者骑自行车出行。而由于当局的拒不让步,使这场抵制运动一直持续了381天,直到全国有色人种协会提交的一项质疑巴士隔离法的诉讼案最终被法庭受理。在美联邦最高法院,法官判原告胜诉并裁定蒙哥马利的种族隔离法违宪,裁定结果在1956年12月20日生效。第2天,黑人开始乘坐公交。

这场抵制运动使罗莎·帕克斯和她的家人的生活陷入困境:她和丈夫雷蒙德都丢掉了原来的工作,而由于经常遭到威胁和恐吓,最终使得雷蒙德患上了神经衰弱症。帕克斯、雷蒙德和她的母亲被迫在1957年搬去了底特律市,在那里她做助理持续了一段时间。但罗莎·帕克斯依然很受大众的欢迎,她被当做民权运动发展的里程碑。

随着帕克斯的名声渐长,她被授予了个荣誉学位,并最终成为底特律议员约翰·康耶斯的工作班子成员。退休后,她仍是一名广受欢迎的演讲者,并成立了罗莎与雷蒙德·帕克斯自主发展学会,致力于为12到18岁的年轻人提供职业培训。

在罹患痴呆症一年之后,帕克斯在2005年10月24日于底特律家中辞世。为向她表示敬意,底特律市和蒙哥马利市的公交系统纷纷在巴士的前4排座位上系上黑丝带,并把这些座位为帕克斯保留至她的葬礼。在蒙哥马利的纪念仪式上,有很多人前来哀悼,帕克斯的灵柩随后被转移至华盛顿的国会山圆形大厅。10月31日,人们为她举行了隆重的总统级仪式,她是享此殊荣的第一位女性,并是仅有的第2个黑人。在底特律伍德劳恩公墓,帕克斯被葬在她丈夫和母亲旁边。依照她的指示,她的墓碑上只写着"罗莎·L.帕克斯,妻子,1913~2005"。

Thirty-four

Luciano Pavarotti, Opera Singer

Who He Is

Who has not been entranced by the majesty and strength of Pavarotti's voice and presence? Few of our heroes exist in exalted and rarified worlds like opera. But this hero is one who transcends that world and makes himself and his art accessible to everyone.

He is a great popularizer but has not traded down. He is approachable without losing his majesty. And he is a singer of such control and majesty that even the uninitiated feel compelled to stop, look and listen when he sings, and they find themselves appreciating his extraordinary talent.

What Made the Man

Pavarotti was born on October 12, 1935, on the outskirts of Modena in northcentral Italy. Pavarotti always portrayed his childhood as being idyllic, but the family was impoverished and crowded four members into a two-room apartment. Pavarotti's father had a fine tenor voice but decided not to pursue performing because of terminal stage fright. Instead, he supported the family as a baker. Pavarotti's mother helped financially by working in a cigar factory—hardly the heady stuff of the operatic world.

Pavarotti was all of 19 when he began studying music in earnest with Arrigo Pola. Pola, a respected music teacher and tenor living in Modena, knew that the family had little money to spare for music lessons, but was so impressed with the young tenor-to-be that he offered to teach Pavarotti for free. Pavarotti soon discovered, to his delight, that he had perfect pitch. This encouraged him to continue his training.

At about the same time Pavarotti was beginning his musical training, he met Adua Veroni, whom he married in 1961. Pavarotti's first teacher, Pola, moved to Japan in 1963, and Pavarotti began studies with Ettore Campogaliani, who had taught Pavarotti's childhood friend Mirella Freni(who was quickly building a reputation as a talented soprano).

Pavarotti supported his new family and his studies
through a series of odd jobs, including returning to
teaching and, of all things, selling insurance.

Pavarotti's early years of study only resulted in performing at a few recitals (without pay); frankly, he did not overly impress anyone. A nodule developed on his vocal cords, and he decided to give up singing. He later said that this decision freed him psychologically from the pressures to succeed. Fortunately, the nodule disappeared. He believed that this was a crucial element in finding his natural voice and creating the type of sound he had been struggling to achieve.

34

鲁希亚诺·帕瓦罗蒂:
歌剧演唱家

他是谁

谁不曾为帕瓦罗蒂那高亢的歌喉所倾倒,谁不曾为他的出场而着迷?我们本书的英雄人物很少有来自歌剧这一高深精妙的殿堂。但是,本文这位英雄却冲破樊篱,让他和他艺术走进千家万户。

他名噪一时,却不因此而媚俗;他平易近人,却又不失威严。他的歌声收放自如、有如天籁,就连那些对歌剧一无所知的人们也不禁为之驻足、侧目、倾听,沉浸在他那不同凡响的歌声中。

是什么造就了他

1935年10月12日帕瓦罗蒂出生于意大利中北部摩德纳的郊区。尽管帕瓦罗蒂经常把童年描述成田园诗般的生活,但是那时家里一贫如洗,一家4口挤在只有两个房间的房子里。他的父亲有着美妙的男高音,因为怯场,只好放弃了表演。他靠烤面包养家糊口。帕瓦罗蒂的母亲在一家卷烟厂做工赚钱,补贴家用——这些行当都与激情荡漾的歌剧相去甚远。

帕瓦罗蒂开始正儿八经学习音乐时已经19岁了。他师从当时居住在摩德纳的受人尊敬的男高音歌唱家艾芮戈·波拉。他得知帕瓦罗蒂家境窘迫,但是被他的天赋深深打动,于是答应不拿报酬免费教他。令帕瓦罗蒂高兴的是,他不久就发现了自己的高音非常完美,这激励着他继续训练。

几乎跟他参加音乐训练同时,他与艾杜娃·维罗妮邂逅,1961年与其结婚。1963年帕瓦罗蒂的第一位老师波拉移居日本,帕瓦罗蒂又师从埃特罗·凯普加利尼学习,后者同样也是帕瓦罗蒂童年好友、现今享誉世界的女高音歌唱家弥芮拉·芙莱妮的老师。

在学习期间,帕瓦罗蒂为了生计不得不边学唱歌边打零工,包括返回讲坛、卖保险等。

最初学习的几年,帕瓦罗蒂不过在几场音乐演奏会上表演(没有报酬)。坦白地说,他并没有给人留下过深印象。之后,他的咽喉上长了一个瘤,他决定放弃继续演唱。他后来说,这一决定使他从心理上脱离了成功的压力。幸运的是,那个瘤消失了。他相信这是发现他自己具有天赋的嗓音并达到自己梦寐以求的境界必不可少的一关。

For whatever reason, Pavarotti post-nodule was a better singer, and he began to receive some recognition. He won the Achille Peri Competition, appearing as Rodolfo in a production of La Boheme. Pavarotti's appearance helped him secure his first agent. With his help, Pavarotti appeared in *La Boheme* in Lucca and later as the Duke of Mantua in *Rigoletto*.

In the 1980s Pavarotti's name became synonymous with opera. He set up the Pavarotti International Voice Competition for younger singers and performed with the winner. He was expanding his repertoire by releasing albums of popular standards. He performed in such huge venues as Hyde Park in London and the Great Hall of the People in Beijing, China.

In 1990, Pavarotti recorded the Puccini aria *Nessun Dorma* as the theme song of the World Cup in Italy. The song would go on to be Pavarotti's trademark song. The same year, he also made his first appearance as part of the Three Tenors (along with Placido Domingo and Jose Carreras) at the Baths of Caracalla in Rome with music director Zubin Mehta. The recording of the concert became the best-selling classical record of all time. Just for fun, he sang with Vanessa Williams in a 1998 *Saturday Night Live* (the only opera singer to ever appear on the show) and with Bono and the band U2 on their 1995 song *Miss Sarajevo*.

The early years of the 21st century saw Pavarotti going through some difficult times, including the breakup of his relationship with his long-term manager Herbert Breslin, the ending of his first marriage and his second marriage to his assistant Nicoletta Mantovani.

Health problems started to beset Pavarotti and limited his ability to perform. At age 69, he announced his farewell tour in 2004. He had to struggle with tax disputes in Italy. He underwent neck and back surgery and was diagnosed with pancreatic cancer in July 2006. After emergency surgery, Pavarotti began to recuperate and is hoping to resume the farewell tour in 2007.

The Legacy of the Man

Luciano Pavarotti will certainly go down in history as one of the most accomplished and popular tenors in classical music. He made the *Guinness Book of World Records* for receiving the most curtain calls (165) following a performance and for the Three Tenors best-selling classical album of all time.

However, Pavarotti was not a perfect performer. Although he was universally praised for his singing, his acting on stage was considered inferior and he struggled most of his early career to try to improve it. He also had to argue throughout his career that he could read music, but sometimes had difficulty following the orchestral parts.

不管原因如何，经历这一关的帕瓦罗蒂歌唱得更棒了，开始逐渐得到认可。他在《拉·波希米》中因饰演罗道尔夫而获得阿基里培利奖。帕瓦罗蒂的表演赢得了他的第一位经纪人。在他的帮助下，帕瓦罗蒂又在卢卡的《拉·波希米》出现。之后，又在《弄臣》中饰演曼都华公爵。

20世纪80年代，帕瓦罗蒂的名字成了歌剧的代名词。他为年轻歌手设立了帕瓦罗蒂国际声乐大赛，并同胜出者同台演唱。他通过发行通用标准的专辑来推广他的保留曲目。他还尝试在伦敦的海德公园和中国北京的人民大会堂这样大的场所演唱。

1990年，帕瓦罗蒂为在意大利举行的世界杯制作了普希尼的《今夜无人入睡》，作为本次杯赛的主题曲。这首歌曲将会继续成为他的代表作。同年，他与另外两名男高音歌唱家多明戈和卡雷拉斯并由祖宾·梅塔担任指挥，在罗马的卡拉卡拉浴场首次演唱。音乐会的唱片在古典音乐中一直是最畅销的。1998年，他(作为节目中第一次出现的歌剧家)跟温妮莎·威廉姆斯在"周末夜直播"节目中合唱，又与波诺和他的U2乐队在他们1995年的歌曲《塞拉耶芙小姐》中合作演唱。

21世纪初，帕瓦罗蒂经历了艰难的时期，包括与他长期合作的经理人赫伯特·布莱斯林关系断裂、第一次婚姻结束以及与他的私人助理尼柯赖特·曼托瓦妮结合。

健康问题开始困扰着帕瓦罗蒂，也限制了他表演的能力。2004年他69岁时，宣布开始他的告别巡回演出。在意大利他不得不纠缠于税收纠纷。他的脖子和背部都做过外科手术，2006年7月被诊断出患有胰腺癌。经过紧急外科手术后，帕瓦罗蒂身体开始康复，期望着能够继续他在2007年的告别巡回演出。

他的遗产
作为古典音乐领域最有成就、最受欢迎的男高音歌唱家，鲁希亚诺·帕瓦罗蒂的名字无疑会载入史册。他由于单场演出收到最多的165次谢幕掌声，以及3大男高音最畅销古典音乐唱片集而被收入吉尼斯世界纪录。

然而，帕瓦罗蒂并非是一个完美无缺的歌唱家。尽管他的演唱得到世人赞誉，但是他的表演实属一般。在他早期的演唱生涯中，他设法改进他的表演。在他整个歌唱生涯中，他不得不承认尽管他能识乐谱，但有时跟不上乐队的节奏。

Thirty-five

Eva Maria Duarte de Peron, First Lady

Who She Is

Eva Peron was our hero because she always seemed larger than life—like Princess Di or Jacqueline Kennedy—and she managed somehow, remotely, to make us feel better about ourselves. She had a fascinating hold on the average person in Argentina and continues to exercise a fascination on the world.

Unfortunately, our heroine is not the stuff of greatness—rather an image of a beautiful, sophisticated, ambitious woman who knew how to manipulate the public.

What Made the Woman

Like many aspects of her life, the facts about Eva's birth are disputed. She was born Eva Maria Duarte on May 7, 1919, at what is believed by some to be the city of Junin in the province of Buenos Aires (other historians think she was born in the nearby village of Los Toldos). Eva, an illegitimate child, grew up with her mother and brothers at La Union farm. Eva arrived in Buenos Aires when she was 15, probably with the help of her mother.

She soon found herself facing the usual problems of any newcomer to a large and unfamiliar metropolis. She had no formal education and no connections in the city, and soon also discovered the rigid class system that ruled Buenos Aires' society. She eventually fell into work as a radio and film actress (many detractors claimed she got these jobs by sleeping her way to the top), and began making regular appearances in B-movies and radio soap operas. Some believe that she dyed her hair blonde during this time so she could look more like her favorite actress, Norma Shearer.

Just as Eva was making a name for herself, she met Colonel Juan Peron at a fundraiser to aid victims of the 1944 San Juan earthquake. The post-World War II government of Argentina was then in constant turmoil. Thanks to his ability to relate to the common people (the descamisados) and his high-profile earthquake relief activities, Peron was considered a possible future president.

His political foes had Peron arrested because of his growing popularity. A widespread myth was that Eva supported Peron on her radio shows and organized a rally of thousands that helped free him from prison. In reality, Eva was still just an actress with no political clout, especially among the powerful labor unions. Her relationship with Peron continued to grow, even though she was not popular with Peron's colleagues.

Eva and Peron corresponded by letters and discussed the possibility of leaving Argentina upon Peron's release. They also had to face the fact that Peron might be killed in prison—not an irrational view, considering the political times.

Finally, a massive rally (actually organized by labor unions) resulted in Peron's release from prison on October 17, 1945. Shortly after his release, he married Eva. The newly freed Peron decided to turn his popularity into a serious bid for the nation's presidency, and he entered the 1946 elections.

35

伊娃·贝隆：第一夫人

她是谁

伊娃·贝隆是我们的英雄，她的身上总带有一丝传奇色彩，就如同戴安娜王妃或是杰奎琳·肯尼迪一样。她总能让我们对自己信心大增。她过去对普通的阿根廷人有着强大的吸引力，今天她对整个世界依然如此。

不过，我们的女英雄不是纯粹意义上的伟大人物，她只是一位美丽、精明而且野心勃勃的女性，她知道如何掌控民众。

是什么成就了她

她的出生同她一生中很多其他事情一样颇受争议。1919年5月7日，她出生于一些人认为是布宜诺斯艾利斯一个叫胡宁的城市，当时取名为伊娃·玛莉亚·杜亚提（其他历史学家认为她出生于罗托尔多附近的一个村庄）。伊娃是个私生女，在母亲的呵护下和几个哥哥在联合农场一起长大。可能是在母亲的帮助下，伊娃15岁时来到了布宜诺斯艾利斯。

不久她便碰到了所有新来到陌生大都市的人们所遇到的问题。她没有接受过正规的教育，在这城市里无依无靠，同时她也很快发现了充斥着整个布宜诺斯艾利斯社会森严的等级制度。最终她成了一名广播电影演员（许多诋毁她的人说她是全凭卖身才一步一步爬到上层社会的），并逐渐大量地拍摄一些二流电影和广播肥皂剧。今天有些人认为她就是在那段时间里把自己的头发染成了棕色，这样看起来就像她最喜爱的女演员诺玛·希拉。

当伊娃逐渐出名的时候，她和胡安·贝隆上校在为援助1944年圣胡安大地震受难者举行的募捐活动上相遇了。当时"二战"后的阿根廷政府正处于水深火热之中。他在普通民众（"无衫者"）当中较强的号召力以及他引人注目的地震救援活动使他成为未来总统的一名候选人。

随着贝隆的受欢迎度日趋上升，他的政治对手将他逮捕起来。有一种流言说伊娃不但在她广播节目上支持贝隆，而且组织上千人集会帮助贝隆出狱。事实上伊娃只是一个普通的女演员而已，并没有什么政治影响力，这点在势力庞大的工会当中尤其如此。虽然贝隆的同事们并不喜欢她，但她与贝隆的感情却是与日俱增。

伊娃和贝隆互相写信给对方讨论他出狱后两人一起离开阿根廷的计划，同时他们不得不面对贝隆有可能在狱中被杀这样一个现实，而考虑到当时的政治情形，这种看法还是很客观的。

1945年10月17日，一场大型集会（实际上是由工会组织的）最终使贝隆从狱中被释放出来。出狱后不久，他便和伊娃结婚了。刚获得自由的贝隆决定将他在群众中的受欢迎度作为一个重要的筹码，竞选国家总统。于是他参加了1946年的总统大选。

Eva used her weekly radio show to extol Peron's virtues,
and tried to show that her own upbringing(poor)
somehow intimated his solidarity with the poor.

After returning to Argentina, Evita changed her style to simpler clothing and her hair pulled back into a bun. She was striving to be seen as a woman of her people. As part of this change of image, Evita began to focus on charity work. She created the Eva Peron Foundation to help build hospitals and orphanages (although some critics believed the foundation funds found their way back to the Perons).

In the general election of 1951, Evita decided to earn a place on the ballot as a vice-presidential candidate. Once she realized that even Juan Peron did not like this idea, Evita formally declined to run for vice president, and devoted her time to supporting her husband.

Part of this decision might also have been based on Evita's increasing physical incapacity. After Peron was re-elected, her health had deteriorated to the point where she could not stand without support from a wire frame worn under her dress. She was also using increasingly heavy doses of painkillers. Evita had developed uterine cancer that had spread and could not be completely removed. The end came quickly and Evita died on July 26, 1952, at the age of 33. The country entered an unprecedented period of national mourning.

The Legacy of the Woman

Eva Peron was beloved by her people and almost universally despised by the ruling classes. Her name appeared almost everywhere during her brief reign; a city and even a star were named after her.

Despite a reputation for being ambitious, she was always careful to stress that everything she said or did in public was inspired by Peron. It is believed that she ultimately made herself subordinate to her husband's political agenda. However, she could be vindictive, and those who insulted or opposed her were often sent into exile.

Despite her shortcomings, Evita remains a beloved figure to millions of Argentines and a popular subject for drama. The most famous version of her life(portraying her mostly as a villain) is the musical Evita by Andrew Lloyd Webber and Tim Rice. No matter her motivations, Eva Peron will be remembered as a popular cultural icon and as a pioneer in combining politics with show business.

伊娃借她每周的广播节目来宣扬丈夫贝隆的美德,并努力向人们证明她的经历(她出身贫寒),这在某种程度上表明了贝隆是站在穷人这一边的。

回到阿根廷之后,埃维塔改变了她的作风,换上了朴素的衣服,并将头发挽成小圆髻。她努力将自己装扮成为民服务的普通女性。在她改变自己形象的同时,埃维塔开始专注于慈善工作。她建立了"伊娃·贝隆基金会",以帮助建立医院和孤儿院(虽然当时一些评论家认为基金会的资金全被贝隆一家收入囊中)。

1951年大选期间,埃维塔决定为自己在副总统的候选名单上赢得一席之位。但当她发现连胡安·贝隆都不喜欢她这种想法时,埃维塔正式决定不参加竞选,而把所有的时间花在支持她丈夫身上。

做出这个决定一方面也可能是因为埃维塔逐渐感到身体上的不适。在贝隆再次当选之后,她的健康状况急剧下降,以至后来只有靠裙子下面的三维线框她才能站得住。同时她服用止痛片的剂量也不断上升。后来她患上了子宫癌,癌症已经发生扩散,因此不能完全移除。不久噩耗传来,埃维塔于1952年7月26日去世,年仅33岁。全国上下进入了空前的哀悼期。

她的遗产

伊娃·贝隆受到她人民的爱戴,但却几乎为所有的统治阶级所鄙视。在她统治全国短暂的时间里,她的名字出现在全国各个角落,甚至命名了一座城市和一颗星。

虽然她的雄心勃勃为人们所熟知,但她非常注意自己的言行,总是强调她在公共场合的言行举动都是受丈夫激励。今天人们相信她最终甘愿为她丈夫的政治前景而退居幕后。不过她似乎很有报复心,那些曾经侮辱过她或是反对她的人经常遭到流放。

虽然她身上有着种种缺点,埃维塔仍然是一个受数百万阿根廷人爱戴的人物,并且成了一个很受欢迎的电影主题。其中由安德鲁·洛依·韦伯和蒂姆·莱斯编写的《贝隆夫人》,就是最著名的一部讲述她一生的音乐剧。不论她活着时的动机是什么,作为一名广受欢迎的文化偶像,并将政治和演艺事业结合起来的开拓者,伊娃·贝隆将永远为人们所铭记。

Thirty-six

Elvis Aaron Presley, Musician

Who He Is

It would be difficult to imagine a more complicated hero than Elvis Presley. Here was a man of humble origins who revolutionized music and the contemporary culture with hip music, good looks, a sexy smile and a swagger. His every movement (many seen on television, including the famous *Ed Sullivan Show*) was followed by millions. His popularity—personal and musical—was unprecedented. So much so that even now, long after his death, his career, his estate at Graceland and his music continue to attract fans—fans who never saw him perform and are not even close to being his contemporaries.

So popular is Elvis that even the former prime minister of Japan, an avid fan, wanted to experience the Elvis legend! President Bush took him to Graceland as part of an official visit to the United States.

In later life, his personal behavior was at best strange, almost as strange as his death. He had turned into an aging rocker with bizarre personal habits, a tendency to gain huge amounts of weight and a serious addiction to drugs—yet all is forgiven and forgotten.

What Made the Man

Reportedly a very shy child, Presley was born in modest circumstances to workingclass parents in East Tupelo, Mississippi. He was an only child(his twin brother was stillborn). The family experienced some very awkward times when Presley's father was convicted of check forgery and sentenced to 3 years in the state work farm.

When he was just 10 years old, Elvis showed his talent for singing when he won second prize in a local contest. A year later, he bought his first guitar and took it with him wherever he went. His pastor gave him basic guitar lessons and set him on his way.

During and after high school, he worked a variety of jobs—from driving a truck to laboring in a machine shop. But that would not be for long—he still had his music and was doing everything possible to absorb the style and tone of the southern blues.

His big break came when he met Sam Phillips of Sun Records. At that time—or so the story goes—Phillips was looking for a white man who could sing the black blues and boogie-woogie music—which Phillips was convinced would be a huge hit for a larger, white audience. In fact, most of Elvis' early efforts were really takeoffs of traditional country and western music, not the rock and roll influenced by the blues musicians that Elvis liked so much. So, naturally, he got a turn at the Grand Ole Opry and appearances on the live country music show *The Louisiana Hayride*.

36

埃尔维斯·亚伦·普莱斯利：
音乐家"猫王"

他是谁

我们很难再找到一个比埃尔维斯·普莱斯利更加复杂的英雄人物。他出生卑微，但却使他那个时代的音乐和文化发生了革命性变化，因为他拥有前卫的音乐，非凡的长相，性感的微笑，就连他身上的那种自命不凡也让人痴迷不已。他的一举一动受到了数百万人的追捧模仿(人们大多数是通过电视看到他的，这包括著名的"艾德·苏利文脱口秀")。无论是他个人还是其音乐的风靡程度都是史无前例的。他的影响之巨以至在他死后及其音乐生涯结束多年后的今天，他在格雷斯兰的别墅、他的音乐一如既往地吸引着众多的歌迷——即使这些歌迷以前没看过他的表演，或根本和他不是同一个时代的人。

埃尔维斯广受欢迎，就连日本前首相也是他的忠实歌迷，想和埃尔维斯一样成为传奇人物！布什总统曾经带这位首相去参观格雷斯兰作为他正式访美的行程之一。

在人生后半期，他的行为变得极其古怪，其诡异程度绝不亚于他的死亡。他是一位逐渐衰老的摇滚乐手，行为习惯很奇特。他的体重不断增加，而且他还有很严重的毒瘾。对于这些，今天的人们选择了遗忘与原谅。

是什么成就了他

普莱斯利出生于密西西比州东土丕洛的一个普通工人家庭里。据说他从小很害羞，是家里的独生子(他的双胞胎哥哥生下来就死了)。由于普莱斯利的父亲被指控伪造支票罪，罪名成立后被判去密西西比州进行3年农场劳动改造，因此全家经历了一段十分困难的时期。

10岁的时候他在当地一个演唱比赛中获得了二等奖，展现出了在演唱方面的天赋。一年后，他给自己买了第一把吉他，无论去哪里，他都会带上这把吉他。他的牧师给他教授了一些基本的吉他课程，把他送上了演艺之路。

无论是在读高中时还是高中毕业后，他都在打各种各样的零工，既开过卡车也在机械加工车间里干过。但这些零工的时间不长，他主要是想着他的音乐，并尽可能地去吸收南方布鲁斯的风格与曲调。

当他碰上太阳唱片公司的萨姆·菲利普斯时，他的音乐生涯出现了重大突破。在那个时候(事情确实如此)菲利普斯在寻找一个能唱黑人布鲁斯和布基伍基音乐的白人，他认为这个会对大多数白人观众有很大的吸引力。事实上埃尔维斯早期创作的音乐大多数是对传统的乡村和西部音乐的尝试，而非一些受埃尔维斯非常喜欢的布鲁斯音乐家们影响的摇滚乐。所以他理所当然地得到了在"大狂欢"上表演的机会，并且在乡村音乐现场秀"路易斯安那大篷车"上多次进行表演。

By 1955, it was time to move up to the big time, and Elvis signed with Colonel Tom Parker, who proceeded to buy out the singer's contract with Sun Records and find him a home with the much larger RCA Victor. While Elvis was certainly talented, most historians and those knowledgeable about Elvis would say that it was the relationship with Parker that really moved his career. The Colonel was a masterful promoter and wasted no time in getting Elvis seen and heard.

However, Colonel Tom was not through. The real money, according to Parker, was in movies. He signed Elvis with MGM studios, with Parker receiving a huge portion of the deal—as much as 50 percent. Nevertheless, Presley made a great deal of money from movies such as *Jailhouse Rock* and *Love Me Tender*—enormous box office hits. The movie business changed Presley's image from a risk-taking (even risqué) singer to a more sedate, wholesome entertainment figure.

However, 1968 would change all of that. This was his comeback year, thanks to very popular television specials and concerts in Las Vegas and other cities. The live Elvis, singing again, demonstrated once and for all that the King still had it. His tours over the next few years would be sold out city after city, including one done in Hawaii that was broadcast all over the world to an enormous audience!

But the return to popularity would not be smooth. By the time of his death in 1977, Elvis had taken on a peculiar persona—overweight, clothed in white jumpsuits and other odd costumes, using heavy makeup and, of course, taking a good deal of prescription drugs. There are countless stories of his odd behavior and even odder eating habits. The hard-edged rock and roller had turned into something very different in middle age(contrast Elvis, for example, with the Rolling Stones, who have never changed what they do).

The Legacy of the Man

Elvis' death exposed the great singer to a good deal of gossip, speculations and outright nastiness. It is very clear that this hero had come down a peg or two. His personal life seems to have been in shambles. At one point, it was suggested that he died of a heart attack, but in reality there were sufficient drugs of different kinds in his system to suggest either an accidental overdose or even suicide. Theories abound.

His personal relationships with various women throughout his life caused considerable scandal—especially his tendency to date very young women. There are those who believe that Elvis was gay, or at least bisexual, supported by longterm relationships with people he had known throughout his career, and his changing and erratic behavior later in life.

　　1955年正是埃尔维斯音乐生涯继续向前发展的时候，于是他和汤姆·帕克上校签下了合同。帕克于是将埃尔维斯与太阳唱片公司的合同买断，并且为他找了一个更好的东家，美国广播唱片公司的分公司维克多。虽然埃尔维斯的演唱天赋毋庸置疑，但大多数历史学家和研究埃尔维斯的专家们却认为，他职业生涯的发展真正得益于他和帕克建立的合作关系。"上校"在宣传包装明星方面是个专家，他抓紧一切时间宣传埃尔维斯，让更多的人接触埃尔维斯和他的音乐。

　　不过汤姆"上校"并不满足这些。在他眼里，拍电影才是最赚钱的行当。于是他让埃尔维斯和米高梅电影工作室签约，自己从中得到了一大笔收入：高达合约的50%。尽管这样，普莱斯利还是从一些像《脂粉猫王》和《温柔地爱我》这样的影片中获得了不菲的收入。这两部电影都十分卖座。电影方面的事业也改变了普莱斯利的形象，从以往一个爱冒险（甚至是有伤风化）的歌手转变成了一个更加低调而健康的娱乐人物。

　　然而在1968年，情况发生了翻天覆地的变化。得益于一些广受欢迎的电视专题节目和他在拉斯维加斯及其他城市举办的一些演唱会，这一年成了他的复出年。埃尔维斯又开始为人们进行现场演唱，永远地向人们证明了"猫王"的演唱天赋依旧。后来的几年里，他在一个接一个城市里举办演唱会，这包括在夏威夷举行的一场演唱会。这场演唱会向全球直播，吸引了广大的观众。

　　但他的复出之路并非十分平坦。在他去世的1977年，埃尔维斯的身体已经超重到十分奇怪的地步。他经常穿白色紧身连衫服和其他一些古怪的服装，并且要化很浓的妆，当然还得服用许多药物。今天有数不清的故事讲述着他那古怪的行为举止和更加离奇的饮食习惯。这位风格鲜明的摇滚乐手在他中年时发生了巨大的转变（举个例子，可以将埃尔维斯和"滚石"乐队比较一下，他们从来没有改变自己所从事的事业）。

他的遗产

　　埃尔维斯的死使他这位伟大的歌手陷入了种种非议、猜测，甚至是彻底的辱骂之中。很明显这位英雄的气势收敛了一些。他的个人生活似乎一直很糟。人们曾一度以为他死于心脏病发作，但事实上，他身体内有许多不同种类的毒品足以证明他要么是吸毒过量致死，要么就是自杀。各种理论解释花样繁多，莫衷一是。

　　他一生中与形形色色的女人们的个人关系引发了相当大的丑闻，特别是他有一种喜欢约会年轻女士的倾向。也有人认为埃尔维斯是个同性恋，或者至少说是个双性恋。他在音乐生涯里和一些熟识的人长期保持着关系，以及他生命后期那些易变而反常的举动可以证明这一点。

Thirty-seven

Ronald Wilson Reagan, President

Who He Is

There was something irrepressible about Ronald Reagan—a smiling, warm and open individual who seemed greater than life. Perhaps he really was the consummate actor and the great communicator. In person, on television, on the radio—and, of course, in all his old movies—he exuded charm and charisma. His supporters were wild in their enthusiasm, just as his detractors found him too smooth, too refined and too rehearsed.

Perhaps not a very complicated man (he could never be accused of overmanaging his cabinet and advisers), he came from a small college (Eureka) and an even smaller town (Tampico) in Illinois. An athlete, sports announcer, Screen Actors Guild president, Democrat turned conservative Republican, he arrived on the political stage at a time when conservatism seemed out of favor with the voters. He redefined that political perspective—so fully, in fact, that he was able to use it as a springboard to national prominence and the presidency.

If nothing else, he was an enthusiastic and optimistic man who came to the nation's attention at a time of tense political and economic problems—high unemployment, inflation and waning international respect for American foreign policy.

What Made the Man

Born on February 6, 1911, the second son of Irish and English immigrants, he lived most of his life in Dixon, Illinois. Before settling in Dixon, the family moved a number of times, including a stint on the South Side of Chicago and Galesburg, Illinois. However, it was Dixon's small-town life that formed the man: student body president in high school, a gifted athlete in basketball, football and track, and a prominent member of the drama club. For 7 years, he worked as a life guard and was credited with saving 77 lives!

The real personality of the future actor, governor and president emerged when he began his collegiate studies at Eureka College. Again, he was elected student body president, and participated in drama, swimming and football. Reagan the activist first came to light at Eureka where he helped organize a student strike.

After graduation, he began his real political life, stumping for Franklin Delano Roosevelt(he was later a staunch defender of Harry Truman). This was a very unexpected political beginning for Mr. Republican.

By 1933, he made a name for himself as the local Des Moines, Iowa, radio announcer for the Chicago Cubs baseball team. His job was to announce Cubs home games—a very tricky task when you are sitting in a radio booth hundreds of miles away from the action! A testament to his cleverness is that using just a simple ticker tape feed, he was able to

37

罗纳德·威尔森·里根：美国总统

他是谁

里根的一生充满传奇，但他看上去总是面带微笑、亲切坦率。或许，他确实是个技艺高超的演员和伟大的交际家。无论是本人、电视上、广播里或者在他早期出演的电影中，他都散发出无穷的魅力和领导气质。他的支持者为他疯狂，而他的诬蔑者却觉得他太平凡，太做作。

里根或许不是一个很复杂的人（他从来没有被谴责过度管理他的内阁和顾问）。他在伊利诺斯州的小镇坦皮科长大，毕业于尤利卡大学。在成长过程中，他当过运动员、体育播报员、银幕演员、协会主席，又从民主党人转为保守的共和党人。他在一个选民都不喜欢保守主义的时代登上了政治舞台。他对政治前景进行了重新全面的定义，并能够以此为跳板进入了白宫甚至登上了总统宝座。

简单地说，这个热情乐观的人在国家面临着紧张的政治和经济问题的时候，进入了公众视线。而那时的美国正面临着高失业率、通货膨胀和全球对美国对外政策的质疑。

是什么成就了他

里根出生于1911年2月6日，是家中的次子，他的父母是爱尔兰和英国移民。他一生大多数时间都住在伊利诺斯州的迪克松市。在迪克松定居之前，里根一家在很多地方都居住过，其中包括伊利诺斯州芝加哥的南赛德和加尔斯堡。然而正是迪克松小镇生活造就了他：高中时的学生会主席，篮球、足球和田径方面的天才运动员，同时又是戏剧社的杰出成员；他还做了7年的救生员，据说救了77条人命。

在尤利卡大学的学习生涯中，他初步展露了一个未来的演员、政府工作者和总统的人格品性。他又一次当选为学生会主席，出演话剧，并参加游泳、足球等活动。在组织了一次学生大罢课后，里根作为积极分子被人们所关注。

毕业后，他才真正开始政治生涯，为富兰克林·德拉诺·罗斯福作政治演讲，后来又是哈里·杜鲁门的坚定支持者。这便是这个共和党人的政治生涯的出人意料的开始。

1933年，他在衣阿华州的德梅因，为芝加哥童子军棒球队播报比赛而扬名。他的工作是播报童子军在家乡的比赛，这是一个务必要反应灵敏的任务，因为你只能坐在离比赛场地百余米远的小隔间里播报比赛。只用一个自动收报机，他却能够为听众创造一个

create a colorful and detailed game for the listeners. He used his vast imagination to fill in the rest—reportedly, he continued his play-by-play description of the game even when the ticker tape went off. He improvised by having the batter hitting a series of foul balls until the ticker tape came back on.

Most biographers, even good friends, would agree that his acting career in Hollywood at Warner Brothers was the stuff of B movies. During his Hollywood days, he first married (and later divorced) Jane Wyman, was active in the Screen Actors Guild, was called to active duty during World War II, and involved himself in local and national politics—particularly interesting was his support, as a Democrat, of Nixon, Eisenhower and other Republicans.

As important as any movie or television role was his marriage to Nancy Davis, the future and sometimes infamous Mrs. Ronald Reagan. By 1962, he had officially changed parties and was now a registered Republican. Many political pundits credit his famous television speech in support of the ultraconservative presidential candidate Barry Goldwater as the true beginning of his political career. The speech brought him into both the local and national limelight. In 1966, his popularity was so strong that he trounced Governor Pat Brown, a Democrat, in the California election.

The Legacy of the Man

The new governor wasted no time in starting to build his political empire, both within California and nationally. He practiced the famous guideline, "do not speak ill of other Republicans", and was generous in his support of not only conservatives but even moderate Republicans.

By the time he was nominated in Detroit in July of 1980, there were few who did not believe that he would trounce the incumbent, Jimmy Carter. In fairness, Reagan's victory owed something to Carter's problems, his public perception, the state of the economy and the Iranian hostage crisis. But the fact remained: Reagan never varied his political agenda and hammered away at it until the American public saw his views as new, refreshing and optimistic. (As every student of history knows, it is one thing to win the presidency; it is another to govern effectively and to show real results.)

The Reagan team was perhaps most famous for its theory of economics, frequently called Reaganomics, or supply-side economics. The essentials of these policies were based on huge tax cuts (which many said benefited the rich), a massive, full-scale assault on inflation, deregulation of business, reduction in interest rates, increased military spending and increased deficits in the national debt (some of the same policies used by John F. Kennedy years before)! Whether critics liked Reagan's economic policies or not, the fact is that they worked. After a short recession, the economy grew at a rate that had not been seen for 25 years.

By the time of his death at age 93, Ronald Wilson Reagan was thought of as one of the most successful and popular presidents since Franklin Roosevelt (oddly, they are often compared to each other, despite their political and government propensities). Personally energetic, loyal to a fault, charming, optimistic and consistent in his conservative message, he and his legacy endure as a great moment in American history.

精彩而详细的比赛,这足以见证里根的智慧。他用丰富的想象来充实比赛的间隙。据说,有一次收报机出了故障停止了工作,他却继续对比赛进行实况转播:他即兴让击球手们连续击出界外球,直到收报机又恢复工作。

很多传记作家,即便是里根的好友都不得不承认,里根在好莱坞华纳兄弟旗下的作品都是二流低成本电影。在好莱坞的日子里,他活跃于银幕演员协会,和一个叫简·怀曼的演员结婚,但是后来又离了婚。他在二战时应招服役,由此进入了地方和国家政治领域。有趣的是,当时他作为民主党人却支持尼克松、艾森豪威尔和其他共和党人。

和他的任何电影或电视角色同样重要的是他和南茜·戴维斯的结合,就是那个偶尔名声不佳的后来的里根太太。1962年,里根正式调换政党,并注册为共和党人。许多政治权威把他支持极端保守派总统候选人巴利·古德沃特所作的电视演讲作为他政治生涯的真正开端。那次演讲让他成为地方和国家注目的焦点。他非常受欢迎,以至在1966年加利福尼亚州的选举中,他以压倒性的优势击败了民主党州长帕特·布朗。

他的遗产

这个新的州长在加利福尼亚甚至全国不遗余力地建造自己的政治王国。他实施了那个著名的指导方针,即"不说其他共和党人的坏话",并大力支持的保守派人士以及温和的共和党人。

1980年7月,他在底特律被提名为总统候选人的时候,很少有人会怀疑他能否击败在任总统吉米·卡特。其实公平的来说,里根的胜利应该归功于卡特的一些管理问题:公共理念、经济状态和伊朗人质危机。但事实仍然存在:如果公众不认同他的观点是新颖、乐观并且令人振奋的,里根就不会变更他的政治议程,并会一直苦心钻研下去。(正如每个学历史的学生都知道的那样,赢得总统大选是一回事,而如何有效管理并得到实际效果是另外一回事。)

里根的政治团队最著名的要数他们的经济理论了,通常被叫做里根经济理论或供应学派经济理论。这套政策最重要的要素便是以大规模的减税(很多人说这为富人造益)、对通货膨胀的全面的大规模压制、解除贸易管制、降低利率、加大军事支出和增加国家债务赤字为基础(一些相同政策在几年前同样被约翰·肯尼迪采用)。尽管批评家们不认同里根的经济政策,但事实上它起了作用。在很短的一个工业衰退期之后,美国的经济开始以25年来最快的速度发展。

在里根93岁去世时,他被认为是富兰克林·罗斯福之后最成功和最受欢迎的总统(奇怪的是,虽然他们二者的政治和管理作风不同,他们还是常被拿来互相比较)。作为个体,他迷人乐观、精力充沛、勇于承认错误,并一贯坚持着保守的理念。他和他的功绩将会成为美国历史的一座丰碑。

Thirty-eight

Venus Williams,
Tennis Star

Why She is Among the *50 plus one Greatest Modern Heroes*

Venus Williams exploded into the tennis scene in the late 1990s' when she won the 1999 French Open doubles with her sister Serena and five other doubles and two mixed doubles grand slams.

On the Way Up

Venus Ebone Starr Williams was born on June 17, 1980 in Lynwood, California. She is the daughter of Richard and Oracene (Brandi) Williams. She and Serena, along with their three older half sisters, grew up in the Los Angeles suburb of Compton, California. Her father, Richard, taught Venus how to play tennis on local neighborhood tennis courts. In 1994, her family moved to Palm Beach Gardens, Florida to train with famed coach, Rick Macci.

Professional Career

Venus turned pro prior to the World Tennis Association (WTA) rule change barring 14-year olds from competing in all tour events, instead favoring a phase-in program instead. During her first 2 years on the pro tour Venus kept a low profile while keeping up with her high school duties. She made her Grand Slam debut at the 1997 French Open. At the Open she became the first unseeded woman ever to reach the tournament's final and the first African-American to do so since Althea Gibson won back-to back championships in 1957 and 1958. Although she lost to Martina Hingis, the No.1 ranking player in the world, Venus saw her own ranking jump from No. 66 to No. 25 in one day.

1998 started well for Venus. She reached the quarterfinals of the Australian Open (defeating sister Serena along the way). She won the mixed doubles championship paired with Justin Gimelstob. She won her first WTA singles title at the IGA Tennis Classic in March. With two big wins against Anna Kournikova of Russia and Martina Hingis, Venus' ranking jumped into the Top 10.

Despite her wins in 1997, Venus had yet to achieve her dream, to secure a Grand Slam victory. A friendly sibling rivalry might have been born when her younger sister, Serena, reached that goal first, when she won the 1999 U.S. Open. Yet, the sisters remained focused and determined to keep winning. In October, Serena beat Venus for the first time in the finals of the Grand Slam Cup in Munich, Germany. Both sisters finished the 1999 season ranked in the top five in the world. Venus was ranked No.3 and was the second-highest paid player in prize money.

The year 2000 got off to a slow start due to injuries. Richard Williams announced that

38

维纳斯·威廉姆斯：
网坛明星

她为何入选《50+1位最具影响力的风云人物》?

维纳斯·威廉姆斯在90年代末占据了网坛,她和妹妹塞雷娜曾获得1999年法国公开赛双打冠军、5项其他双打冠军和两项混双大满贯。

成长之路

1980年6月17日,维纳斯·艾博恩·斯塔·威廉姆斯出生于加利福尼亚林伍德。她的父亲是里查德·威廉姆斯,母亲是奥西恩(布兰地)·威廉姆斯。她和妹妹塞雷娜及3个大半岁的姐姐成长在加利福尼亚州洛杉矶近郊康普顿市。她父亲在当地邻里网球场教她打网球。1994年,全家搬到了佛罗里达州棕榈滩花园,在那里,她可以接受著名教练瑞克·马奇的训练。

职业生涯

维纳斯在女子职业网球协会(WTA)取消14岁少年不得参加任何巡回赛规定之前就已成为职业运动员,并在分段训练计划中受益。在参加职业巡回赛的头两年,维纳斯成绩不佳,因为要顾及高中学业。自1997年法国公开赛,她便开始了自己的"大满贯"生涯。公开赛中,她成为第一位"非种子选手"闯入锦标赛决赛,也是继阿尔西·吉布森1957年和1958年蝉联冠军后的第一位美国黑人冠军。虽然败给了世界排名第一的玛蒂娜·辛吉斯,维纳斯在一天之内亲眼目睹自己的排名从第66名升至第25名。

1998年是维纳斯良好的开端。她进入澳大利亚公开赛1/4决赛(击败妹妹塞雷娜)。她与搭档贾斯汀·吉美尔斯托布获得混双冠军。3月,她获得了生平第一个WTA单打冠军——IGA网球精英赛。维纳斯打败玛蒂娜·辛吉斯和俄罗斯的安娜·库尔尼科娃,这两大胜利让她一跃排名第10。

虽然1997年连续夺冠,维纳斯仍要实现梦想:捍卫大满贯。当她赢得1999年美国公开赛时,她那友好的竞争对手——妹妹塞雷娜率先实现了这一梦想。这对姐妹花仍然决心继续夺冠。10月,塞雷娜在德国慕尼黑大满贯杯决赛中首次战胜维纳斯。结束1999年赛季时,姐妹俩已排名世界前5。维纳斯名列第3,在高额奖金运动员中排名第2。

2000年,她因受伤而推迟开赛。里查德·威廉姆斯宣布维纳斯正考虑退役,但是几个

Venus was contemplating retirement but just a few months later Venus was on a winning streak all the way through to Wimbledon where she grabbed the Grand Slam title beating Hingis, Serena and Davenport. One day later, Venus and Serena teamed up to win the Wimbledon doubles title.

Venus' 2005 season began poorly as well. At the French Open, Venus lost to 15-year old Bulgarian Sesil Karatantcheva. The following month Venus reached the 2005 Wimbledon finals defeating defending champion Maria Sharapova in the semi-finals in straight sets. In the longest Wimbledon final in history, Venus, with a win from behind, triumphed over top seed Lindsay Davenport 4-6, 7-6(4) 9-7 to win the 2005 Wimbledon Championship—her third Wimbledon in 6 years. This marked the first time in 70 years that a player had won after facing match point during the women's championship. William was also the lowest seed (14th) to win the title in Wimbledon history.

In 2005, *Tennis* Magazine placed her 25th in its list of 40 Greatest Players of the Tennis era.

About the Woman Herself

Despite the inevitable rivalry, the Williams sisters remain close friends. Raised as devout Jehovah's Witnesses, both were home-schooled by their mother, and have received their high school diplomas. In 1999, Serena joined her sister at the Art Institute of Florida, where they studied fashion design.

Venus is a businesswoman and CEO of her interior design firm V Starr Interiors, located in Jupiter, Florida. Williams' company gained recognition by designing the set of the *Tavis Smiley Show* on PBS; designed the Olympic Athletes' Apartments as a part of the U.S. bid package for New York to host the 2012 Games; and designed residences and businesses in the Palm Beach, Florida area.

◀ **Venus Williams, Tennis Star**

月后，维纳斯在温布尔登大赛中扬眉吐气，打败了辛吉斯、塞雷娜和达文波特，捧回大满贯。一天后，维纳斯和塞雷娜获得温布尔登双打冠军。

2005年赛季刚开始时，维纳斯成绩不佳。在法国公开赛中，维纳斯输给了15岁的保加利亚选手卡拉坦捷法。下个月，维纳斯在2005温布尔登半决赛中直落盘数击败卫冕冠军玛丽娅·莎拉波娃，直闯决赛。在这次史上最长时间的温布尔登决赛中，维纳斯后来者居上，以4-6,7-6(4)9-7战胜了头号种子选手达文波特，摘得2005温布尔登桂冠——这是6年中第3次赢得温布尔登冠军。这是70年来第一位在女子锦标赛出现赛点后获胜的选手。威廉姆斯也是温布尔登历史上夺冠排名最低(第14名)的选手。

2005年，《网球》杂志将她评选为"网球时代40位最伟大球员第25名"。

关于此人

虽然威廉姆斯姐妹俩是无可避免的竞争对手，但是两人关系亲如朋友。两人是虔诚的耶和华见证会成员，从小由母亲进行家庭教育，并获得高中文凭。1999年，塞雷娜进入姐姐就读的佛州艺术学院，两人一起主修时装设计。

维纳斯是佛罗里达州丘比特室内设计公司V Starr Interiors的女商人，也是首席执行官。威廉姆斯的公司因设计PBS台《塔维斯·斯麦里秀》的布景而闻名；为纽约申办2012奥运会设计了奥林匹克运动部门；还在佛州棕榈滩设计了住宅及商店。

Thirty-nine

Jackie Robinson, Athlete

Who He Is

Many of us would think ill of a world so segregated that there were actually two major league baseball organizations—one for whites and the other for blacks. However, it was not just baseball that was out of bounds for promising African-Americans—it was most of contemporary life, including the majority of other sports, business, education and employment.

Finding yourself the only black athlete in the major leagues is hard to imagine. What must it be like to be shunned by fellow athletes and fans alike? Imagine traveling across the United States and being forced to take different accommodations from the rest of your teammates? Try to think of the courage it took to stand up against such social customs. Not only did Jackie Robinson need to break the color barrier, he had to do it as a better, faster and stronger player than the rest of his teammates—and the rest of the National League.

What Made the Man

Jack Roosevelt Robinson was born on January 31, 1919, in Cairo, Georgia. His mother, Mallie, moved the family to Pasadena, California. Robinson and his four older siblings grew up in a working-class neighborhood where racial prejudice was common. As a child, he was most comfortable playing sports and tried his hand at just about anything: baseball, basketball, dodgeball, football, golf, marbles, soccer and tennis.

Starting in 1939, Robinson attended the University of California, Los Angeles(UCLA) after excelling in sports at Pasadena Junior College. He continued his athletic success at UCLA, where he was a star player on the football, basketball, track and baseball teams. Robinson was the first athlete in the university's history to letter in four different sports.

In 1944, Robinson played shortstop for the Kansas City Monarchs in the Negro American League. He caught the attention of a scout who worked for Branch Rickey, the Brooklyn Dodgers' president and general manager. Rickey soon decided that Robinson had the strength, courage and, of course, skills to become the first African-American professional baseball player. In 1946, Robinson was assigned to play for the Montreal Royals, the top minor league affiliate of the Dodgers. He played second baseman and led the International League with 0.349 batting average, while also stealing 40 bases and carrying the team to the Little World Series championship. The team as well as the fans in Montreal respected and welcomed Robinson almost overwhelmingly during his stay in their city. But that kind of support would soon come to an end for him—for a while, anyway.

In 1949, Robinson was named the National League's Most Valuable Player after completing a fantastic season. He led the league both in hitting with 0.342 and steals with 37, all while batting in a career high of 124 runs. Although he played his rookie season with the Dodgers as a first baseman, he spent most of his career at second base. Throughout his 10 seasons with Brooklyn, Robinson saw the team win six National League

他是谁

我们中很多人都会认同，这个世界的种族隔离非常严重，以至于真实存在于两个棒球大联盟组织：一个为白人而设，一个则属于黑人。然而，不只是棒球界超越了允诺给非洲裔美国人的界限，而是大部分的当代生活，包括了其他大多数体育运动、商业活动、教育和就业。

发现你自己竟是大联盟中唯一的黑人运动员，这是难以想象的。被其他运动员和球迷躲避注定会是什么样呢？想象一下在穿越美国的时候，却被迫住在和其余队友不同的房间。试着想想这是何种的勇气来对抗着如此的社会风气啊。杰克·罗宾逊不仅需要打破肤色障碍，他还要作为一个更高更快更优于其余队友甚至国家联盟的运动员去完成。

是什么成就了他

杰克·罗斯福·罗宾逊1919年1月31日出生于佐治亚州的凯罗。他的母亲玛利亚把家搬到加利福尼亚州的帕萨迪纳。罗宾逊和他的4个兄弟姐妹成长在一个种族偏见很普遍的工人阶级居住区。作为一个孩子，他在运动时最舒适快乐，并用他的双手去尝试几乎任何运动：棒球、篮球、躲避球、橄榄球、高尔夫、弹珠、足球和网球。

1939年起，由于在帕萨迪纳专科学校体育方面表现出色，罗宾逊进入加州大学洛杉矶分校(UCLA)。在那儿，他延续着在体育上的成功，他在橄榄球、篮球、田径和棒球队中都是明星队员。罗宾逊是大学历史上第一个在4项不同运动上被登记在册的运动员。

1944年，罗宾逊在美国黑人棒球联盟中作为游击手效力于堪萨斯城君主队。他引起了一个为布朗·瑞奇工作的球探的注意。而布兰奇·瑞基，则是布鲁克林道奇队的会长兼总经理。瑞奇很快认定罗宾逊有力量、勇气，当然还有技能，足以让他成为第一个非洲裔美国人职业棒球手。1946年，罗宾逊被指派为蒙特利尔皇家队效力，那是加入道奇队的首屈一指的小联盟。他担任二垒手，并以0.349的平均打击率领先国际联盟队，40次盗垒，带领球队赢得小世界职业棒球锦标赛冠军。球队以及蒙特利尔的球迷在他停留在他们的城市期间，空前尊敬并欢迎罗宾逊。但这种支持对他来说很快就结束了，虽然情况很快出现了转机。

1949年，在完成了一个梦幻般的赛季后，罗宾逊获得国家联盟最有价值球员称号。他以0.342的安打率和37个盗垒领先，同时开创了高达124分的职业新高。尽管在他效力

pennants as well as the World Series in 1955 against their long-time rival, the New York Yankees. Robinson played in the last game of his professional career on September 30, 1956. He finished his career with a batting average of 0.311, 137 home runs, 734 runs batted in and 19 steals home.

In 1997, 50 years after Robinson's first season with the Dodgers, Major League Baseball(MLB) permanently retired his uniform, No. 42, from all of its teams. And in 2004, it named April 15 Jackie Robinson Day, to be celebrated each year in every league ballpark.

The Legacy of the Man

Robinson appeared as himself in the 1950 movie The Jackie Robinson Story, and wrote an autobiography called I Never Had It Made: An Autobiography of Jackie Robinson, which was published in 1972.

Shortly before his death in 1972, he was asked to throw out the first pitch at that year's World Series. That same year, Rachel started the Jackie Robinson Development Corporation, which builds low- and moderate-income housing. In 1973, she founded the Jackie Robinson Foundation, a not-for-profit national organization that helps deserving underprivileged minority youths by providing them with 4 year scholarships. In October of 2002, Robinson was posthumously awarded the Congressional Gold Medal, which Rachel accepted in a ceremony in the Capitol rotunda. Robinson, who also received the Presidential Medal of Freedom from Ronald Reagan in 1984, is only the second baseball player to receive the Congressional Gold Medal.

Jackie Robinson's legend continues through his family as well as through his memorable performances on the field of baseball and in the field of life.

于道奇队的首个赛季他是作为一垒手完成比赛的,但他大部分时间是在二垒上。在整个布鲁克林的10个赛季,罗宾逊见证了球队6次获得国家联盟冠军,并在1955年世界职棒锦标赛击败他们的凤敌纽约扬基队。罗宾逊职业生涯的最后一场比赛是在1956年9月30日。他以0.311的安打率,137个本垒打,734分和19个本垒盗垒结束了他的职业生涯。

1997年,即罗宾逊在道奇队的首个赛季的50年后,棒球大联盟从所有联盟球队里永久封存了他的42号球衣。2004年,棒球大联盟将4月15日命名为杰克·罗宾逊日,并每年都在所有联盟棒球场上庆祝。

他的遗产

杰克·罗宾逊于1950年在电影《杰克·罗宾逊的故事》中扮演他本人,并于1972年出版了自传,名为《我从未真正成功:杰克·罗宾逊自传》

在他1972年去世不久前,他被邀请在当年的世锦赛上投出第1球。同年,雷切尔开办了建造低价平价房屋的杰克·罗宾逊发展公司。1973年,他成立了杰克·罗宾逊基金会。这是一个通过颁发少数贫困青年4年奖学金来给予他们帮助的非赢利性的全国组织。2002年10月,罗宾逊被追认获得国会黄金勋章。雷切尔在美国国会大厦圆形大厅的一个仪式上接受了这一奖项。罗宾逊曾在1984年从罗纳德·里根那儿获得了总统自由勋章,同时是第2个获得国会黄金勋章的棒球运动员。

杰克·罗宾逊的传奇故事不仅通过他的家庭,还通过他在棒球世界和个人生活中的令人难忘的成绩继续着。

forty

The Rolling Stones, Musicians

Who They Are

If there are entertainment heroes with more lives than a cat, this is the group. Year after year, no matter how old they get, they appear at major venues throughout the world and entertain their ever-aging audiences with some of the greatest songs from the 1960s and 1970s. Even though the band, creatively, belongs somewhat to the past, fans love them anyway. Perhaps they represent the nostalgia that everyone craves—our time was the best, after all.

Why are they are heroes, despite their bad-boy image, drugs and decadent life? Well, they are heroes probably because they are bad boys, wild and decadent—and very entertaining. If nothing else, fans love the high energy level of Jagger on stage, even though he is in his 60s!

What Made the Group

The Rolling Stones are one of the most famous and popular rock and roll bands in history, making music for over 40 years and still going strong. The band's consistent members are Mick Jagger, Keith Richards and Charlie Watts. Other members included, and in some cases still include, co-founder Brian Jones, Mick Taylor, Ron Wood, Bill Wyman and keyboardist Ian Stewart(who was also the group's tour manager).

A fateful meeting between British schoolmates Jagger and Richards with Brian Jones began what would be the Rolling Stones(Jones came up with the idea of using the title of a Muddy Waters song as the name of the band). The band recruited Ian Stewart on piano and Bill Wyman as the bassist. After a series of drummers, the band brought in jazz-influenced Charlie Watts, who would stay with the group throughout its history.

The group was originally more interested in rhythm and blues(R&B) music, rather than what was considered rock and roll music at the time. The Stones quickly made a name for themselves, appearing at the Marquee Club in London, and soon had their own permanent club, The Crawdaddy Club in Richmond.

> They were considered one of the best live acts in London
> and even the Beatles stopped by to check them out.

Thanks to a tip by George Harrison, Decca Records signed the Stones to a recording contract. Their first single was a cover version of *Come On* by Chuck Berry. The band was establishing a following for R&B, a music form that was still largely unfamiliar to the broader American rock audience. Their anti-Beatles street-tough and dangerous look also made them a fan favorite.

The success of the band was leading to discord between Jagger and Richards in the late 1960s, but this period would see the Stones return to their R&B roots and record

滚石乐队：
歌星

他们是谁

　　如果有娱乐英雄能永葆魅力，胜过家猫九命，那么它非滚石乐队莫数。年复一年，不论年龄几何，他们总会在世界各地的重大场合出现，为他们同样在日渐老去的观众演唱一首又一首20世纪60、70年代的经典老歌。虽然从创作上来看，这支乐队似乎属于过去的岁月，但歌迷一如既往地喜爱他们。也许是因为他们代表着众人渴望的怀旧之情。毕竟，自己的时代才是最美好的。

　　尽管他们一副坏男孩的形象，吸毒、生活颓废，可为何还能成为英雄呢？或许，正是因为他们坏男孩的形象，加上狂野与颓废，才让他们格外有趣。其他暂且不论，歌迷喜欢舞台上精力充盈的贾格尔，即使他已经年过六旬！

是什么成就了他们

　　滚石乐队是史上最负盛名最受欢迎的摇滚乐队之一，从事音乐40多年，如今仍备受青睐。乐队的老成员有米克·贾格尔、凯斯·理查兹和查理·沃兹。其他成员有乐队合伙创办人布赖恩·琼斯，还有米克·泰勒、荣恩·伍德、比尔·怀曼和键盘手伊恩·斯图尔特(同时也是乐队的巡回演出经理人)，而其中有些人仍在滚石麾下。

　　贾格尔和理查兹与英国校友布赖恩·琼斯的一次相遇，成就了滚石的雏形(琼斯想用慕迪·华特的一首歌名作为乐队的名称)。乐队请来伊恩·斯图尔特做钢琴手，比尔·怀曼则做贝斯手。在试用了很多鼓手后，乐队最终迎来了查理·沃兹，这位爵士乐风格的鼓手从始至终都在乐队中效力。

　　比起当时的摇滚，滚石乐队最初对节奏与R&B更感兴趣。滚石乐队在伦敦的马奎夜总会进行了演出，立刻名声大噪。很快，他们就有了自己的永久俱乐部，即里士满克劳戴迪俱乐部。

　　他们的现场演出是伦敦最为出色的表演之一，甚至连披头士也前来驻足，看个究竟。

　　经过乔治·哈里森的指点，德卡唱片公司跟滚石乐队签下了唱片合同。他们的首张单曲翻唱了查克·贝里的《来吧！》。在当时美国的摇滚听众中，R&B这种音乐形式还鲜为人知，而滚石乐队正在为它建立起一支拥趸队伍。他们的形象与披头士截然相反，像极了街头恶棍，凶狠的样子也让他们成为歌迷的最爱。

　　20世纪60年代末，乐队的成功引起了贾格尔和理查兹间的龃龉，但在此期间，滚石乐队又回归到了R&B的根本，并录制了一些单曲，结果大受追捧，如《跳跃的杰克·弗莱

some of their most popular songs, including *Jumpin' Jack Flash*, *Street Fighting Man and Sympathy for the Devil*. The Rolling Stones were now being referred to as the world's greatest rock and roll band.

Some critics began dismissing the Stones as irrelevant by the late 1960s and were enamoured of the new guitar bands such as Cream, Free and Led Zeppelin. To offset this image of being over the hill, the band planned a major concert tour of the United States. The tour culminated in a free concert at the Altamount Music Festival near San Francisco. The concert promoters had hired members of the Hell's Angels motorcycle gang for security, and the intoxicated guards beat up several concertgoers and reportedly stabbed and killed one man.

Even with this tragic incident, the 1969 tour was a triumph and the Stones were playing some of their best music. As the group progressed into the 1970s, it began to fragment. Disagreements between Jagger and Richards increased. Mick Taylor left the band because he believed he was not being properly credited for his work. And Jagger became less interested in the music than in traveling in jet-set social circles. The little music they produced during this period reflected this drifting.

The band was in danger of completely falling apart and, although they remained fan favorites, critics in the 1970s were increasingly dismissing their new music. This changed with the release of *Some Girls,* widely considered the best Rolling Stones album. Richards was making a concerted effort to kick his drug habits. The band again started achieving critical and audience success with the release of albums like *Tattoo You,* but the relationship between Jagger and Richards remained tenuous at best. Ron Wood was developing his own drug problems and would be fired from the band, and Jagger was attempting to record as a solo artist(with mixed success).

The death of long-time band member Ian Stewart in 1985 started motivating the band to reconcile their differences and make music again. The group released more albums, such as *Bridges to Babylon, Steel Wheels and A Bigger Bang,* and started touring extensively in the 1990s and into the 21st century (without Bill Wyman, who had retired). The band continues to tour the world, much to the delight of millions of fans.

The Legacy of the Group

The Rolling Stones are still a vital rock band, creating new music and rocking the house. Even though they are entering their 60s, Jagger and company continue to put out some of the most energetic music of any rock band.

Whether they were really the world's greatest rock and roll band is certainly open to debate, but their output in the 1960s and 1970s contains some of the most influential and covered rock songs in history. They managed(for the most part) to survive the costs of fame and fortune, as well as a creatively dry period in the 1990s, to once again emerge as a rock band that still has something to prove.

Who can say how long they will continue to perform? The band has forged a strong bond with their older fans, while still attracting younger fans who enjoy the band's sound and bad-boy image. Perhaps they are such a long-lived band simply because they and their fans agree that they know it's only rock and roll, but they like it.

什》、《大街上战斗的人》和《同情魔鬼》。当时，滚石乐队就被称作全球最出色的摇滚乐队。

20世纪60年代，一些评论家开始抛弃滚石乐队，认为他们互不协调，转而对新兴的吉他乐队移情别恋，如克里姆、弗里和莱德·齐柏林。为了弥补正在走下坡路的形象，滚石乐队计划在美国进行一场的大型巡回演出。在旧金山附近的阿尔塔音乐节，他们举办了一场免费演唱会，成了巡演的最高潮。演唱会的组织方请来"地狱天使"摩托车帮的成员担任保安，结果醉酒的保安们痛打了几个观众，据说还有一位观众被害。

尽管发生了这样的悲剧，1969年的巡回演出还是大获成功，滚石乐队开始推出他们最优秀的歌曲。但进入70年代后，乐队开始分裂。贾格尔和理查兹之间的矛盾日渐激化。米克·泰勒觉得自己虽努力工作，但得到的回报远远不够，于是离开了乐队。贾格尔也对音乐兴趣渐失，转而钟情与自己的一圈朋友乘飞机旅行。他们在这一时期毫无建树，正反映了他们二人之间的疏离。

滚石面临着分崩离析的危机，尽管他们仍旧是歌迷的最爱，但70年代的评论家对他们的新歌愈发不以为然。《一些女孩》的发行改变了这个状况，而大家普遍认为这张唱片是滚石最精彩的一张专辑。理查兹不懈努力，意欲摆脱毒瘾。在发行了《为你纹身》等一些专辑之后，滚石乐队开始重新得到评论界和观众的赞赏，而贾格尔和理查兹的关系充其量称得上不即不离。伍德也开始吸毒，不久就被乐队开除了。而贾格尔正在尝试以独立音乐人身份录制唱片(尽管成就是乐队共有的)。

1985年，乐队老成员斯图尔特与世长辞，这激励了滚石乐队开始弥合分歧，重新创作。他们发行了更多的专辑，如《通向巴比伦的桥》、《钢轮》和《石破天惊》，并在90年代开始在各地进行巡回演出，一直延续到今天(除了退休的怀曼)。滚石现在继续在世界各地巡演，这令数百万歌迷感到十分惊喜。

他们的遗产
滚石乐队仍然是当今一支至关重要的摇滚乐队，他们创作新歌，赢得满堂喝彩。尽管他们纷纷步入6旬，贾格尔和他的团队还能继续创作出一些最具激情的歌曲，这让其他任何一支摇滚乐队都望尘莫及。

他们是否真是世上最伟大的摇滚乐队，这一点有待讨论，但他们在20世纪60和70年代的作品中包含着历史上一些最具影响力、最流行的摇滚音乐。他们经受住了名声与金钱的种种考验与消磨，在90年代创作的干涸期中坚持下来，再次作为摇滚乐队出现，并证明了自己仍然不乏价值。

谁能说他们还能继续表演多久？这个乐队与老歌迷之间已经铸就了坚固的纽带，同时凭着他们独特的噪音和坏男孩的模样，吸引着更年轻的歌迷。也许他们就是这样一支长盛不衰的乐队，原因很简单，他们和歌迷都承认，他们知道这只是摇滚，但他们就是喜欢摇滚。

forty-one

Franklin Delano Roosevelt, President

Who He Is

Franklin Delano Roosevelt was an odd contradiction as a man and politician. The 32nd president of the United States was both one of the most popular presidents of all time and seemingly one of the most complex. Here was a man who had unlimited compassion for the common man but could be aloof and distant when it came to matters of refugees.

How do we understand this man? Was he the great political genius or, as some would suggest, simply the right man in the right place at the right time? How are we to really know a man who managed to keep his personal life secret from the nation—rumored extramarital affairs, his handicap from polio and even his off-again, on-again relationship with his own wife, Eleanor Roosevelt, a growing political luminary in her own right.

Despite all the questions, Franklin Roosevelt has survived the rigors of investigation and the ebb and flow of historical criticism not only to be hailed as a great hero but to be truly idolized for the next 50 years for his accomplishments—no matter how they were perceived.

What Made the Man

Born in January of 1882, Franklin was the only child of a wealthy Democratic New York family from which he gained all the privileges of life—including trips to Europe and the finest private education: the Groton School, Harvard and Columbia Law School. He learned German and French, and was highly influenced by both his mother, Sara, and his vibrant, crusading Republican uncle, Theodore Roosevelt, president of the United States.

Roosevelt married a distant cousin, Eleanor. They seemingly were an odd couple: He was popular, outgoing, charming and sociable while she was shy, introverted and did not like social occasions. Her early wish was to stay home and raise children. They ended up having six children, five of whom survived into adulthood.

What really complicated Roosevelt's early adult years was the affair that he had with his secretary, Lucy Mercer, and the very poor relationship between his wife and mother. After a time, the Roosevelts started living apart, although they remained married— seemingly as political allies and friends, rather than as husband and wife.

A measure of the man is the fact that when he contracted polio in 1921, he desperately resolved not to let the resulting paralysis affect his life, his career or the public's perception of his abilities and personal strengths. The Roosevelt era was one in which a public figure, like a president, could actually acquire sympathy and support from the media, and thus hide, or at least manage, his handicap in public.

In an effort to assist others suffering from the ravages of polio and paralysis, Roosevelt went on to found what is now known as the March of Dimes.

富兰克林·德拉诺·罗斯福：美国总统

他是谁

富兰克林·德拉诺·罗斯福是一个普通人和政治家相结合的古怪的矛盾混合体。这位美国的第32任总统既是有史以来最受欢迎的总统之一,同时又是最复杂难懂的总统之一。他对大众充满了无限同情和怜悯;但是,当提到难民问题,他却变得疏远而难以亲近。

那么,我们应该怎样来了解这个人呢?他是伟大的政治天才吗?抑或是如许多人所认为的"时势造英雄"?他试图对国家保守个人生活保密(无论是谣传的还是虚构的事件),他因小儿麻痹症而落下残疾,他甚至与在政界愈发闪耀的妻子伊琳诺·罗斯福之间的关系分分合合。而这一切,我们如何去理解?

尽管面对种种质疑,富兰克林·罗斯福还是从严酷的调查以及历史评论的浮浮沉沉中挺了过来,并荣升到了伟大英雄的位置。在未来50年里,人们还会因他取得的政绩(不管从何得知)而将他奉为偶像。

是什么成就了他

1882年1月,富兰克林出生于纽约的一个富裕的民主党派家庭。作为家里的独子,他享受了所有的生活特权,其中包括去欧洲旅行,去格罗顿学校、哈佛大学以及哥伦比亚大学法学院接受最好的私人教育。他会说一口流利的德语和法语,并且深受母亲萨拉和同样为美国总统的叔叔、精力充沛的共和党人西奥多·罗斯福的影响。

罗斯福和一位远房表亲伊琳诺结了婚。他们看上去是一对古怪的夫妻,富兰克林深受欢迎、外向迷人并且善于交际,而他的妻子却腼腆内向,不喜欢社交场合。她早期的梦想就是待在家里抚育孩子。这对夫妻一共生了6个孩子,其中的5个存活下来并长大成人。

罗斯福成年后的早期岁月异常复杂:他和女秘书露西·密尔西亚之间有一段婚外情,又与妻子和母亲之间的关系糟糕透顶。不多久,罗斯福夫妇就分居了,尽管他们还保持着婚姻关系,但他们之间看上去更像是政治盟友和朋友,而不是丈夫和妻子。

在1921年,富兰克林经历了一个考验,那就是在他确认染上了小儿麻痹症的事实之后,他非常强烈地下定决心不让这即将造成的残疾影响到他的生活,他的事业以及公众对于他的能力和个人优势的看法。在罗斯福时代里,一个公众人物,如总统,能够实际地从媒体得到同情和支持,那么这样就能够隐瞒,或者至少能够控制他的残疾这一事实在公众里的传播程度。

为了努力帮助其他的因患小儿麻痹症和瘫痪而遭受痛苦的人,罗斯福成立了国家小儿麻痹基金会,也就是现在为人们所熟知的"积分累角会"。

His first taste of Washington came when he was appointed assistant secretary of the Navy in the Wilson administration. His first attempt at national office was in 1920 when he was nominated for vice president on the Democratic ticket, which was soundly defeated by the Republican Warren G. Harding. Politics over, he moved back to New York state to practice law and retire from public life—or so he said!

By 1928, the fire was back in him and he ran as a reform governor in New York—ironically with the help and support of Tammany Hall, his avowed enemy. This was just one of the many political compromises Roosevelt was to make over his long career. His tinkering with greater government involvement in social and economic affairs would begin in New York and would ultimately find greater and more expansive expression in Washington.

Campaigning during the Great Depression, Roosevelt was the candidate for less government, sound currency and tight fiscal responsibility—an amazing irony considering the New Deal that was to come. Roosevelt defeated Hoover, winning the 1932 election. Government would never be the same. Throughout his terms in office, he enjoyed large pluralities in the popular polls and had the strong backing of an increasingly Democratic Congress—making his plans and programs all that much easier.

The Legacy of the Man

The Roosevelt administration concentrated on finding ways to bring immediate relief to the general public—as much as 25 percent of the American work force had no employment or marginal employment at best. The banking system was in chaos, commodities prices were the lowest in years, farmers were forced off the land and industrial production by any measure had plummeted to new lows.

While it is fairly clear, with hindsight, that the various New Deal programs did not end the depression of the 1930s, it is also the case that war, or rather preparations for war, did end the depression. By 1941, approximately one million people were out of work—a fraction of the unemployment of 10 years earlier.

If Franklin Roosevelt is truly a hero, it is for his efforts and leadership before and during the Second World War. He clearly understood the importance of reversing 20 or more years of isolationism in light of the international threats of fascism. He saw an impending change in the balance of power in the world, one that would ultimately hurt the United States and its interests, domestically and internationally.

So, how do we judge Roosevelt? He was president for longer than any other man, and had been on center stage through some of the most tumultuous times in modern American history. He was the eternal optimist, the leader, the wartime president, the grand statesman and a larger-than-life figure. He came from wealth, yet challenged traditional notions of the responsibilities and rights of the rich—increasing income and excise taxes to the highest in the nation's history.

The other Roosevelt was seen as arrogant, prejudiced(having done little in the arena of civil rights, for example), obsessed with control and power, a profligate with the public's wealth, and a believer in big government, bigger budget deficits and higher taxes. He shaped modern American government, its role in everyday life, like no other president. His legacy, like Social Security, continues—a little shaky at times, but still monumental.

他初次品尝国家权力是他被任命为威尔逊内阁海军秘书助理。1920年,在民主党的候选人名单中,他被提名为副总统,这是他第一次试图获得国家总统或副总统的职位。而那一次他却被共和党候选人沃伦·哈里惨痛地击败了。在政坛受挫之后,他转而回到纽约州去实践法律并淡出公众生活,至少罗斯福这么说过。

1928年,激情在他的内心重新燃起。而且最具讽刺意义的是,他接受了曾经公开承认过的敌人坦马尼·霍尔的帮助而重回政界,并成为纽约州的州长,倡导改革。这当然仅仅是罗斯福在他漫长的政治生涯中不得不做的众多妥协之一。他希望凭借政府的强大力量参与到社会和经济的各项改革事业中的想法,从纽约州开始并且最终在华盛顿找到了更辽阔的发展空间,形成了更为繁荣的局面。

在经济大萧条期的总统大选中,总统候选人罗斯福主张政府管得尽量少、实行稳健的货币政策和从紧地财政政策,而考虑到即将开始的"新政",这简直是一个让人吃惊的讽刺。罗斯福击败了胡佛政府,赢得了1932年的总统大选。理所当然,内阁又有了新的变化。纵观他的整个白宫生涯,他既能在公众选举中赢得多数的投票又拥有一个最强大的并且处于不断扩展的民主党国会的支持,这样,他的计划以及各种改革方案就能很顺利地执行。

他的遗产

罗斯福政府集中注意力于寻找能够给大众带来立竿见影效果的缓解措施。因为当时有多达25%的劳动力失业或者处于就业不足状态。银行金融体系一片混乱,商品产品的价格降至历年来的最低点,农民面临着不得不离开土地的残酷现实,而工业生产无论如何努力都难免跌到了新的低谷。

如今回头再看,事实已非常清楚:罗斯福各种各样的新政措施并没有阻止1930年的大萧条;同时也证明,是战争,或者是为战争做的各种准备结束了大萧条。截止到1941年,仍有一百万的人民处于失业状态,但这仅仅是十年前失业总人口的一个零头。

如果说富兰克林·罗斯福是一位真正的英雄,那么其原因要归功于他在二战前和二战中的不懈努力和杰出的领导才能。他能够清楚地明白在法西斯成为全球性的公敌时,废除二十多年来坚持的"中立政策"的重要性。他能够预见原有的世界格局又要被打破。这样一来,最终会影响到美国以及美国在国内外的各种既得利益。

既然这样,那么我们怎么来评论罗斯福呢?他是有史以来任期最长的总统,并且在美国的现代史里,他是能够历经最动乱的年代还屹立于国家中心的人物,他是永久乐观的人,是领航人,是战争时期的总统,是伟大的政治家,是传奇的人物。他来自富裕阶层,尽管这样,他仍旧挑战富人对于社会的责任和权利的传统观念,他提高人民收入,并在美国历史上实行了最高比率的税收。

从另一方面来看,罗斯福骄傲自大并怀有偏见(比如说在民权领域,他鲜有举动)。他迷恋掌控权力,对于公共财产挥霍无度,是大政府主义的信奉者,支持巨大的财政赤字和高税收。他塑造了现代美国政府及其在日常生活中的作用,这一点,无人能企及。他遗留下来的财富,比如说社会安全保障体系,尽管偶有动摇,仍在继续发挥着巨大的作用。

forty-two

Anwar Sadat, President

What Made the Man

Sadat was born December 25, 1918, in the village of Mit Abul Al-Kum, Al-Minufah, to an impoverished family. His father was Egyptian and his mother was Sudanese. He eventually graduated from the Royal Military Academy in Cairo in 1938 as a signal corps officer. Before the start of World War II, Sadat joined the Free Officers Movement, a group of military officers who worked to remove the British from control of Egypt.

While in the Royal Academy, Sadat met a man who would have a profound effect on his life and the entire country, Gamal Nasser. Many Egyptian army officers were sympathizers with the Nazi armies fighting in northern Africa, hoping their victory would be a catalyst for Egyptian independence. After the Axis powers invaded Libya and made a push into Egypt in 1941 to attempt to seize the Suez Canal, Sadat plotted with German spies to help expel the British (his actions included trying to send sensitive information to German General Erwin Rommel).

Sadat's efforts were discovered and he was imprisoned by the British. He escaped from prison in 1944 and, with the help of freedom sympathizers, successfully hid from the British through the war. He resurfaced into public life in 1945 and immediately resumed his actions against British rule.

Sadat was now a part of the new Egyptian government of Nasser, but his early assignments were not impressive. He edited the new regime's newspaper, and served as secretary-general of the Islamic Congress and National Union, the forerunner of Egypt's only political party. The importance of Sadat's jobs grew and he was a major advocate of Egypt's involvement in the disastrous Yemen civil war.

Soon after, Nasser's government started the 1967 Six-Day War with Israel. Egypt suffered a staggering defeat by the Israelis, almost destroying Nasser's regime. Recognizing his time in office might be growing short, Nasser appointed Sadat vice president. Nasser died of a heart attack in 1970 and Sadat was quickly confirmed as his successor. He cemented his hold on power in the Corrective Revolution of 1971, and signed a treaty of friendship with the Soviet Union.

Sadat's first years as president were full of surprises. He extended a cease-fire with the Israelis on the Suez front and announced plans to reopen the canal. Because he could not secure Soviet military support for a showdown with Israel, he expelled all the Soviet advisers from Egypt, hoping to gain some assistance from the United States.

The United States did not pay enough attention for Sadat's liking, and, along with Syria, he attacked Israel in 1973. At first, Egyptian forces were more successful than before

安瓦尔·萨达特：埃及总统

是什么成就了他

萨达特于1918年12月25日出生在密铁·安布的一个小村子。他家里非常穷。他父亲是埃及人，母亲是苏丹人。1938年他从皇家军事学院毕业。在学校里，他担任信号员的职务。在二战前，萨达特加入了自由军官运动。参加的人员都是军官。他们都想使埃及摆脱英国的统治。

在皇家军事学院期间，萨达特遇到了影响他一生的人。这个人对整个国家也产生了深远影响。他就是加莫·纳塞尔。许多埃及军官都支持他们在北非与纳粹作战。他们希望这次战争的胜利能加速埃及的独立。在轴心国政权入侵利比亚，并于1941年试图侵占苏伊士运河后，萨达特和德国间谍秘密谋划，想赶走英国人。(他的行动包括送一些重要的信息给德国的埃尔温·隆梅尔将军。)

萨达特的行踪暴露了，他被英国人关押起来。1944年，在自由组织运动的帮助和支持下，他从监狱逃了出来。由于战争的影响，他成功躲过英国人的搜捕。1945年，萨达特重新投入工作中，又开始了反抗英国统治的斗争。

萨达特现在已是埃及纳塞尔政府的一员，但是他早期的运动并没有给人们留下深刻印象。他出版了新的有关社会制度的报纸，并且担任伊斯兰教会和国会这两个埃及政党先驱组织的总书记。萨达特的地位在逐步提高，他支持埃及参与也门的特大国内战争。

不久，纳塞尔政府开始了1967年与以色列的6天大战。难以置信，埃及被以色列打败了。战争的失败几乎毁掉了纳塞尔政府。纳塞尔感到自己从政的时间在慢慢变短，就任命萨达特为副总统。1970年，纳塞尔因心脏病去世，萨达特很快被任命为他的接班人。他上任后，就加强了自己对1971年修正革命的控制，并且与前苏联签订了和平共处的条约。

萨达特在任职总统的第一年，发生了很多令人惊奇的事。他下达了与以色列在苏伊士运河上的停火命令，并且宣告重新开启苏伊士运河。由于在和以色列正式摊牌时，萨达特没有得到苏联军队的支持，他就开除了所有苏联驻埃及的顾问，希望这样可以从美国得到些帮助。

美国对他的愿望并未多加理睬。于是他联合叙利亚于1973开始发起了对以色列的进攻。起先，由于埃及军队比以前更强大，可以毫不费力渡过苏伊士运河，但是，他们却迅

and crossed the Suez Canal. However, they were quickly repulsed by an Israeli counterattack and Sadat found himself in a precarious position until intervention by the United States and Soviet Union led to a cease-fire.

At this time, Sadat took a chance by aligning himself
with the United States, hoping shuttle diplomacy would
lead to a long-term peace agreement with Israel.

Sadat surprised the world by visiting Israel and addressing the Knesset in 1977. U.S. President Jimmy Carter stepped in personally to move along the peace talks by bringing Sadat and Israeli Prime Minister Menachem Begin together at Camp David. The diplomatic efforts led to two major agreements for permanent peace and Palestinian autonomy. The final agreements were signed in 1979. Other Arab countries saw the agreement as being detrimental to Arab interests and withdrew their ambassadors from Egypt.

By the late 1970s, Sadat's open-door economic policies and peace efforts with Israel caused disillusionment among many Egyptians.

In 1981, he arrested hundreds of politicians and silenced the media in an effort to keep power.However, it was too late. On October 6, 1981, as Sadat was reviewing a military parade, he was assassinated by Muslim radicals. The murder shocked the West, which sent prominent government figures to his funeral. In contrast, the Egyptian public reaction to Sadat's death was tepid and the president of the Sudan was the only Arab head of state to attend his funeral.

速被以色列击退。萨达特在遭到美国和苏联干涉时,才认识到自己正处在一个危险的境地,于是不得不实现停火。

这时,萨达特抓住了机会,与美国结盟,希望穿梭外交可以与以色列达成长期和平协议。

访问过以色列并且在1977年致函以色列国会后,萨达特使全世界都为之震惊。美国总统吉米•卡特以个人名义参与了这件事。他让萨达特与以色列总理梅纳赫姆•贝京在戴维营进行和平谈话。这次谈话产生了两个重要的协议。一个是永久的和平,另一个是巴勒斯坦的自治权。后一项协议在1979年签署。另一个阿拉伯国家看到这个协议对阿拉伯的利益产生了危害,就从埃及撤回了他们的大使。

20世纪70年代后期,萨达特的开放经济政策及与以色列和平共处的努力,使许多埃及人幻想破灭。

1981年,他逮捕了几百个从政者,并设法让媒体平息这件事,借此来巩固自己的权力。但是,一切都太迟了。1981年10月6日,萨达特在阅兵时,被穆斯林极端分子暗杀。这起谋杀案震惊了整个西方国家,它使一个著名的政府领导走向了自己的葬礼。相反,埃及社会对萨达特之死的反应不太强烈。苏丹总统是唯一一位参加萨达特的葬礼的阿拉伯国家元首。

forty-three

Charles Monroe Schulz, Cartoonist

Who He Is

How can a man who draws cartoons, and simplistic ones at that, be one of our heroes? The reason is quite simple: He both made us laugh out loud and had a keen insight into human behavior, especially our foibles.

Charles Schulz communicated to the world through a protagonist who just could not win, a dog who wanted to be an aviator, a sometimes mean-spirited girl, a boy who dragged a blanket around and a bunch of birds that lived their lives on top of a dog house. Anything unusual about all of this? Seemingly not. His humor was insightful, cute, at times mean and frustrating, but always ultimately warm and supportive.

Yes, Charles Schulz was a genius, a rich man(who refused to allow the comic strip to be written by anyone else) and a daily feature of our lives. But just as importantly, he knew our nature and took a great deal of pleasure in poking fun at us through his characters. And we adored him for it!

What Made the Man

Schulz was born on November 26, 1922, in Minneapolis, Minnesota, to Dena and Carl Schulz. He actually grew up in St. Paul. From an early age, Schulz might have been destined to be a cartoonist: He got the nickname Sparky from one of his uncles, Sparky being a character in the then-popular Barney Google comic strip. The name stuck; Schulz would be called Sparky by family and friends for the rest of his life.

He was a good student and skipped two half-grades in elementary school. This might have worked against him when he entered high school, where he was the youngest student attending Central High. Schulz became more and more shy and had few friends. He kept himself entertained by taking correspondence courses from the Art Instruction Inc. school.

He discovered he had a knack for cartooning.

By now, Schulz was considering creating a comic strip that would center on the lives of ordinary children. It would not feature cartoon-like, larger-than-life characters or storylines. Instead, it would draw its humor from the struggles of everyday life as seen through the honest eyes of articulate children.

The first version of Schulz's vision was called *Li'l Folks* and ran from 1947 to 1949 in the St. Paul Pioneer Press. The name Charlie Brown was first used in these strips, but the character had not been defined yet. Four different characters were given the name

查尔斯·门罗·舒尔茨：漫画家

他是谁

一个画卡通画的人——而且是那种过于简单化的卡通画——如何会成为我们的一个英雄？原因很简单：他让我们开怀大笑，对于人类行为，尤其是我们那些小毛病有着敏锐的洞察力。

查尔斯·舒尔茨向人们展示了一个不断失败的主角，一只想当飞行员的狗，一个有时有点刻薄的女孩，一个到处拖着条毯子的男孩，一群住在狗宅屋顶上的小鸟。这些有什么异乎寻常吗？似乎并非如此。他见解深刻，思维敏捷，有时不乏尖刻又令人惘然，但总体上却是温暖人心，令人振奋。

没错，查尔斯·舒尔茨是个天才，一个富有的人(他不允许别人创作其连环漫画)，也是我们生活中的一个凡人。但同样重要的是，他深知我们的天性并乐于通过他的漫画里的角色来开我们的玩笑，我们还就是喜欢他这样。

是什么成就了他

1922年11月26日，舒尔茨出生于美国明尼苏达州的明尼阿波利斯市，父亲卡尔·舒尔茨，母亲蒂娜。他的成长地在圣保罗市。或许在幼年时期舒尔茨就注定了要成为一个漫画家吧：他的一个叔叔曾给他取了个小名斯帕基——当时风行一时的连环漫画《巴尼·古葛》中的人物——那个名字被沿用了下来，从那以后亲友们就一直这么叫他。

上学期间他的成绩很好，小学时曾连跳两级。上中学时他是中央中学年龄最小的学生，这可能成为阻碍他性格发展的原因。舒尔茨变得越发腼腆了，他的朋友也寥寥无几。他就把兴趣投向艺术指导公司学校的函授课程的学习。

他发现自己很有画漫画的天分。

此时，舒尔茨正考虑创作一部反映普通儿童生活的连环画，它不再以卡通的英雄人物或故事情节构成，而是通过会说话的孩子们天真无邪的眼睛，打量人们在日常生活中的奋斗，并由此体现出连环画的幽默。

舒尔茨这个构思的第一个版本的作品叫《小家伙》，于1947年至1949年间由圣保罗先锋出版社出版。在这部作品里首次使用了查理·布朗这个名字，但人物个性尚未界定。有

Charlie Brown. Another recurring character in the strip was an unnamed dog that looked very much like an early version of Snoopy.

Schulz approached the Newspaper Enterprise Association in 1948 to have the strip nationally syndicated to other newspapers, but the deal, which would have made Schulz an independent contractor, fell through. The next year, Schulz took his best strips to the powerful United Features Syndicate. United Features liked the work, but changed the name of the strip(for reasons still unknown) to *Peanuts*.

During the 1960s and 1970s, Peanuts would grow from a popular comic strip into a true pop cultural phenomenon. During this time, Hallmark began the first series of Peanuts-themed greeting cards; the book *Happiness Is a Warm Puppy* appeared on the New York Times' best-seller list; and the strip was featured on the cover of Time magazine. An off-Broadway musical called *You're a Good Man, Charlie Brown* debuted. The strip also has inspired numerous television specials and two feature films. Snoopy's battle with the Red Baron was made into a topselling pop record and, in 1969, the Apollo X astronauts named their command module Charlie Brown and the Lunar Excursion Module Snoopy.

Mostly on his own, Schulz worked on the *Peanuts* strip uninterrupted for almost 50 years. The work came to a stop in 1999 when Schulz suffered a stroke. Doctors later discovered he had colon cancer that had metastasized to his stomach. Chemotherapy side effects restricted his vision and he announced his retirement later that year at the age of 77. Schulz died of a heart attack on February 12, 2000. The last original strip ran the next day.

The Legacy of the Man

Charles Schulz redefined how humor could be expressed in comic strips, and firmly believed that wisdom could come from the mouths of babes. The public responded to this and made the strip a tremendous success. Schulz received two Reuben Awards for his cartooning; won a Peabody Award for one of his television specials; was honored with a star on the Hollywood Walk of Fame (next to Walt Disney's); and was posthumously awarded the Congressional Gold Medal, the highest honor the U.S. Congress can give a civilian.

Schulz was saddened by his inability to continue his strip, telling people that "it was taken away from him". However, older strips are still appearing in newspapers and Schulz's estate continues to earn substantially from the merchandising of the characters. Not long ago, Forbes magazine called Schulz the highest-paid deceased person in America.

4个不同的人物都叫查理·布朗。同一部作品里,另一个经常出现的人物是一只没有名字的狗,看上去很像早期版本的史努比。

1948年,舒尔茨找到报业协会,试图通过报业辛迪加在全国其他报纸上发行该作品,如果谈妥,舒尔茨就会成为一位独立的承包商,但这笔交易终成泡影。次年,舒尔茨携其最佳作品来到美国联合菲彻辛迪加公司,后者对他的作品甚为满意,但却该作品更名为《花生》(原因不得而知)。

20世纪六七十年代,《花生》由一部流行漫画成长为一种真正意义上的流行文化现象。其间,霍马克发行了首批以《花生》为主题的贺卡系列;《幸福是一只温暖的小狗》一书出现在《纽约时报》的畅销书目上,该漫画还上了《时代》周刊的封面。一部名为《你是个好人,查理·布朗》的百老汇新式音乐剧也首次登场。该书还启发人们制作了很多电视特别节目和两部长片。史努比与红爵士之战被制作成一张畅销的流行音乐唱片,1969年,阿波罗10号的宇航员将飞船的指令模块起名为查理·布朗,将登月飞船叫做史努比。

《花生》漫画主要都是舒尔茨亲自制作,将近50年从未间断。1999年,一次中风让他不得不停下工作。医生后来诊断出他患上了直肠癌,并已转移到胃部。化疗的副作用影响到了他的视力,当年77岁的他只好宣布退休。2000年2月12日,舒尔茨心脏病发作去世。次日,他的最后一部原创作品就发表了。

他的遗产

查尔斯·舒尔茨重新界定了幽默如何可以通过连环漫画表现出来,且坚信智慧可以出自于儿童之口。公众的回应造就了这部漫画的巨大成功。他的连环画曾两度荣获"鲁本奖";一部电视特辑获得了皮博迪电视奖;在好莱坞星光大道上,他被授予一枚星形奖章(紧挨着沃特·迪士尼);并于死后获得国会金奖——是一项美国国会赋予公民的最高荣誉。

因为无法继续创作漫画,他伤心至极,说漫画已远离他的生活。然而,他原先的作品还在各报纸上出现,他塑造的形象常被广告商采用,因此舒尔茨的财产继续以惊人的数目递增。不久前,福布斯杂志宣布舒尔茨是美国收入最高的已故人士。

forty-four

Frank Sinatra, Entertainer

Who He Is

Why is Frank Sinatra one of our modern heroes? Because he could sing and entertain us like no one else. Four generations of music and movie fans have placed Frank Sinatra on the top of their hit parade. No matter what music is in style, Sinatra is always in style. In recent years, his mellow voice and famous lyrics have been the background to some of the classiest parties and best restaurants and watering holes worldwide. There is not a single country where his songs are not played and where his reputation as a singer and entertainer is not exalted.

His career spanned seven decades and, with few exceptions, his style was bigger than life—literally above the crowd and almost untouchable. He was not an innocent hero; nor was he known for his great charitable works. He ate, drank, smoked and partied his way through life—married a number of times and was part of the famous Rat Pack. He associated with politicians and gangsters, and not necessarily in that order.

He is our hero because he made us feel good(or sad or blue) in song, through movies and in his life. He was blue-collar, brash and absolutely a man with wisdom. And we loved him for it all.

What Made the Man

Francis Albert Sinatra was born on December 12, 1915, in Hoboken, New Jersey—a classic blue-collar town, though his family was solidly middle class. His first musical break came when he appeared with his group, The Hoboken Four, on *Major Bowes Amateur Hour*. The group won top honors and Frank's career was begun, including a stint as a singing waiter—can you imagine Old Blue Eyes delivering the main course with a song?

His first national break came with a stint with the famous bandleader Harry James, and then with the even more popular bandleader, Tommy Dorsey.(The famous scene in *The Godfather*—"*I'll make him an offer he can't refuse*"—*is a vague reference to Sinatra's getting out of a contract with a bandleader to pursue his own, individual career.) The 1940s were the beginning of a tremendous long success story—particularly with teenage girls—again The Godfather,* when the Sinatra-like character comes to entertain the bride and groom, and the young girls swoon.

So what had been a slight pause turned into full-blown success as his movie exposure revitalized his singing career—so much so that he had his own label, Reprise Records, with Capital in the early 1960s. It was in this unique role that the famous moniker, Chairman of the Board was born. For whatever reason, Capital refused to renew his contract, making

44

弗兰克·辛纳屈：
歌唱家

他是谁

为什么弗兰克·辛纳屈能够成为我们这个时代的英雄之一？因为他的歌声以及他给我们带来的愉悦无人可以取代。整整4代的乐迷和影迷都把弗兰克·辛纳屈列在流行排行榜的首位。不论是哪种风格的音乐大行其道，辛纳屈总能成功走在潮流前沿。近年来，他那圆润的嗓音以及耳熟能详的歌词常常作为背景音乐在世界各地一些顶级宴会和一流饭店、酒吧中使用。没有哪个国家不曾传唱过他的歌曲，也没有哪个国家没有听闻过他作为歌手和艺人的声名。

他的演艺生涯延续了70多年。同样绝无仅有的是，他的风格影响已经远远超越了有限的生命——完全凌驾于众人之上，几乎无人可以企及。他并不是一个没有污点的英雄；也并非仅因他那伟大的慈善事业而为人称道。他也曾暴食、酗酒、抽烟，终生都在寻欢作乐——他曾多次结婚，并曾经是著名的"鼠帮"成员之一。他与黑白两道人物都有来往，却也未必与他们属于一丘之貉。

他是我们的英雄，因为他用他的歌曲（或悲伤或忧郁）、他的电影乃至他的生命给我们带来了一种美好的感觉。他是一名蓝领，轻率鲁莽而又绝对聪明。我们爱他就是因为爱他这一切。

是什么成就了他

1915年12月12日，法兰克·阿尔伯特·辛纳屈出生于新泽西州的霍博肯——一个典型的蓝领城镇，尽管他的家庭属于稳固的中产阶级。当他和他的乐团霍博肯4人组出现在"鲍斯少校的业余时段"电台节目上时，他迎来了音乐事业上的第一次突破。他们的组合获得了头奖，弗兰克也就此展开了他的演艺生涯，其间他曾经当过歌唱服务生——你能想象弗兰克眨着他那蓝色忧郁的眼睛唱着歌上菜的情形吗？

他首次蜚声国内是在著名乐队哈里·詹姆斯担任主唱期间，之后，又与更加流行的汤米·道尔希乐队合作，担任主唱。（电影《教父》中有一句经典台词："我提出的条件将使他无法拒绝。"这句话从某种程度上解释了辛纳屈为什么会与乐队解约，不再担任主唱，转而开创属于自己的事业。）从20世纪40年代开始，辛纳屈开始了自己长久的辉煌，特别是与无数少女之间的浪漫故事，又重现了《教父》中的经典画面：当辛纳屈式的人物走上舞台为新郎新娘表演助兴的时候，无数少女为之倾倒。

辛纳屈的银幕生涯也使他的歌唱事业出现转机，在短暂休歇之后又取得全面辉煌。60年代早期，他与卡普托公司合作，创立了自己的公司"重显唱片公司"。正是这一独特的角色，使他赢得了"董事局主席"的绰号。不知由于何种原因，卡布托公司拒绝与辛纳屈续

perhaps one of the biggest blunders in recording history. Be that as it may, there was no limit for this popular, roughedged star and singer.

Next stop, Las Vegas and continued fame and fortune!

Of course, the Vegas lifestyle and his movie career were not terribly compatible with a stable home life. Frank was not particularly faithful. Enter wife number two: actress Ava Gardner, whom he married in 1951 and subsequently divorced in 1957. Wife number three was Mia Farrow, in 1968. She was substantially younger than Sinatra; not surprisingly, that marriage ended 2 years after it had begun. Finally, wife number four enters the picture in 1976; her name was Barbara Max and she would be Frank's wife until he died.

A very strange episode in Sinatra's life took place in 1963 when his son, Frank Jr. was kidnapped. A ransom was paid and his son was returned safely. The kidnappers were eventually caught and punished. A story circulated around this time that Sinatra started carrying around a roll of dimes because the kidnappers would talk to him only on public pay phones. Even after the kidnapping was resolved, Sinatra continued to carry the roll of dimes around with him—it became a lifelong habit.(In fact, he was buried with a roll of dimes in his pocket!)

He continued to perform and wow audiences almost up to his death. In the 1990s he recorded the *Duets* album with U2's Bono.

The Legacy of the Man

How does the world look upon the life and work of Frank Sinatra? It is hard to imagine any performer who was able to retain his popularity for so long, even at a time when he seemed to be in decline. He managed two or three times to reinvent himself through his music, movies and Las Vegas performances. He has created a library of music so popular, so classic in its tone, that almost every generation to come will listen to Sinatra music in some form during their lives.

While he hated the publicity and the accusations, including several unauthorized biographies, he made no bones about the fact that where he grew up (during Prohibition and in New Jersey) there were illegal saloons run by gangsters. If you wanted to work—as a singer—you had to associate with gangsters. He insisted to his dying day that he was not and was never a part of the Mafia.

In any case, throughout his life, his personal comings and goings—marriages, children, lifestyle, known associates—filled newspapers and magazines with speculation, fact, fiction and nonsense. He not only survived this chaos, he thrived in its midst. And to his credit, he was absolutely opposed to segregation and the treatment of his friend Sammy Davis Jr. He used his power to work against such discrimination.

约,这也许是唱片史上犯下的最严重的错误。尽管如此,到现在已经没有什么力量可以阻止这位深受人们喜爱、棱角分明的影星兼歌手的发展了。

下一站,拉斯维加斯,名利跟进!

当然,拉斯维加斯的生活方式和他的演艺生涯根本无法与拥有稳定的家庭生活相比。弗兰克并非是一个很忠诚的人。他的第2个妻子是演员艾娃加德纳,他们于1951年结婚,但不久就在1957年分道扬镳了。1968年,他又和米亚·法罗开始了他的第三段婚姻。米亚·法罗的年龄比弗兰克小许多,因此2年之后这段婚姻走到尽头也就不足为奇了。最终,他的第4任也是最后一位妻子巴巴拉·马克思走进了他的生活,并陪伴他走到生命的尽头。

1963年,弗兰克的生活中发生了一个特别的小插曲,他的儿子小弗兰克被绑架了。最终在支付了赎金之后,他的儿子安全回到他的身边。而绑架者也最终被抓捕归案并受到制裁。当时流传着一个故事,辛纳屈会随身带着一卷硬币,因为歹徒只通过公用电话与他联系。结果,即使当绑架事件结束之后,他依然会随身携带一卷硬币——这已经成为他一生的习惯。事实上,他下葬时口袋里仍装着一卷硬币。

辛纳屈坚持自己的演艺生涯一直到生命结束,给观众带来无数欢笑与感动。90年代,他和U2乐队联合录制了唱片《二重唱》。

他的遗产

世界将会如何看待弗兰克·辛纳屈的一生及其成就呢?很难想象还有哪一位艺人像他一样取得如此持久的名声,即使在他事业处于低潮期。他通过音乐、电影以及赌城表演,给我们塑造了不同的形象。他的音乐是如此流行又如此经典,以至无论哪个时代的人在其一生之中都会以某种形式聆听。

他极为痛恨炒作宣传和一些空穴来风的指责,包括几本未经许可的传记。他毫不掩饰地承认,在他成长的地方(美国禁酒法令实施期间的新泽西州)有许多黑帮控制的非法沙龙。如果你想有一份工作,尤其是作一名歌手,你就不得不和这些黑帮打交道。他至死都一直强调他不是也永远不会是黑手党成员。

无论如何,辛纳屈的一生沉沉浮浮,他的婚姻、子女、生活方式、社会交往都经常见诸报端杂志,其中有猜测,有事实,有虚构,也有胡言乱语。他不仅安然度过这些嘈杂之声,而且于其中筑就了辉煌。另外值得赞扬的是,他坚决反对种族隔离制度以及对他朋友小山姆·戴维斯的不公对待。他利用自己的力量反抗这种歧视。

forty-five

Superman, Comic Strip Hero

Who He Is

Can Superman really be our hero? Absolutely. In fact, he has been a hero for generations, and with a movie that came out in 2006(with others to follow, no doubt), his reputation as an invincible doer of good deeds will live on. Superman, of course, is merely one of a pantheon of comic book heroes.

What Made the Man

Superman is arguably the most famous comic book superhero, with a 70-year history that has moved the character through countless battles and relationships with supervillains, friends and family.

Superman was created by a Canadian artist, Joe Shuster, and an American writer, Jerry Siegel, in 1932. Superman was one of the first major characters for what was known at the time as Detective Comics (now DC Comics) in a series called Action Comics. The character was an immediate hit and became DC's franchise persona, following success in the comic books with stage, movie and television appearances.

Over the years, the history of Superman has evolved, but the basics remain the same. Superman is actually an alien named Kal-El, born on the planet Krypton to renowned scientist Jor-El and his wife, Lara. When Jor-El realizes that Krypton is going to be destroyed, he places his infant son in an intergalactic spaceship and sends him to Earth(for reasons that are still being debated).

His Kryptonian parents realize that Kal-El will have abilities beyond any that normal Earth people possess, including the ability to fly, invulnerability to injury, X-ray and heat vision, and incredible strength. However, the child does not know this—yet. Kal-El's spaceship crashes on Earth in rural farm country near the town of Smallville. He is rescued from the ship by an older Earth couple, John and Martha Kent.

The Kents raise the boy as a normal human named Clark, and as he grows into his teens he discovers some of his superpowers. After the death of his adopted parents, Clark travels to the far north and uses Kryptonian technology to build the Fortress of Solitude, which will be Superman's headquarters. There he finally learns who he is and why he was sent to Earth. He decides to use his powers to fight for truth, justice and the American Way, and moves to the large city of Metropolis.

Clark Kent goes to work as a reporter for the Daily Planet (originally called the Daily Star), which gives him the opportunity to find out about any threats to humanity. He makes friends with fellow reporter Lois Lane (a friendship that will develop into a love affair), cub reporter and photographer Jimmy Olsen and the newspaper's acerbic editor, Perry White. He is now poised to be the savior of mankind.

Superman became a franchise whose demands the original creators could not meet. Although Shuster's and Siegel's bylines stayed with the comics for many years, other artists

45

超人：
连环漫画英雄

他是谁

超人真的能成为我们的英雄吗？答案是肯定的。实际上，他的确已是几代人心目中的英雄了。而且，随着2006年一部电影的上映(毫无疑问，其他几部电影也紧随其后)，他战无不胜、能力超群、帮助弱小的形象将会一直流传下去。当然，在所有漫画所塑造的英雄人物中，超人也只不过是其中之一。

是什么成就了他

超人在争议中成为最著名的漫画类超级英雄人物。在70年的历史中，他经历了无数次的战斗，周旋于超级坏人、朋友和家庭之间。

《超人》由一位名裘·舒斯特的加拿大艺术家和一位叫杰瑞·西格尔的美国作家于1932年共同创作而成。在系列"动作漫画"的侦探漫画(即DC漫画)中，超人成为首批主要角色之一。接着，超人这一形象很快便在社会上掀起了一阵狂热并成为侦探漫画的特许虚构人物，接着又成功出现在了各类漫画、电影及电视荧幕上。

在过去的这些年里，超人的故事一直在不断发展着，但基本内容仍旧保持原样。超人其实是一个名叫卡尔·埃尔的外星人，出生在一个叫克利普顿的星球上，与著名科学家约·埃尔和妻子拉腊生活在一起。在约·埃尔意识到克利普顿星球面临毁灭这一事实后，他把他那还是婴儿的儿子放入一个太空舱中并由太空舱将他送入地球(因为一些仍有争议的原因)。

超人的父母知道卡尔·埃尔将拥有超出正常地球人的超能力，其中包括：飞翔、抵御伤害、X光及热能的令人难以置信的超能力。然而，这个孩子自己起先并不知道这些。他的太空船撞在地球上，被美国斯莫威尔附近农场里的一对老夫妇约翰和玛莎·肯特从船舱中救出并收养。

肯特一家把这个男孩当作一个正常小孩来抚养并给他取名叫克拉克。就在克拉克十几岁时，他意外地发现自己拥有一些超能力。在他的养父母去世后，克拉克开始到遥远的北方旅行并利用克利普顿星球上的技术建立了孤独堡垒作为超人总部。在那里，他终于知道了自己的身份、来历以及他被送到地球上来的原因。于是他决定利用他的超能力为真理、正义以及美国方式而斗争并移居到大都市。

克拉克·肯特在"每日星球"报社(原名叫"每日之星")做了一名记者，这份工作让他有机会发现任何一个对于人类的威胁。他和他的同事罗伊斯·兰妮(他们之间的友情之后发展为爱情)、新闻记者兼摄影师吉米·奥尔森以及尖刻的新闻编辑派瑞·怀特成为好朋友。他坚信自己能成为人类的拯救者。

原创者已经难以满足《超人》独家专有权的要求。尽管多年来舒斯特和西格尔的名字一直在报纸上伴随《超人》，但其他一些艺术家和作家已经慢慢开始接手创作这一漫画作

and writers slowly began to take over the series and flesh out Superman's backstory and add to his abilities.

Other characters became essential to the Superman universe as both villains and allies. The most famous of them are the evil genius Lex Luthor, childhood sweetheart Lana Lang, Supergirl(a cousin of Superman from Krypton), the younger Superman character known as Superboy and perhaps the strangest in Krypto, a superdog companion. Superman also became a member of the Justice League of America, which united him with other superheroes such as Wonder Woman, Green Lantern and Aquaman.

Despite all the changes, one thing remained certain: The world knew that when danger threatened, they could look up and say:"It's a bird, it's a plane...no, it's Superman! "

The Legacy of the Man

Whatever their influence, Superman's creators came up with something that has touched people's imaginations for decades. Life was not so great for the creators themselves, who had a troubled relationship with their publishers and had to go to court to get a fair share of the huge profits generated by their creation. Thanks to their efforts and the passion of their fans, any use of the name Superman in any version has to include the citation that he was created by Jerry Siegel and Joe Shuster.

Superman, of course, became much more than just a comic book figure. He is one of those rare fictional characters that have succeeded in a variety of different media. Among them are cartoons by the Max Fleischer studios (there have been many other animated versions of Superman and the Justice League of America), a 1940s movie serial starring Kirk Alyn, the popular 1950s television series starring George Reeve, and a Broadway musical. The character has remained in the public eye through four film appearances by Christopher Reeve, the television series *Lois and Clark* starring Dean Cain and Terri Hatcher and *Smallville,* the early story of Superman, starring Tom Welling. The Superman story was brought back to the big screen in *Superman Returns,* directed by Bryan Singer and starring Brandon Routh.

品并充实超人的背景故事,增强他的超能力。

　　加入其他一些或丑恶或善良的角色对于扩充超人世界是很有必要的。其中最有名的要数罪恶天才莱克斯·卢瑟、童年好伙伴拉娜·朗、超级女孩(来自克利普顿星球,是超人的表妹)、以超级男孩著称的更为年轻的超人以及一条超级狗伙伴,这条狗可能是克利普顿最奇怪的一个角色了。超人还是美国正义联盟中的一员,该联盟将他和其他诸如奇迹女子、绿色灯笼以及水人等超级英雄联合在一起。

　　虽然有了这么多变化,但其中有一点是肯定的,那就是:全世界都知道,当危险来临时,他们会抬起头高喊:"那是一只鸟,那是一架飞机……不,那是超人!"

他的遗产

　　无论影响力如何,这几十年来,超人的创作者们激起读者的丰富想象。那些创作者们的生活并不总是一帆风顺,他们可能会和出版社的关系不和,因此不得不通过法律途径来获得他们创作所应得的报酬。多亏了他们的努力和超人迷们的热情,在任何译本中对于超人这一名字的使用都必须注明超人由杰瑞·西格尔和裘·舒斯特共同创作。

　　当然,超人远不是一个漫画人物那么简单。在众多媒体成功塑造的人物当中,超人是其中之一。其中,超人的形象出现在了马克思·弗莱舍电影制片厂的动画片(该厂已经制作了许多其他有关超人和美国正义联盟的动画片)、20世纪40年代柯克·艾兰主演的一部电影中、20世纪50年代的一部乔治·里夫主演的电视连续剧,以及一出百老汇音乐剧中。超人这一形象一直吸引着公众眼球,其中包括克里斯洛夫·里夫出演的4部影片、丁·凯恩和泰莉·哈琪主演的电视剧《路易斯和克拉克》、《超人前传》,以及由汤姆·韦林出演的超人的早期故事。超人的故事在《超人归来》中被重新搬回荧幕,此片由布莱恩·辛格和布兰登·鲁斯共同导演。

forty-six

Mother Teresa, Missionary

Who She Is

Mother Teresa is surely one of the most famous names of the last 50 years, having garnered almost every honor and award for her tireless work with the homeless and poor in India. So great is her personal and spiritual renown that the Roman Catholic Church began the process of beatification almost immediately upon her death—in fact, she is now Blessed Teresa of Calcutta—and ultimately she may be canonized as a saint of the church.

Is it possible for someone who has done so much good—who has received the Nobel Peace Prize and who is beatified by her church—to be controversial? Perhaps it is the fate of all great heroes to be controversial in some way. In the case of Mother Teresa, some— including more liberal Catholics—consider her views and interpretations of doctrine and Catholic practice far too conservative and strict. She was absolutely and fundamentally against abortion and contraception, and equally vocal on the immorality of divorce.

The confidante of popes and presidents, she was awarded a state funeral in India upon her death. But it was her life, not her death, that continues to motivate and inspire men and women of good will to care for the homeless, children with HIV and victims everywhere.

What Made the Woman

Mother Teresa has so long been associated with India that many forget that she was actually born in what is now part of modern Macedonia, of Albanian parents in 1910. From an early age, she was active in Catholic youth groups and showed interest in working in the missions. By age 17, she had joined the Sisters of Loretto, an Irish order of sisters, and eventually was assigned to Calcutta as a teacher of geography and catechism at St. Mary's High School. In 1944, she became the principal of St. Mary's. Soon, Sister Teresa contracted tuberculosis, was unable to continue teaching and was sent to Darjeeling for rest and recuperation. It was on the train to Darjeeling that she received her second calling.

> Mother Teresa recalled later:*"I was to leave the convent and work with the poor, living among them. It was an order. I knew where I belonged, but I did not know how to get there."*

In 1948, the Vatican granted Sister Teresa permission to leave the Sisters of Loretto and pursue her calling under the jurisdiction of the Archbishop of Calcutta. Mother Teresa started with a school in the slums to teach the children of the poor. She also learned basic medicine and went into the homes of the sick to treat them. In 1949, some of her former pupils joined her. They found men, women and children dying on the streets, rejected by local hospitals. The group rented a room so they could care for helpless people otherwise

特雷莎嬷嬷：
传教士

她是谁

特雷莎嬷嬷无疑是过去50年中最著名的人物之一，她在印度为那些无家可归的穷人孜孜不倦地工作，获得了几乎所有的荣誉和奖章。她的人格和精神上的声誉是如此之高，以至于罗马天主教堂在她去世的那一刻就立即着手为她行宣福礼，事实上现在人们称颂她为神圣的"加尔各答的特雷莎"，她死后还被追封为天主教的圣徒。

一个做了许多善事的人，一个获得过诺贝尔奖的人，一个教堂为之行宣福礼的人，还会有可能引起人们的争论吗？也许，从某方面来说伟大的英雄注定会引发人们的争论。对于特雷莎嬷嬷，有些人，包括更为自由化的天主教徒，认为她对天主教义和习俗的看法和阐释过于保守和严格。她完全彻底地反对流产和避孕，并且同样直言离婚是不道德的行为。

作为教皇和总统的知心朋友，特雷莎去世后享受了印度国葬的礼遇。但是，不是她的死，而是她的一生仍然激励和鼓舞着善良的人们关心无家可归者、感染艾滋病病毒的儿童和世界各地的受难者。

是什么成就了她

特雷莎很长时间都是和印度联系在一起，所以许多人忘了她1910年出生时的地方是现代马其顿的一部分，她的父母是阿尔巴尼亚人。从很小的时候她就开始活跃在天主教青年团体中，对在传教机构中的工作表现出极大的兴趣。到17岁时，她已经加入了洛雷托姐妹会，那是一个爱尔兰天主教修女会，并且她最终被派往加尔各答圣玛丽中学任地理和教学法老师。1944年她成为圣玛丽中学的校长。不久，特雷莎感染上肺结核而不能继续教书，她被送到印度大声岭去修养和康复。在去大声岭的火车上她又一次接到了人们对她的召唤。

特雷莎嬷嬷后来回忆说："我当时即将离开女修道会去为穷人工作。和穷人们生活在一块，这是天意。我知道我属于哪儿，只是我不知道如何才能到达那儿。"

1948年，特雷莎修女得到梵蒂冈教会的允许，离开了洛雷托姐妹会，在加尔各答主教管辖下重新开始她的工作。特雷莎的工作从在贫民窟中的一所学校教穷人的孩子开始。她还学了基础医学到病人家中治疗。1949年，她以前的一些学生加入到她的行列。他们看到被当地医院拒绝的男人、女人和孩子躺在街头等死。她的小组租了一间房用来

condemned to die in the gutter. In 1950, the group was established by the church as a Diocesan Congregation of the Calcutta Diocese. It was known as the Missionaries of Charity.

There was not a group of downtrodden individuals that the Missionaries and Mother Teresa did not try to help. Much of her early work focused on the homeless and dying of Calcutta, especially those of the so-called untouchable class. But not satisfied with that, she helped lepers, AIDS victims, refugees, the handicapped, orphans, victims of natural disasters and just about anyone who needed help. By 1965, Mother Teresa was granted permission to expand her ministry outside of India, to other parts of Asia, Africa and South America, and even the Bronx in New York City. At the end of the 20th century, more than 500 missions, hospices, orphanages and other institutions were founded and operating for the benefit of millions. It is estimated by one source that nearly one million workers are employed by the Missionaries of Charity for charitable work.

What is extraordinary is that her work attracted so many women and men to a life in a religious community, when orders of nuns, brothers and priests throughout the world have been in precipitous decline for decades. As her fame increased, so, too, did the accolades heaped upon her—including the Nobel Peace Prize and the Presidential Medal of Freedom. Such honors had little effect on her work or her views of the world and the church she served. She refused to compromise in her beliefs.

After suffering deteriorating health for a number of years, she died in September of 1997 just after her 87th birthday. Almost immediately, the process for beatification and canonization began.

The Legacy of the Woman

How should we understand this woman and her views of the world and beyond? By any measure, Mother Teresa has fascinated the world by being a complete and utter contrarian. No modern-day view of the church and its mission for her; rather, a strong, simplistic approach to charity and to religious works. Her heroism is based on the belief of the dignity of the individual, no matter how poor, how sick or how low on the social pecking order he or she may be.

One controversial practice, common in the Catholic Church, was to baptize the dying—the notion being that once baptized they have an opportunity to be with God. The problem is that many people felt that Mother Teresa and her followers had no right to make that decision, especially in societies like India that are not primarily Christian. Also, there were some who criticized the quality of health care being provided at the various clinics run by the sisters.

照料无助的人,不然,这些人就只能死在贫民窟里。1950年,这个团体被教堂确立为加尔各答主教管辖的教区委员会,就是人们所知的"仁爱修道会"。

"仁爱修道会"和特雷莎嬷嬷愿意帮助任何一群被压迫的人。她早期的大部分工作致力于帮助加尔各答的无家可归者和垂死者,尤其是那些被称为贱民的阶层。但她并不满足于此,她还帮助麻疯病人、艾滋受害者、难民、残疾人、孤儿、自然灾害受难者以及任何一个需要帮助的人。到1965年的时候,特雷莎嬷嬷获准在印度以外拓展她的传教事业,在亚洲其他地方,非洲和南美,甚至纽约的布朗克斯区都留下了她的足迹。20世纪末,500多个救助站、收容所、孤儿院和其他的公共机构建立起来并为数百万人的福祉而工作。据某方面的估计,"仁爱修道会"雇有将近一百万人来做慈善工作。

不同凡响的是当全世界的修道院、修士和牧师数量已数十年急剧锐减时,特雷莎的工作吸引了这么多的人在宗教团体中生活。当她的名字越来越为人所知的时候,她也获得了满身的荣誉——包括诺贝尔和平奖和总统自由勋章。这些荣誉很少影响她的工作及她的世界观抑或她对所服务的教会的看法。她拒绝在信仰上妥协。

在遭受多年的健康衰退之后,特雷莎于1997年9月辞世,当时刚刚过完87岁生日。几乎同时,为她行宣福礼和正式宣布她为圣徒的程序开始了。

她的遗产

我们应该如何理解这位女性、理解她的世界观以及其他更多的东西呢?按照任何一个标准,特雷莎嬷嬷都以一个完全彻底的背道而驰者吸引世人。她没有现代社会对教会及其使命的看法,而是通过执著而又简单化的途径来从事慈善和宗教事业的。她的大无畏精神是基于对个人尊严的尊重,不管他或她有多穷,多不健康或在社会权势等级上多么低下。

在天主教中有一个有争议的习俗,也是很常见的,那就是给快要死的人施以洗礼,其目的是他们一旦被施以洗礼,就会有与上帝同在的机会。而问题在于许多人认为特雷莎嬷嬷和她的信徒没有权利做那个决定,尤其是在印度这样一个基督徒不是多数群体的国家。还有一些人批评女子修道会主办的各种诊所所提供的健康护理的质量。

forty-seven

Desmond Mpilo Tutu, Bishop

Who He Is

Many would consider religion and politics a volatile mixture, one that almost never works. One ends up corrupting the other. But Desmond Tutu is our hero because he is truly one of the outstanding exceptions to this rule. He used neither his religious nor his political influence to impose an orthodoxy on the rest of South Africa.

Rather, he made his pulpit a conscience for the nation and the world. He used his religious position to make men and women free and able to live in their own country without the hated apartheid system. He used his prestige not for his own benefit, but to remind the world that so much injustice must not be ignored.

What Made the Man

Tutu was born in Klerksdorp, Transvaal, on October 7, 1931. He moved to Johannesburg with his family when he was 12. His father was a teacher and, after Tutu realized his family could not afford to send him to medical school (to follow his dream of being a physician), he decided to take up his father's career and also become a teacher.

Tutu became more and more politicized during this establishment of apartheid and sought a way to help his repressed people. His bishop encouraged Tutu to study for the Anglican priesthood and Tutu was ordained a priest in 1960. At the same time, the government further expanded apartheid by instituting the forced relocation of blacks from newly designated white areas. Millions of black South Africans were moved to the homelands and permitted to return only as officially designated guest workers.

By now, Tutu was the chaplain of the University of Fort Hare, one of the few good colleges for blacks and a center of protest against apartheid. Tutu decided to pursue his studies out of the country and attended King's College in London from 1962 until 1966, receiving a master's degree in theology. He returned to South Africa in 1967 and taught theology for the next 5 years before returning to England to serve as an assistant director of the World Council of Churches. In 1975, Tutu came back to South Africa as the first black to serve as dean of St. Mary's Cathedral in Johannesburg. He served from 1975 to 1978 as the bishop of Lesotho. Finally, in 1978, Tutu was named the first black general secretary of the South African Council of Churches.

Tutu immediately used his new position to denounce apartheid, calling for equal rights for all South Africans. He promoted nonviolent opposition to the white government and the use of economic boycotts. The government responded by revoking his passport, but international protest led to his privileges being restored.

德斯蒙德·图图：
大主教

他是谁

许多人将宗教与政治看成是一个几乎无法运作的不稳定的混合物，以一方将另一方腐蚀掉而告终。但是德斯蒙德·图图是我们的英雄，因为他是一个真正杰出的人，从不受这一规则影响。他没有利用其宗教和政治影响力将正统强加于南非其他地区。

相反，他用传教呼唤人们对于国家和世界的责任心。他利用他的宗教地位解放人民，使他们在自己国家免受种族隔离政策。他凭着自己的声望不为个人利益，而是去提醒全世界不要忽视社会的不公正。

是什么成就了他

图图于1931年10月7日出生在克拉克多普·德兰士瓦。在他12岁时全家人搬到了约翰内斯堡。他的父亲是一位教师，当了解到家里无法支付他上医科大学的费用时(去实现成为医生的梦想)，他决定继承他父亲的事业，成为了一名教师。

随着种族隔离政策的建立，图图越来越积极地投入到政治活动中，他试图寻找途径帮助受压制的人民。他的主教鼓励他去深造成为圣公会教士，并于1960年任命他为教士。与此同时，政府强制将黑人从最新划定的白人地区调到另一区域，以此进一步推行种族隔离政策。数以万计的南非黑人被迫转移到"黑人家园"。只有当他们成为被指派的工人才被允许回去。

现在，图图是福特哈尔大学的牧师，这是一所为数不多的黑人名牌大学之一，也是抗议种族隔离政策的中心。图图决定出国继续深造。1962年到1966年，他进入了伦敦的国王学院，并获得神学硕士学位。1967年，他返回南非，教授了5年的神学。之后，他又回到伦敦，成为世界宗教委员会副理事。1975年，图图再次返回南非，成为约翰内斯堡圣玛丽教堂的第一位黑人主教。1975到1978，他担任莱索托王国主教。1978年，图图被任命为南非宗教委员会的第一位黑人总书记。

图图立即利用他的新职位公开指责种族隔离政策。为所有南非黑人争取平等的权利。他号召人们对白人政府进行非暴力抵抗以及经济联合抵制。于是政府撤销了他的护照，但这一举动遭到了国际社会的抗议，图图的特权又被取消。

In 1984, Tutu was awarded the Nobel Peace Prize not only as a gesture to his efforts but as an acknowledgement of the oppression of black South Africans. Two years later, he was elected archbishop of Cape Town.

One of Mandela's first appointments after gaining power was to make Tutu the chair of the newly created Truth and Reconciliation Commission. The commission was charged with investigating human rights violations under the apartheid government of the past 34 years. Tutu was chosen for this important position because of his advocacy of forgiveness and cooperation—rather than promoting acts of revenge for past injustices.

Tutu retired as the archbishop of the Anglican Church in 1996, but maintained his political activism. He was named archbishop emeritus and is now a professor of theology at Emory University in Atlanta, Georgia.

The Legacy of the Man

Desmond Tutu will be remembered as a brave activist against a corrupt system and as a proponent of change without violence, making forgiveness and reconciliation the primary way to effect political change. While he may have retired from the church, he has maintained his interest in social causes both in his native country and around the world.

Tutu was an outspoken critic of President George W. Bush's decision to invade Iraq as part of the global war on terror. He called the act mind-boggling and was appalled that the British government of Tony Blair would support the invasion. As part of this protest, he criticized imprisoning suspected terrorists without trial in Guantanamo Bay, Cuba.

Besides the Nobel Peace Prize, Tutu has been honored by receiving Marymount University's 2004 Ethics Award and the Sydney Peace Prize and by giving the commemoration oration as part of the King's College's 175th anniversary (the students' union nightclub is named Tutu's in his honor).

Perhaps Tutu's life and work were best described by Nelson Mandela when he said: "Sometimes strident, often tender, never afraid and seldom without humor, Desmond Tutu's voice will always be the voice of the voiceless."

在1984年,图图被授予诺贝尔和平奖,不仅是对他努力的肯定,更是对南非黑人受压迫状况的承认。两年后,他当选为开普敦大主教。

在获得政权后,曼德拉首先提名图图为新成立的"真相与和解委员会"主席,这个委员会负责调查过去34年中白人政府违背人权的事件。图图被选任这一职位,是因为他提倡宽恕与合作而不是对过去的不公正采取复仇。

在1996年,图图作为圣公会大主教退休了,但是他仍然继续活跃在政坛。他被授予荣誉主教,现在是亚特兰大佐治亚州埃默里大学的一位神学教授。

他的遗产

人们会永远记住德斯蒙德·图图,一位与腐败体系勇敢斗争的积极分子,一位用宽恕和解来影响政治变化的倡导者。虽然他已退休,但他依然热衷于国内外的社会事业。

对乔治·布什总统决定侵略伊拉克来作为其全球反恐的一部分的行为,图图坦率直言这次行动实在令人难以置信,并对英国首相托尼·布莱尔对美国的入侵行为给予了支持感到惊骇。作为抗议的一部分,他还批评了未经审判就在古巴关塔那摩海湾随便关押恐怖分子嫌疑人的行为。

除了诺贝尔和平奖,图图还被授予2004年玛丽蒙特大学伦理道德规范奖、悉尼和平奖、并因在国王学院175周年纪念上所做的纪念演说而受人称颂(学生会午夜俱乐部还以图图的名字命名)。

也许图图的生活和工作正如曼德拉描述的那样,"时而尖锐,时而温柔,从不畏惧,不乏幽默,德斯蒙德·图图的声音将永远代表弱势人群的心声。"

forty-eight

Oprah Winfrey, Entertainer

Who She Is

If there is an archetypal rags-to-riches story, one that has inspired millions of adoring fans, it belongs to Oprah(as she is affectionately called). She has become one of the richest women in American, frequently showing up on Fortune's list of the wealthy. She has hosted a television show that is a must for millions of people, founded a production company, starred in full-length movies and is a mover and shaker for writers who dream of being included in her book club. A mere mention by Oprah through any of her media holdings assures prominence and instant fame.

Yet at the same time, there is an enduring quality about this woman who goes to great efforts to expose the hardships and problems within society—particularly those that affect women.(It does not hurt that the controversial subjects help television ratings!)

She is highly admired, consistently appearing on lists of the most popular as well as the most respected. She has been on the cover of Time magazine and enjoys the confidence of dozens of well-respected politicians, entertainers and businesspeople.

What Made the Woman

Oprah Gail Winfrey was born in 1954 in Kosciusko, Mississippi, to barely workingclass parents. Most people who have watched her television show know that she had a very difficult childhood, having spent time with her mother, grandmother and her father—some of whom were supportive, some not. Her grandmother taught her to read at a very early age and was very helpful to the small child. At some point, the decision was made to send Oprah to Milwaukee to live with her mother, who seemingly was less supportive and less concerned about the child and her development.

Despite her lackluster family life, Oprah channeled her energies into getting good grades. While in high school, she is reported to have rebelled against her mother, and was sent to Nashville to live with her father, who was stricter but also more encouraging. Education, again, was a priority and she earned honors in high school. She joined the high school speech team and won a national oratory contest, which was instrumental in her advancing her education at Tennessee State University, one of the fine historically black colleges.

To no one's surprise, the outgoing co-ed majored in communications and had her start in the broadcast industry at just 17 years of age working at a local radio station. This experience and her degree from Tennessee State helped her land her first television job in Nashville as a news anchor. Her career moved right along—next to Baltimore as a news anchor and a co-host for a talk show, called *People Are Talking*.(This move, of course, set the stage for the future *Oprah Winfrey Show* from Chicago!)

The move to Chicago to host a very mediocre talk show, AM Chicago, was a real challenge for both her and the station. To this day, Winfrey regards the risk taken by the

欧普拉·温弗丽：
节目主持人

她是谁

说起白手起家的原型故事，欧普拉(人们这样亲切地称呼她)的故事就是其中一个，它激励了数以百万的仰慕者。她是最富有的美国女性之一，经常上财富排行榜。她主持着拥有千万观众群的电视脱口秀节目，创立了一家制片公司，演过电影。作家们梦想作品能被纳入她的读书俱乐部，她在作家心目中的地位举足轻重。凡在欧普拉媒体中报道过的人都会一夜成名。

与此同时，这位女性竭尽所能揭露社会中的苦难和问题，尤其是女性问题(有争议的话题会提高电视收视率，但这并不是她成名的原因)。

她深受观众喜爱，不断出现在最受欢迎和最受尊敬的人物名单中。她上过《时代》杂志的封面，深得许多受人尊敬的政治家、演艺人员和生意人的信任。

是什么成就了他

1954年，欧普拉·温弗丽出生于密西西比州科休斯科小镇的一个普通工人家庭。多数看过她节目的人都知道她的童年坎坷跌宕。她曾分别与母亲、外祖母以及父亲生活过，他们有的关注欧普拉的成长，有的从来不闻不问。很小的时候，外祖母就教她认字读书，这一点对她的成长大有帮助。有一段时间，家人把欧普拉送往密尔沃基与母亲居住，而她的母亲似乎很少关心和支持孩子的发展。

尽管家庭生活并不幸福，欧普拉把精力转移到了学习成绩上。高中时，有报道她曾经反抗母亲，后又被送往纳什维尔和父亲一起生活。父亲对她更加严厉，但也给予了更多鼓励。在欧普拉的生活中，教育重新被放到了首位，她也在高中取得了优异的成绩。她加入高中演讲队并在全国演讲比赛中获胜，这次经历帮助她进入了历史悠久的黑人大学——田纳西州立大学继续深造。

果然不出所料，这个善于交际的通信专业女大学生从17岁就开始在当地的广播台工作，进入了播音行业。由于有了这段广播经历以及田纳西州立大学的文凭，她在纳什维尔电视台得到了第一份工作——新闻主播。接着，她又去了巴尔的摩电视台，在那里，她主持新闻并联合主持脱口秀节目"人们在说话"。(这一步无疑为后来的芝加哥"欧普拉·温弗丽脱口秀"节目提供了一个良好的平台。)

欧普拉调到芝加哥分部后主持了一档毫无特色的脱口秀节目"芝加哥早晨"，这对她和电视台来说都是挑战。至今，温弗丽把WLS电视台制作人的那次冒险看做她人生中一

producer at WLS-TV in Chicago as the great moment in her life. Simply stated, it was not good business to hire a slightly overweight black woman to host a talk show. Further, she was competing with the very popular and established Phil Donahue, who had the highest rankings in daytime talk at the time.

Not only did she succeed in raising the ratings for AM Chicago, but it was expanded to a full hour and renamed *The Oprah Winfrey Show*—and she never looked back from there. With national syndication in 1986, the show topped all others of its kind, hit new records in viewership and became the standard against which all other similar shows were judged.

Because she changed the format of her show to a less controversial and confrontational, more reasoned and thoughtful style, she increasingly became the spokesperson on many issues that involved those not in the mainstream: gays, lesbians, AIDS, fate of women in the Third World and more. Her middle-aged audience responded well to such changes and seems to mirror her own personal interests and charitable concerns.

The Legacy of the Woman

Oprah is our hero because she is, and will continue to be, successful in spite of poverty and a less-than-stable upbringing. She is our hero because she is willing to take risks, to bring people on the show in order to raise consciousness about events and forces that might not be controllable, but which at least need to be understood.

Those who have worked for her know that she is a tough taskmaster—but most great businesspeople do not get to the top being shy or laid back. And there is a puzzling part of her personality that just cannot shake her physical image: much of her personal effort over the years has revolved around her obsession with her weight and general wellness.

Oprah Winfrey certainly is not the typical television personality and entertainer. She is complicated, outspoken, liberal(but not always), a believer in personal responsibility, rich, influential, strong-willed, insightful, popular and strangely aloof. She seemingly has an endless appetite for new projects, media and otherwise, shows no interest in winding down the television show (although she has threatened several times to quit TV on a regular basis) and seems highly motivated to make a personal and professional difference in the world.

Oprah is our hero because she has made, and continues to make, a difference in the way we think and feel about our world, about the people with whom we interact and about ourselves. She is our hero because she expects the best from us, no matter our circumstances and background. And she is our hero because throughout it all, she is forever the entertainer. The stage is hers.

The Resources

Oprah has co-authored a number of books. Visit *www.amazon.com* or other online resellers. The most recent of these books was published in 1999.

段重要的事件。简单说,启用一个身体发胖的黑人女性主持脱口秀节目,这显然不是明智之举。况且,她的竞争对手是备受欢迎和尊敬的菲尔·多纳修,他的脱口秀节目在白天排行榜中名列榜首。

然而,温弗丽不仅成功提高了"芝加哥早晨"的收视率,而且节目还延长到一小时,并重新命名为"欧普拉·温弗丽脱口秀"——从此,她的事业蒸蒸日上。1986年的全国收视统计显示,"欧普拉·温弗丽脱口秀"在同类节目中的排名跃居第一,创下了收视率新高,成为所有同行的标杆。

温弗丽将节目的模式转变为少争议、多理性的风格,从此,她逐渐成为非主流事件的代言人。这些事件包括男性同性恋、女性同性恋、艾滋病、第三世界女性的命运,等等。她的中年观众群对节目的改动反映良好,节目的内容也能体现她本人的兴趣和对慈善的关注。

她的遗产

欧普拉是我们的英雄,是因为尽管她出身贫寒、童年坎坷,但她取得了成功并会将成绩延续下去;她是我们的英雄,是因为她甘愿担当风险,通过节目让人们关注那些失控发生的,但至少需要得到理解的事件,以提高人们的觉悟。

在她手下工作过的人知道,她是一个强硬的老板,不过最成功的商人如果害羞畏惧或者退缩不前就难以达到事业的高峰。另外,她的外表也是困扰她的一个方面——多年来她一直试图能摆脱体重和健康问题的困扰。

欧普拉·温弗丽无疑不是电视名人和娱乐工作者的典型代表。她复杂难懂、性格直爽、没有城府(有时也不然)、责任心强、富甲一方、影响力大、意志坚定、富有远见、受人欢迎、超然自若。她似乎对新项目、媒体等的兴趣永无止境(尽管她已不仅一次地提出要离开电视),积极进行个人和职业的变革。

欧普拉是我们的英雄,因为她已经并将持续改变我们对世界、人际交往以及对自我的思考与感受方式。她是我们的英雄,因为不管环境背景如何,她都希望我们能展现最好的自我。她是我们的英雄,因为经历了这一切,她永远是我们心中的娱乐工作者。舞台是属于她的。

相关资源

欧普拉与人合作撰写了多部佳作。有关信息请登录www.amazon.com 或其他网上转卖网站查询。大部分近期作品于1999年出版发行。

forty-nine

Tiger Woods, Athlete

Who He Is

He is our hero not just for his good looks,   personable public image and incredible skill as a golfer,   but also because he represents a whole new generation of athletes who see his success and are motivated to emulate it in their own sports.

He is our hero because Tiger Woods had one of the most respected amateur careers in the history of golf, and has continued this into his professional career. He is a latter-day version of Arnold Palmer—wildly popular with golfers and nongolfers alike.

What Made the Man

Eldrick(Tiger) Woods was born on December 30, 1975, in Cypress, California. His father,   Earl,   a retired lieutenant colonel in the U.S.   Army,   nicknamed him Tiger after a Vietnamese soldier and friend,   Vuong Dan Phong.   Phong,   who had also been given the nickname Tiger by Earl, saved Earl's life during the Vietnam War.

Woods was practically born with a golf ball in one hand and a putter in the other. When he was 6 months old,   he reportedly watched his father hit golf balls into a net and imitated his swing.   And at age 2,   he made an appearance on the *Mike Douglas Show,* playing golf with comedian and golfer Bob Hope.   He shot 48 for nine holes when he was only 3 years old and featured in Golf Digest when he was 5.   He was a six-time Optimist International Junior tournament winner at ages 8-9 and 12-15. However, although golf was important in his family,   education always took precedence as Woods was growing up.   He attended Western High School in Anaheim, California, where he maintained high grades.

In the 2 years that he played for Stanford, he won 10
collegiate events to clinch the NCAA title at the end
of his second season.

The week after he won his third U.S. Amateur title, Woods played his first tournament as a professional. Since he started late in the season, there were only seven events left for him to try and finish among the top 125 money winners and earn a PGA Tour player's card. He did that with a flourish, winning two tournaments and ranking among the top 30 money winners while qualifying for the Tour Championship.   Woods finished 25th with $790,594 and was the first rookie since 1990 to win twice and the first player since 1982 to finish in the top five a total of five consecutive times.

In 1997,   Woods achieved No.1 on the Official World Golf Ranking—the most rapid

泰格·伍兹：
运动员

他是谁

他是我们的英雄,不仅因为他帅气的外表,个人的社会形象以及作为高尔夫选手的令人难以置信的球技,还因为他代表了所有那些目睹他成功的新一代运动员,他们纷纷在自己的运动中竞相效仿。

他是我们的英雄,因为泰格·伍兹有着高尔夫历史上最受尊敬的业余生涯,这份荣誉也延续到他的职业生涯当中。他被誉为阿诺·帕玛的现代版,深受高尔夫爱好者和非爱好者的喜爱。

是什么成就了他

厄尔德里克(泰格)·伍兹于1975年12月30日出生在加利福尼亚州的塞普雷斯。他的父亲厄尔是一名退役的美国陆军上校。泰格(老虎)一名来自厄尔的一位越南士兵朋友王丹凤的绰号,他曾在越战中救了厄尔一命,这个绰号也是当年厄尔为他取的。

伍兹是一名天才高尔夫球员。据说他在6个月大时看到父亲击球入网,就开始学习挥棒打球。他在2岁时就在麦克·道格拉斯脱口秀中露面,与身为喜剧演员和高尔夫选手的鲍勃·霍普一起打球。他3岁时取得9洞48杆的好成绩,5岁时上了《高尔夫文摘》。他曾6次赢得了国际少年高尔夫锦标赛中8至9岁和12至15岁年龄组的冠军。但是,在伍兹的成长过程中,教育永远比打高尔夫球重要。他就读于加利福尼亚州的安纳海姆西部高等学校,成绩一直名列前茅。

在代表斯坦福大学参赛的2年里,他赢得了10项大学生赛事,在第2赛季末获得NCAA(美国全国大学生体育协会)锦标赛冠军。

在他第3次赢得美国业余高尔夫锦标赛后的一周,伍兹开始了他职业生涯的第一场赛事。因为参加这个赛季的时间晚,他只能在7项比赛中与125名顶尖选手决一胜负并获取参加PGA巡回赛的资格。他在比赛中表现出色,赢得了两项比赛,排名在前30名奖金获得者中,并取得参加冠军赛的资格。伍兹在第25届冠军赛中获得790 594美元,成为自1990年来第一个获胜2次和自1982年来第一个连续5次名列前5名的新生选手。

1997年,伍兹在官方世界高尔夫选手排名中名列第一,成为有史以来向这个冠军迈

progression ever to that position—and on June 15 of that year, during his 42nd week as a professional golfer, he became the youngest No. 1 golfer in history. He was 21 years, 24 weeks old when he claimed that status, beating out the previous youngest from 1986 by more than 8 years.

Woods' record is astonishing. He won the 1997, 2001, 2002 and 2005 Masters Tournaments, the 1999 and 2000 PGA Championships, the 2000 and 2002 U.S. Open Championships and the 2000 and 2005 British Open Championships. He also became the first major championship winner of African or Asian heritage. Woods holds records for 270 (18 under par) in the Masters, 272(12 under par) in the U.S. Open and 269(19 under par) in the British Open. He also shares the PGA Championship record of 270 (18 under par) with Bob May.

Woods is a 5-time PGA Tour money leader and PGA Tour Vardon Trophy winner as well as a 3-time member of the U.S. Presidents Cup team and a 4-time member of the U.S. Ryder Cup team. Here is a list of some of the other awards that he has procured throughout his career as a professional golfer:

O Jack Nicklaus Award, also known as the PGA Tour Player of the Year Award (1997, 1999 to 2003, and 2005)

O Player of the Year Award, PGA of America(1997, 1999 to 2003 and 2005)

O Player of the Year Award, Golf Writers Association of America (1997, 1999 to 2003 and 2005)

O Male Athlete of the Year Award, ESPY(1998—co-winner, 2000 to 2002)

O Sportsman of the Year Award, Sports Illustrated(1996 and 2000)

O World Champion of Champions Award, L'Equipe magazine, France(2000)

O Male Athlete of the Year Award, The Associated Press(1997, 1999 and 2000)

O Sportsman of the Year Award, Reuters(2000)

O World Sportsman of the Year Award, World Sports Academy(1999 and 2000).

进最快的人。同年6月15日，在他成为职业高尔夫选手的第42周里，他成为历史上最年轻的排名第一的选手。那时他只有21岁零24周大，比先前1986年最年轻的选手还要小8岁多。

伍兹的成绩振奋人心。他赢得了1997、2001、2002和2005年的大师巡回赛，1999和2000年的PGA冠军赛，2000和2002年的美国公开赛和2000年及2005年英国公开赛的冠军。他甚至成为第一个有亚非血统的冠军赛获得者。伍兹保持着大师赛270分（比标准杆数少18杆），美国公开赛272分（比标准杆数少12杆），英国公开赛269分（比标准杆数少19杆）的纪录。他还和鲍伯梅同时保持着270分的PGA冠军赛的纪录（比标准杆数少18杆）。

伍兹是5届PGA巡回赛获得奖金最多的人、瓦尔顿杯（授予美国职业选手巡回赛的胜利者）获得者、3次美国总统杯队员之一，以及4次美国莱德杯队员之一。以下是他在职业生涯中取得的其他奖项：

○ 杰克·尼科莱斯奖项，也被称为PGA巡回比赛奖（1997，1999～2003，2005年）
○ 美国PGA年度队员奖（1997，1999～2003和2005年）
○ 美国高尔夫作家协会年度队员奖（1997，1999～2003和2005年）
○ "年度卓越体育表现奖"颁发的年度男运动员奖（1998年并列获奖者，2000～2002年）
○ 运动解说协会的年度运动健将奖（1996和2000年）
○ 法国《队报》杂志评定的世界顶尖冠军奖（2000年）
○ 美联社评定的年度男运动员奖（1997，1999和2000年）
○ 路透社评定的年度运动健将奖（2000年）
○ 世界体育协会评定的世界年度运动健将奖（1999和2000年）

World War Ⅱ Armed Forces, Warriors

Who They Are

They are literally millions of men and women, living or dead, who fought in Europe, Africa and Asia to preserve American freedom and the American way of life. They are the veterans, many still living, who risked everything for a country in need and a world desperate for help to fight and destroy inexpressibly nefarious political systems.

They were ordinary people, most drafted from their daily lives and routines, who were asked to travel overseas, live in miserable and terrifying conditions, and destroy an enemy they had never seen. They did everything that was asked of them, including suffering and dying. And they did it with tremendous heroism. They are the eternal symbols of all members of the armed forces, before and after, who have served their country.

What Made Them

Although hundreds of medals were awarded to deserving service men and women, the real heroes of World War Ⅱ are...verybody. Unlike World War Ⅰ, this was total war, involving a drastic change in the way an entire country conducted its life. And it was a war in which not everyone wanted the United States to become involved.

U.S. President Franklin Roosevelt knew that it was only a matter of time before the United States would be involved in the war. He faced heavy opposition from many who believed the United States should not enter what was perceived as a European war. Roosevelt skirted around this issue at first by simply sending needed supplies to the embattled British in a program called Lend-Lease. Then the Japanese attacked the U.S. naval base at Pearl Harbor, Hawaii, without warning on December 7, 1941. Congress quickly declared war and the United States was finally involved in World War Ⅱ.

However, the U.S. military was in no condition to fight a war. Between World War Ⅰ and World War Ⅱ, the United States had cut substantial funding from the military. There were not even enough supplies to train an army. A few professionals had stayed in the armed services, but for the United States to fight the war adequately, it would have to enlist (or draft) citizen soldiers.

The soldiers came from all walks of life. Upper classes fought next to the people who normally would have been working for them. And the armed services comprised ethnicities of all kinds mixed. The U.S. military took a crash course in building up its training capacity, emphasizing physical conditioning in preparation for what would be an exhausting war.

Two often-neglected parts of the military effort were the Coast Guard and the Merchant Marine. The Coast Guard helped patrol the waters off the U.S. coastlines and

---

220   www.ahstp.net

二战美军：
勇士

他们是谁

他们是数以百万的男性和女性,有的活着,有的已经死去。他们曾经为了维护美国的自由和生活方式,在欧洲、非洲和亚洲浴血奋战。他们是那些依然健在的退伍军人,曾为祖国奉献一切,帮助陷入绝境的世界人民,并为摧毁无比残酷的政治体系而英勇战斗。

他们是普通人,其中大部分从原本平静安定的生活中应征入伍。他们被迫出征海外,在艰苦卓绝的环境下,去摧毁从未谋面的敌人。他们服从命令,包括苦难和死亡。他们以极大的英雄气概完成了祖国交予的神圣使命,他们是那些献身祖国的整个军队的不朽象征!

是什么成就了他们

尽管有上百枚勋章授予了参战的男女,但二战的真正英雄是每一个人!与一战不同,二战是一场彻头彻尾的战争。它剧烈地改变了整个国家的生存方式。这也是一场不是每个人都希望美国卷入的战争。

美国总统富兰克林·罗斯福意识到,美国迟早会陷入战争。但当时,他面临着巨大的反对压力,一些人认为美国不应该卷入这场欧洲战争。所以,罗斯福开始只是通过租借法案给处境困难的英军提供所需物资,并以这种方式来回避矛盾。然而1941年12月7日,日本突袭美国夏威夷的珍珠港海军基地。美国国会立即对日宣战。至此,美国最终被卷入二战。

然而,美国的作战实力并不强大。在一战与二战之间,美国已经削减了大量军费,他们没有足够的补给训练军队,部队中也没有足够的军事专家。美国需要大量人员参与战争,因此,必须征募平民士兵参战。

这些士兵来自美国的各个阶层。上层社会的人同平日为他们服务的人一起并肩战斗。部队由不同种族的人组成。美军为提高他们的训练能力开设了速成课程,课程的重点是培养士兵应对激烈的持久战所应具备的体能。

在军队中,两个经常被忽视的部分是海岸警卫队和商船。海岸警卫队帮助巡查美国海岸线附近的水域和操作将潜艇运往太平洋作战的运兵车。商船在保证欧洲战区供给充

also manned the personnel carriers that took Marines into combat in the Pacific. The Merchant Marine was instrumental in keeping the European theater of war supplied and took heavy casualties from German submarines. The Merchant Marine has been referred to as the forgotten arm of the service and finally received an official memorial in 1988.

Women were instrumental in both the services and the home front. Members of the Women's Army Corps(WAC) did not see actual combat but were vital in supporting jobs. A special group of the women's military called the WASPs was responsible for transporting aircraft over the United States to whatever bases they were needed. Women also entered the workplace in unprecedented numbers, helping to create the iconic character of Rosie the Riveter, who symbolized their dedication and hard work.

The average American family also had to undergo hardships to help the war effort. There was rationing of rubber, gasoline, sugar and coffee. Many civilians joined the Civil Defense Corps and helped in air-raid training. Even children learned how to spot aircraft in case they saw an enemy plane in the skies.

The Legacy of the World War II Heroes

The war took a heavy toll, with more than a million Americans killed or wounded. The heroes of World War II both at home and abroad have been referred to as The Greatest Generation. The war has sometimes been called The Good War because of its clear distinction between good and evil.

As is often the case, many veterans suffered debilitating physical and mental problems (now identified as post-traumatic stress syndrome) that would haunt them all their lives. They were often forgotten and neglected, assigned to a series of Veterans Administration hospitals and facilities—in other words, housed for the world never to see again. Despite the problems and heartaches, most Americans during World War II were justly proud of what they did to protect their country and free people from brutal dictatorships.

足和从德国潜水艇上运送伤员方面起了重要作用。商船曾是战时服务机构中被遗忘的一支。直到1988年,它们才得到一块正式的官方纪念碑。

女性在后勤服务和大后方中也发挥着重要的作用。女兵们并没有真正上场杀敌,但她们在后援方面作用甚大。妇女空军辅助飞行员是女子军团中很特殊的一支,她们的任务是负责把飞机从美国运送到所有需要的基地。在那段时期,参加工作的女子数量也是空前的,她们创造了铆钉工人罗茜所代表的勤奋和奉献的经典形象。

一般的美国家庭为了协助作战,也经历了那段艰难岁月。橡胶、石油、糖和咖啡是定量配给的。许多市民加入了民防组织并参加了空袭训练。甚至连孩子也学习怎样去发现敌机。

他们的遗产

这场战争造成了重大的损失:美国人的伤亡人数超过了一百万。二战的英雄们被描述成是世界上最伟大的一代。二战有时也被称为正义的战争,因为它在善与恶之间做了清晰的界定。

战后,老兵身心衰竭(现在被确诊为创伤后精神紧张性障碍综合征)是普遍的现象。但他们却经常被忽视和遗忘。他们被分派到一系列的老兵政府医院和地方;换句话说,为老兵提供住处的时代已经一去不复返了。尽管遭受身心的严重创伤,大多数二战老兵还是为保卫祖国和解放独裁专政中的人民所做的一切感到骄傲和自豪!